RELIGION, STATE
AND THE
BURGER COURT

RELIGION, STATE AND THE BURGER COURT

by Leo Pfeffer

Prometheus Books

700 East Amherst St. Buffalo, New York 14215

Library of Congress Card Catalog No. 84-43056
ISBN: 0-87975-275-0

Table of Contents

v

Introduction

In a sense, the title of this book is misleading. One might reasonably infer from it that when Warren E. Burger took his oath of office as Chief Justice of the United States Supreme Court a new institution came into existence, one that should be distinguished from the Earl Warren Court and those of the twelve other Chief Justices who had presided over the Court before President Nixon appointed Burger to serve as its Chief Justice. Nixon had the constitutional power to disregard the recommendations or to dismiss any or all of the members of his cabinet. Burger has no comparable power over his eight colleagues on the Court; his vote carries no more weight than that of its most recent appointee. The only power accorded to him and not shared by his colleagues is that of presiding over the Senate when it considers whether or not the president should be removed from office by impeachment.

The most significant power exercised by the Chief Justice and not shared by his colleagues (since Sandra Day O'Connor's appointment to the Court, the traditional use of the term "Brethren" would seem to be inappropriate) is to designate the member of the Court who is to draft its opinion in each case. But even that is limited to cases in which the Chief Justice's vote is in the majority; if he dissents, the majority member of seniority designates the draftsman of the Court's opinion and the Chief Justice designates who is to write the dissenting opinion. In either case, other members of the Court can write concurring opinions on one side or the other.

Why then is this book entitled "Religion, State, and the Burger Court?" The answer is simply one of convenience; it is a practicable method of treating a particular subject within a necessarily limited number of pages. Although the cases dealt with in this book were decided after October 1, 1969, when Burger joined the Court, an understanding of them requires brief summaries of prior decisions and these therefore are included.

This book is not written for constitutional lawyers, or at least not for them alone. It is written for a much wider audience, encompassing those whose interests lie in, among other fields, politics, sociology, religion, and journalism. Or, to put it another way, it is written for those who, on occasion, read the text of a Supreme Court opinion as it appears, necessarily abridged, in the *New York Times* and other newspapers or unabridged in periodicals (for example, the *Journal of Church and State*). The fact that the *Times* prints Supreme Court opinions in this area of constitutional law indicates not only a recognition of widespread interest extending beyond the field of law but also that the decisions are readable and understandable by a substantial number of nonlawyer readers.

Because of the audience to which this book is addressed, footnotes are not used—an avoidance impracticable in court opinions and law books. Instead, there is frequent use of brackets as a means of presenting matter related to but not directly encompassed in the opinion being discussed. For the same reason, legal terminology is avoided when practicable; when not, a brief explanation is given the first time a technical word or phrase is used. An example of this is the use of the Latin term *de minimus non curat lex* (meaning, the law does not concern itself with trifles). It is used because it can be helpful to an understanding of some of the Court's decisions, as for example in the case of *National Labor Relations Board v. Catholic Bishop of Chicago* in Chapter 6.

Another example is the form of law decision titles. Probably in all state courts, and in all federal courts below the United States Supreme Court, when Jones sues Smith the title of the case is *Jones v. Smith*, and it retains that title until the litigation reaches its final disposition in the courts. But not so if the case gets to the Supreme Court. In such an instance the title might still be *Jones v. Smith*, but it might have become *Smith v. Jones*. What this titling tells us is not who was suing whom but who won and lost in the court just below the Supreme Court: the loser's name comes first whether he was the plaintiff or the defendant. Should you ask why this is so, I can do no more than refer you to the anonymous person speaking to Dr. Fell.

> I do not love thee, Dr. Fell
> The reason why I cannot tell
> But this I know and know full well
> I do not love thee Dr. Fell.

In relating how the Burger or other courts decided cases dealt with in this book I have tried, as far as possible, to be nonpartisan. What I have not done, even if it were possible, is to make any effort to exclude my own partisan judgment as to the significance and correctness of the decisions discussed in the book.

Lawyers and scholars cognizant in the field of the free exercise of religion and church-state separation are aware that I consistently defend a position called absolutist or extremist or doctrinaire or unrealistic or uncompromising. Perhaps the most charitable name is the term *strict separationist* in contrast to what is called "accommodationist." The standard response to absolutists is the quotation from *Cantwell v. Connecticut* (1940): "the First Amendment embraces two concepts, freedom to believe and freedom to act. The first is absolute, but in the nature of things, the second cannot be."

If you find this quotation near the beginning of a court's opinion in an establishment case you can safely assume that the decision will not be in favor of the strict separationists. (Ironically, the decision handed down in the *Cantwell* case, which involved police action against Jehovah's Witnesses who verbally attacked Roman Catholicism, was in favor of their absolutist, etc., claim.)

To the extent that the *Cantwell* quotation is true, it is a platitude, and to the extent that it is not, it is meaningless. Of course freedom to believe is absolute; for, as the old adage goes, the devil himself knoweth not the thoughts of men. It is only when belief is translated into action (which encompasses verbal action, else all incitement to riot prosecutions and slander lawsuits would be unconstitutional) that law can intervene.

Those defending the strict separationist interpretation of the First Amendment's Establishment Clause recognize that the absolute separation of church and state is not possible, but what does that prove? Does the reality that no person is immortal mean that the medical and pharmaceutical profession should be abolished? Realistic separationists recognize that the absolute separation of church and state cannot be achieved, else what's a secularist heaven for? Nevertheless, that is the direction they would have constitutional law relating to the Religion Clause take, fully aware that perfection will never be reached.

Measured by realistically attainable goals, how, in the eyes of realistic absolutists, has the Burger Court done so far? On the whole, with respect to the Free Exercise Clause, I think it has done quite well. It has, for example, upheld the right of Amish to discontinue secondary school attendance after graduation from elementary schools. It has ruled that prisoners are protected by the free exercise guarantee, a decision that has had substantial effects upon treatment of cultists in penitentiaries. It has upheld a claimant's right to receive unemployment compensation notwithstanding his rejection of an available position in an arms factory because acceptance would violate his religious conscience.

It has, however, not become absolutist. Thus, for example, it rejected a claim that the Free Exercise Clause protects the religiously mandated practice of selling printed material on the grounds of a state-operated fair.

The history of the Establishment Clause during the Burger period has been different. Indeed, it is as if there were two Burger Courts: Burger Court I in the seventies and Burger Court II in the eighties. In 1970 the Court upheld the constitutionality of the tax exemption privilege accorded to churches. In view of the reality that the privilege had long existed when the Constitution was adopted and that it has continued to exist without interruption in the federal government and in all the states in the Union, it would have been completely unrealistic to have expected the Court to decide otherwise.

More important, in his opinion upholding the statute, Chief Justice Burger interpreted the Establishment Clause in a way that delighted the most doctrinaire of separationists. The clause, he said, invalidated a law if its purpose was to advance religion or if it resulted in excessive governmental entanglement with religion. The decisions in the next decade of Burger Court I indicate that in the *Walz* case it had meant what it said and not what it did. During that period, with only one or two rather minor exceptions, it uniformly struck down under the Establishment Clause a variety of statutes enacted with the purpose of finding some way to finance parochial schools that the Court would accept.

This was the first time in American history that the Supreme Court ruled unconstitutional laws appropriating funds to finance the operations of religious schools. At the beginning it seemed that even Byron A. White, the most stalwart of the Court's defenders of aid to religious schools, would go along. He added a footnote at the end of his partial dissent in the *Lemon-DiCenso* cases (1971) reading:

> As a postscript [he said] I should note that both the Federal and State cases are decided in specified Establishment considerations, without reaching the questions that would be presented if the evidence in any of these cases showed that any of the involved schools restricted entry on racial or religious grounds or required all students gaining admission to receive instruction in the tenets of a particular faith. For myself, if such proof were made, the legislation would to that extent be unconstitutional.

During the seventies, this is exactly what Burger Court I did. The White minority, which by the eighties became a majority, blandly ignored it with respect to the religion aspect. (In the case of *Bob Jones University v. United States* [1983] he did not dissent from the Court's decision that a college having a racially discriminatory admissions policy does not qualify for tax exemption.) One can only speculate as to what induced White to add the footnote. Taken seriously and adhered to there would have been no controversy in the arena of aid to religious schools. Imagine, if you can, a religious school accepting equally all applicants for admission irrespective of religion, or one that does not require students to receive religious instruction. Were this to come about, there would be no need for church-state litigation with respect to financing.

At the turn of the present decade Burger Court II began handing down decisions pointing in the direction exactly opposite to that of the preceding decade. With only two exceptions, one dealing with the posting of the Ten Commandments in public schools and the other a very minor one dealing with the proximity to churches of restaurants serving intoxicating liquors, Burger Court II (which came into existence by reason of Lewis F. Powell's conversion from absolutism to accommodationism) handed down rulings that made the separationists grieve and the accommodationists smile. Like probably all other strict separationists I suffered a period of despondency, convinced that all that had been achieved in the seventies would be vitiated case by case in the eighties. President Ronald Reagan appointed Sandra Day O'Connor to the Court after he made sure that her positions on religion and state, whether they involved abortion, prayer in the public schools, or aid to parochial schools, coincided with his own. The two most ardent separationists today on the bench, William J. Brennan and Thurgood Marshall, are likely to retire within a short period of time and it can safely be assumed that if Reagan is reelected, their successors will be required to pass his accommodationist test; indeed, he made it quite clear that this was his intention.

Surprisingly, Burger Court II did not overrule the absolutist decisions of Burger Court I. It did not, for example, overrule decisions ruling unconstitutional tax credits for parochial school tuition costs or appropriations to finance instruction in those schools. Instead, it limited itself to applying the accommodationist approach to fact situations that had not been passed upon by Burger Court I (e.g., allowing tax deductions for parochial school tuition payments, or prayer on college rather than elementary and secondary school premises, or financing a crèche during the Christmas season).

One can only speculate why Burger Court II contented itself with this compromise rather than overruling the unhappy decisions of Burger Court I. Perhaps compromise was the price that had to be paid for Powell's conversion from absolutist to accommodationist. Perhaps the

Court did not want to emulate the recklessness of the Roosevelt-packed New Deal Court in overruling the decisions of its conservative predecessors. Indeed, it is even possible (but to political scientists, not likely) that the majority really believed that the Burger Court I cases were correctly decided and so too were those of Burger Court II.

Whatever the explanation, the rulings of Burger Court I are still the supreme law of the land. Of course strict separationists are not happy with this compromise. But then neither are protagonists of tax credits for parochial school tuition or school-sponsored prayers at the elementary and secondary school level, or teaching of creationism in the public school, or the prohibition of abortions. These pro-strict separationist decisions still stand intact.

It may well happen that the reluctance of the 1980 Burger Court to overrule the 1970 Court decisions will not be shared by a new majority in which O'Connor-type Republicans will replace Brennan and Marshall, and Burger Court III may follow the practice of the Roosevelt-packed Court in not hesitating to overrule prior decisions it does not like. For the time being, however, the situation is not as tragic as we strict separationists have thought it to be.

CHAPTER

1

Tax Exemption

WORSHIP PROPERTIES

Tax exemption of church-owned property may be as old as taxation itself. The Bible relates that, when Joseph bought the Egyptians' land for the food he had stored during the seven years of plenty, he turned back to each Egyptian his land and "made it a law over the land of Egypt unto this day that Pharaoh should have a fifth part [of the produce]; except the land of the priests only, which became not Pharaoh's" (Genesis 47:26). Later, when Ataxerxes, King of Persia, authorized Ezra to levy a tax for the rebuilding of the Temple, he specifically directed that "touching any of the priests and Levites, singers, porters, Nethinim, or ministers of the house of God, it shall not be lawful toll, tribute, or custom, upon them" (Ezra 7:24). (Today's tax lawyer, familiar with our Internal Revenue Code, will recognize what might be the original statutory repetitive language and listing endemic to tax statutes.) Still later, in the fourth century, when Constantine was in the process of establishing Christianity as the state church of Rome, he accorded the privilege of exemption to church buildings and to the land about them that was used for church purposes.

Without doubt most of those who dictated exemption were sincerely committed to religion and sought to secure a status for priests enabling them to devote all their efforts and concerns to their divine duties. Yet, as contemporary events in the life of Pope John Paul II and as all history preceding them can testify, those who have been entrusted the keys of the heavenly kingdom possess great power over the people of the worldly kingdoms, notwithstanding their lack of armies and nuclear weapons. It is therefore quite understandable that governments should afford special privileges such as tax exemption to religious institutions.

Most nations extend privileges to churches considerably further than

1

the United States Constitution, as interpreted by the Supreme Court, will allow ours to do. Even Marxist governments, such as those in Poland and Hungary (but not the Soviet Union), actually finance the operations of church schools and pay the salaries of priests and nuns who teach in them. Superficially this seems surprising; it was Karl Marx who declared that religion was the opiate of the people and therefore obviously their enemy. Realistically, however, the political rulers in the heavily Catholic East European countries recognized that for the time being the masses must be appeased and decided that the error made by Pharaoh in not allowing the Hebrew slaves a three-day furlough to worship their God in the desert (Exodus 5:3-41) should not be repeated.

In the United States, the First Amendment to the Constitution prohibits laws "respecting an establishment of religion or prohibiting the free exercise thereof." This provision forbids outright subsidization of religion; but the next best thing was to emulate Joseph, Ezra, and Constantine by granting tax exemption to churches with respect to the land owned by them and the contributions they receive from their parishioners. To Frederick Walz, a no-nonsense, no-compromise atheist who owned a piece of real estate in New York City, this was not good enough. Accordingly, he instituted a suit challenging the law that accorded exemption to churches in regard to real estate used for religious purposes. This law, he said, violated the First Amendment no less than one according outright subsidies to churches.

In *Walz. v. Tax Commission* (1970), the Supreme Court, with only William O. Douglas dissenting, rejected the challenge and upheld the constitutionality of exemption. Looked at objectively, it is difficult to justify the decision in light of accepted constitutional principles relating to church-state separation. In *Everson v. Board of Education* (1947), and in many later decisions, the Court had ruled against the validity of government aid to churches, and exemption from taxation would seem to fall in that category. In other cases, the Court held unconstitutional statutes having the purpose or primary effect of advancing religion, and here too exemption would appear vulnerable. James Madison, who as chief architect of the First Amendment would be presumed to know what it meant, deemed unconstitutional laws exempting churches from taxes imposed on laymen. Nor can exemption be easily justified on the *quid pro quo* or fair-exchange rationale that might justify exemptions to charitable institutions that relieve the state of financial burdens it otherwise might have to bear. Since the First Amendment forbids government to provide religious services (except in special circumstances, as will be discussed later), there is no *quid* for the *quo*.

Yet history, if it does not entirely justify exemption, does explain it; not the history of Joseph, Ezra, or Constantine (they did not rule under constitutions mandating the separation of religion and state), but that of the generation which adopted the First Amendment. Never mind what Madison may or may not have had in mind when he drafted the First Amendment, which forbids government financing of religious institutions; it was not he but the states that made it the supreme law of the land, and without exception all thirteen of them accorded tax exemption to churches to the same extent that Section 501(c)(3) of our Internal Revenue Code accords it to nonprofit hospitals, libraries, playgrounds, and scientific, professional, historical, and patriotic groups.

A plausible case could be made that in financing churches, which constitutionally can and do furnish secular benefits such as hospital care, soup kitchens, and homes for the aged, the infirm, and the orphaned, the government is not aiding or advancing religion but providing compensation for services the government would otherwise have to provide. But Chief Justice Warren E. Burger, who wrote the Court's opinion in the *Walz* case, may have implicitly recognized the danger of relying upon this "good works" rationalization. Churches do have the constitutional right to exclude from membership or employment persons of other or no religion; a right not shared by other "good works" organizations. Moreover, some churches do not at all engage in "good works" but apply their income entirely to finance preaching and propagating their faith. Recognizing this, Burger made it clear that exemption was not to be justified on "good works" (although some of the briefs submitted in the case emphasized the charitable services that churches offered the community); to do so, he said, would require the state to evaluate the worth of particular social welfare programs, thereby producing the kind of continuing day-to-day entanglement of religion and state that the Establishment Clause seeks to minimize.

Realistically, an unfavorable decision by the Court would have been an act of futility. The universality of exemption and its uninterrupted history from ancient times made it practically a certainty, recognized by all members of the Court, including Douglas, that in the shortest possible time the Constitution would be amended to restore exemption to the churches. The net effect of the decision was that it made the amendment process unnecessary. But, as later transpired, protagonists of government aid to religious institutions, particularly schools, paid a high price for their victory in the *Walz* case. Within a year after the decision, the Chief Justice would write another opinion, making the pro-aid forces quite unhappy.

History has an often unfortunate way of repeating itself. A year after the Court, to the delight at least of the Catholic church, handed down its decision in the *Everson* case upholding government financing of transportation to parochial schools, in large measure because its principal purpose was the secular one of protecting children from the perils of traffic, it ruled in *McCollum v. Board of Education of Champaign, Illinois,* that religious instruction in the public schools was unconstitutional aid to religion. So, too, as we shall see later, a year after the *Walz* decision came down, the Court would decide *Lemon v. Kurtzman,* substantially invalidating government financing of church-related schools. In both instances the author of the first decision (Hugo Black in *Everson* and Burger in *Walz*) also wrote the second, respectively (*McCollum* and *Lemon*), and in both a new dimension was added to existing law—no-aid in *Everson-McCollum* and entanglement in *Walz-Lemon*. In several decisions in the period between *Everson* (1947) and *Walz* (1970) the Court, while relying primarily on the no-aid test, simultaneously held that a law having a purpose or primary effect of aiding (or inhibiting) religion also violated the Establishment Clause. Burger, in the *Walz* decision, added entanglement as a third factor, so that it applied a three-pronged "purpose-effect-entanglement" test, meaning that in order to be valid a law must have a secular legislative purpose, its principal or primary effect must be one that neither advances nor inhibits religion, and it must not foster an excessive entanglement of state with religion.

Beginning a year after the *Walz* decision the Court did strike down statutes that entailed excessive entanglement, but in *Walz* itself the Court did not find that fatal flaw. Indeed, the Court said, were exemption not permissible the government would become excessively entangled in church affairs through tax valuations of church property, tax liens, tax foreclosures, and direct confrontation in the legal process.

The logical implication of this reasoning is that exemption is not merely a privilege but a constitutional mandate, for were there no exemption, the consequence would be impermissible entanglement. The claim of a constitutional right to exemption under the Free Exercise Clause had been urged, on a different rationale, in *amicus curiae* (friend of the court) briefs submitted separately by the National Council of Churches (whose religious liberty director, Dean Kelley, later wrote a book, *Should Churches Be Taxed?,* expanding it), by the Baptist Joint Committee on Public Affairs, speaking for some twenty-three million congregants strongly committed to church-state separation, and by the Synagogue Council of America representing the three branches of American Judaism, Orthodox, Conservative, and Reform.

These organizations predicated their contention on the First Amendment, not primarily on the Establishment Clause but rather on the Free Exercise Clause. The power to tax implies the power to destroy, and since the latter clause forbids government from destroying churches, so does it forbid it to tax them. The argument is cogent if taxation is merely an attribute of unlimited sovereignty requiring no other justification. The difficulty with that argument lies in the fact that Article I, Section 8, does not confer upon government an unrestricted right to tax as a sovereignty but only to make effectual the "power to provide for the common defense and general welfare." Since churches, as all others, benefit from such protection, it would seem at least permissible to require them to share the costs. (It bears noting that the *amicus* brief submitted by the United States Catholic Conference did not go as far as the other religious organizations but contented itself with arguing only that exemption was constitutionally permissible.)

One might assume that state governments would welcome the decision sought by Walz, for it would not only enable but require them to tax churches and thereby increase their treasuries without incurring the wrath of the churches. ("We didn't want to do it; the Supreme Court made us.") Nevertheless no state attorney general submitted a brief supporting Walz; on the contrary, thirty-six joined in a brief drafted by New York's attorney general opposing him. The *amicus curiae* support he received was, as to be expected, from the American Civil Liberties Union, the dauntless atheist Madalyn Murray O'Hair, and the Society of Separationists, Incorporated.

One would also expect Protestants and Other Americans United for Separation of Church and State (now known as Americans United for Separation of Church and State) to submit a brief in support of Walz, and indeed its lawyer did prepare such a brief. At the last moment, however, the organization's officers directed him not only to cancel the brief but to submit one on the other side, that is, sustaining constitutionality of exemption. This was a complete 180-degree change of direction, which as will be seen later was at least to some extent emulated by President Ronald Reagan in the *Bob Jones University* case. It is a fair guess that the explanation for the organization's turnabout lay in the reality that its major constituency and financial contributors were to be found among Protestant clergymen and congregations who also would suffer financially were Walz to prevail.

INCOME PRODUCING ASSETS

A question left open in the *Walz* decision was the constitutionality of taxing churches' income from businesses and other purely secular commercial enterprises owned by them. In the 1940s a professor of law at New York University advised the university that under the federal tax law, as it then read, it could acquire the stock of the Mueller Spaghetti Company and pay no tax on the profits earned by the sale of spaghetti, so long as all of the profits were used for educational purposes. The university accepted the advice and entered into business in a position to undersell non-tax-exempt competitors. Hardly surprising, it was not long before other tax-exempt organizations followed suit.

The ensuing hue and cry raised by non-tax-exempt corporations forced Congress in 1950 to change the law so as to limit the exemption to income earned from enterprises directly related to the purpose of the exempt organization. The change would, for example, continue the exemption on profits of university presses (assuming university presses make profits) but not of spaghetti factories, for there is no visible direct relation between spaghetti and scholarship. The church lobbies, however, proved more powerful than those of educational and charitable institutions and even the Treasury Department itself: at the last moment the bill was amended to continue the exemption on unrelated business activities of churches.

The result of this was that a church could operate a girdle business (which one did) or an apartment house or a department store without paying a federal income tax on the profits, although nobody else could. In time even the major religious groups could not accept this. In its *amicus curiae* brief in the *Walz* case, the United States Catholic Conference stated:

> In arguing that houses of religious worship constitutionally may be afforded exemption from State real estate taxation, this *amicus* does not defend exemption from taxation accorded church properties used or operated for commercial purposes and has so advised Congress and the Public. [Joint Statement of the National Council of Churches and the United States Catholic Conference, *Hearings on H. R. 13270 (The Tax Reform Act of 1969)* before the Senate Committee on Finance, 91 Cong. 1st Sess. 83 (May 2, 1969) (unofficial print)]

In view of this position adopted by the major American religious organizations and the widespread protest of nonreligious groups, Congress had no choice, and in the Tax Reform Act of 1969 it put the word "religion" back into the law. Churches were thus placed in the same category as other tax-exempt institutions, except that they received a five-year grace period during which they continued to be exempt on the unrelated businesses they owned when the amendment was enacted into law. (The churches' conscience did not impel them to reject this privilege not accorded to nonreligious exempt institutions.)

Many states followed suit in repealing their own tax laws to end exemption in relation to income received by churches from unrelated business sources. On the other hand, many did not. One of these was Florida, where a Baptist congregation owned nearly a square block of land in downtown Miami occupied by its church building and an off-street parking lot. On Sunday, parking was supplied without charge to persons attending the church for worship, but during the rest of the week the lot was operated pretty much as any other commercial parking lot in a city business district.

Some taxpayers brought a suit challenging the exemption to the extent that it applied to income earned during the six business days. Before the Supreme Court heard argument in the case, *Diffenderfer v. Central Baptist Church of Miami* (1972), the Florida legislature amended its statute to limit the exemption to the extent that the parking lot and other church-owned properties were used by worshippers during religious services. The Court, after hearing argument, dismissed the appeal on the ground of mootness, that is, since the taxpaying plaintiffs had achieved their purpose through legislation, there was no need for the Court to pass judgment on their complaint.

As of now the Court has not explicitly ruled that government, state or federal, may constitutionally tax the income that a church receives from purely commercial enterprises but used exclusively for religious purposes. It has universally been assumed that it may; were it not so, the Central Baptist Church could have claimed its right to exemption, notwithstanding the amendment.

Nevertheless, so eminent an authority as Harvard Professor Laurence Tribe, author of the oft-cited *American Constitutional Law*, states (on p. 846) that exemption should be permitted "because of the church-state entanglement that could be encountered in any attempt to tax religion, including religiously owned commercial enterprises."

Were the Court to accept this proposition, it is a good guess that a host of religious organizations (including perhaps even the United States Catholic Conference and the National Council of Churches) would not be able to resist the temptation to press for exemption and that before long most if not all states (and probably even Congress on the urging of

President Reagan) would yield to the pressure for extension of exemption to encompass church-owned commercial enterprises. The inevitable consequences would be an added burden upon the majority of taxpaying citizens who believe that their contributions to religious institutions should be entirely voluntary.

Serious constitutional issues arise when the courts are faced with conflicts between First Amendment claims to the free exercise of religion and the Fourteenth Amendment guarantee of equal protection under the law. Although, as will be indicated in a later chapter, in most instances the claims to exemption that reach the courts involve church-related schools, they may also arise, for example, in tax exemption of church-related camps that admit only applicants of a particular faith, or hospitals that will not permit even lawful abortions or that exclude or segregate patients on the basis of race.

The conflict between tax laws and sincerely held religious beliefs in the arena of education came to the Supreme Court in the 1983 companion cases of *Bob Jones University v. United States* and *Goldsboro Christian School v. United States*. The Goldsboro Christian School was established to give "special emphasis to the Christian religion and the ethics revealed in Holy Scriptures." Its founders believed that race is determined by descent from one of Noah's three sons, Ham, Shem, and Japheth. Based on this interpretation Orientals and Negroes are Hamitic, Hebrews are Shemitic, and Caucasians are Japhethetic. Cultural or biological mixing of the races was regarded by the school officials as a violation of God's command. Accordingly, they maintained a racially discriminatory admission policy in not accepting any but Caucasians, although it occasionally admitted children of mixed marriages if one of the parents was Caucasian. The sponsors of Bob Jones University were likewise genuine in their belief that the Bible adjudges interracial dating and marriage to be sinful, and they forbade, under penalty of expulsion, students to commit that sin.

The role of the federal government in this litigation was rather unusual; there are few other instances in American legal history in which a government, federal or state, instituted a suit and before its final conclusion turned around and identified itself with the opposite side. The federal government's stance in relation to exemption-nonexemption of religious schools discriminating against blacks reminds one of many things: the quadrille in *Alice in Wonderland*; the change-your-partner call in square dances; the on-again, off-again matrimonial pattern of Elizabeth Taylor and the late Richard Burton; and the oft-repeated you're hired–you're fired relationship between George Steinbrenner and his oft-time manager, Billy Martin.

There must be something in the tax-exemption arena that gives rise to this affliction. As noted earlier, counsel for Americans United for Separation of Church and State initially prepared a brief in the *Walz* case urging the Supreme Court to rule exemption unconstitutional, and then at the last moment discarded it and submitted a new one urging the opposite. In the *Diffenderfer* case, Dade County had originally attempted to tax the portion of the church property used as a parking lot, but by the time Diffenderfer sued it had changed its position and defended the exemption. So was it too with the government in the *Bob Jones University-Goldsboro School* litigation, only much more so. Here is how it happened.

In *Green v. Connally* (1971) parents of black public school children sued to enjoin the Internal Revenue Service from according tax-exempt status to private schools in Mississippi that discriminated against blacks. The Internal Revenue Service defended its policy, arguing that racially segregated private schools were entitled to tax exemption. Richard Nixon was then president and was expected to run again the following year. As l'affaire Watergate was later to disclose, he was not one who allowed fine technicalities of constitutional law to stand in the way of the overriding priority of reelection. Through the efforts of Martin Luther King and the National Association for the Advancement of Colored People (NAACP), the Negro vote was something to be reckoned with. (Even arch-segregationist George Wallace, who physically sought to block the door at the admissions building of the University of Alabama when two black applicants tried to enter, later recognized this during his presidential election efforts in 1972.) So, as the trial judge noted, "in the midst of the litigation," the Internal Revenue Service reversed its position and urged the trial court to rule against exemption. The trial court did and the Supreme Court later affirmed its decision. So ends chapter one.

The law then rested for ten years. During that decade the Internal Revenue Service uniformly denied exemption to private schools, religious as well as secular, that discriminated against blacks in admission or instruction procedures.

However, notwithstanding the *Green v. Connally* decision, the exodus from public to private schools not only continued but increased and is continuing to do so substantially beyond the extent manifested in the statistics set forth in Chapter 2. The reason for this is twofold: first, fundamentalists' (Evangelicals') dissatisfaction with the secularism of public school education and, second, fear engendered by the increasing number of blacks entering public schools in white residential neighborhoods by reason of federal courts' rulings that busing must be resorted to if necessary to achieve full integration in public schools.

The *Bob Jones University* and *Goldsboro School* cases raised the issue of whether application of this public policy exclusion could justify denial of tax exemption to schools based on the sincerely held belief that race mixing was against God's will. The schools argued that it could not, since public policy could not override the First Amendment's guarantees of church-state separation (which forbids inhibition of religion) and the free exercise of religion. Their contention was rejected by the lower courts; hence their appeal to the Supreme Court, and it was at this step in the quadrille that Reagan exercised his change-partners privilege. During his election campaign he had promised that he would direct restoration of tax-exemption to Bob Jones University, since he agreed with its president that denial of exemption violated the First Amendment. Accordingly, after inauguration he directed the Internal Revenue Service to restore exemption and no longer defend suits seeking restoration of exemption.

This action was highly satisfactory to North Carolina's Senator Jesse Helms, whose political influence was respected by Reagan, and to the evangelical schools in the South, since it was predicated on the premise that tax exemption of churches and church schools was a constitutionally protected right rather that a revocable privilege. On the other hand, it infuriated or dismayed blacks, most northern Protestants and Jews (even those who had argued in the *Walz* case that exemption was a constitutionally protected right), the majority of the attorneys on the staff of the United States Department of Justice, liberals generally, and even Republicans in states with substantial numbers of black voters.

It was clear that the time had come for another change-your-partners step in the quadrille. The president, his spokesmen said, had been misunderstood. He did not mean that Congress could not withdraw exemption from schools practicing racial discrimination, but only that it had not done so and that until it does Bob Jones University and Goldsboro Christian School could not be denied exemption. Were Congress to pass such an amendment to Section 501(c)(3) of the Internal Revenue Code the president would of course gladly sign it, because he was sure it would not be in violation of the First Amendment. (The difficulty with this solution lay in the likelihood that Helms and those who agreed with him would engage in a filibuster that could not easily be overcome.)

That was the position urged by the government in its brief to the Burger Court in the *Bob Jones University* case, but it persuaded only William H. Rehnquist. To the relief of most members of Congress, the Court, in an opinion by the Chief Justice, ruled that it would be wholly incompatible with the concept underlying tax exemption to grant the status to racially discriminatory private educational institutions. Exemption is predicated on a fair exchange concept; the community as a whole benefits by what the exempted taxpayer does for the public at large, and it cannot be said that racially discriminatory institutions benefit the public. Moreover, said Burger, denial of exemption would not violate either the Establishment or the Free Exercise clauses of the First Amendment, since eradication of racial discrimination in education substantially outweighs the burden that denial of exemption would place upon religious schools (even though this compelling governmental interest was not recognized until the *Green v. Connally* decision was handed down). Finally—and this was the crux of the controversy—it was not necessary for Congress to enact a law expressly endorsing that ruling (assuming Helms' filibustering and other tactics could be overcome); its nonaction had the practical and judicially recognizable effect of making the ruling the law of the land.

Thus, at least until the present writing, ended the quadrille, and legislators, national and state, breathed a deep if inaudible sigh of relief. As with the issue of abortion, one function of judicial review is to do what has to be done but cannot be by timid legislators whose primary obligation is to get reelected.

TAXATION AND "CULTS"

Just as grant of exemption can be utilized to reward favored churches or religions, denial can be the price paid by those that are feared or hated—those groups called "cults." As will be more fully discussed in Chapter 7, cults, or more accurately their leaders, have become the subjects of intense persecutory treatment by agencies of government—legislative, executive, and judicial—and one of the instruments utilized has been the resort to tax laws.

Cultists have not been the only or even the first subjects of such treatment. In the 1920s "Scarface" Al Capone was implicated in brutal murders, assaults, blackmailing, and prohibition violations but the law-enforcement officials, including the vaunted and revered J. Edgar Hoover, apparently felt unable to effect successful prosecution for these crimes. What they did, therefore, was resort to trials for tax evasion, on the theory that no matter how tainted Capone's money might be the Internal Revenue Service was entitled to its share and had not received it.

When in 1787 the framers of our Constitution authorized Congress (in Section 8 of Article I) to "lay and collect taxes" in order "to pay the debts and provide for the common defense and general welfare of the United States," it is a fair assumption that their purpose was to raise revenue rather than to punish criminals and eliminate them as a source of anti-social activities. There is no doubt that in Capone's case the government was successful in achieving the latter purpose; when released from prison eight years after his conviction he was a seriously sick man, physically and mentally, and though he lived eight years longer it is safe to assume he committed no further crimes.

Success evokes emulation, so it is not surprising that prosecutions for revenue-law violations should be resorted to as a means to destroy unpopular religions. For two decades Jehovah's Witnesses were as feared and hated as present-day cults, and prosecutions for tax-law evasions became one of the many devices resorted to in efforts primarily aimed at eliminating them as an enemy of the people rather than collecting revenue. The Witnesses, however, proved considerably less vulnerable than Capone and other racketeers. In a series of decisions the Supreme Court ruled that the Free Exercise Clause of the First Amendment guaranteed the Witnesses' freedom from a license tax with respect to practices that are primarily religious, such as the sale of religious tracts, even though they produced income which accrued in part to the benefit of the colporteurs.

Present-day cults have not yet won the general acceptance finally achieved by Jehovah's Witnesses, and resorting to tax-law enforcement has become a popular means of restricting their free exercise of cultism. The most prominent or perhaps notorious cults, such as the Holy Spirit Association for the Unification of World Christianity, popularly known as the Unification Church (its believers are usually called "Moonies"), the Church of Scientology, the Worldwide Church of God, and the Hare Krishna groups, have achieved legal recognition as valid churches in the eyes of the federal and most state courts and are therefore deemed to be entitled in principle to the same exemptions from taxation enjoyed by the well-established religions.

As has been noted, both the National Council of Churches and the Synagogue Council of America have urged the courts, so far unsuccessfully, to rule that tax exemption is not merely a revocable privilege but a constitutionally protected right. The National Council has been faithful to this principle, and by *amicus curiae* briefs and otherwise has urged that cults enjoy the same tax privileges accorded the Protestant, Catholic, and Jewish religions. Not so the Synagogue Council and its constituents. They have consistently refused to support the efforts of cults to achieve equality of treatment under tax laws, state or federal.

Rigid enforcement of tax laws can be an effective weapon against cults. With the possible exception of traffic regulations, tax laws are probably the most frequently violated statutes in the United States. Very few of us can truthfully say that we have never in the least underestimated our income or overestimated our deductions in filling out our IRS 1040 and similar forms. Were the revenue authorities to prosecute every such violation, there would not be enough prisons to house us, even if all other criminal laws were repealed. Realistically, selective prosecution is the only practical solution to this problem, but the selective process may be vulnerable to judicial attack.

The record in the case of *United States v. Moon* bears witness to this. Moon was indicted and tried in a federal court for income-tax evasion. The amount in question was a relatively small one, not merely with respect to Moon and his church but also when viewed in light of the tax liabilities of multimillion-dollar business corporations. An objective consideration of the factual situation would seem to justify, at least in part, Moon's complaint in a speech he made in front of the courthouse that "I would not be standing here today, if my skin were white and my religion were Presbyterian." The judge who presided at the trial agreed. "Let me say," he said in a conference with the attorneys outside the presence of the jury, "that I think Reverend Moon is *sui generis* (exceptional). I don't think there is anyone in this country similar to him. . . . I am not so naive as to believe that if Reverend Moon was a noncontroversial person whose religion was Pollyannish, who nobody took exception to, that the government would not have had as much interest in looking at his taxes as they did. . . ."

The *Moon* case will be discussed more fully in Chapter 7, which deals with disfavored religions. Here it is sufficient to note that Moon was found guilty by a jury and his conviction was upheld by all courts, including the Supreme Court.

Tax-enforcement problems relating to religious groups are not limited to those that are now hated and feared by the people at large. The Amish have for far too long been members of the American family of accepted religions to be deemed a cult, such as the Unification Church and the Jehovah's Witnesses were. As discussed in Chapter 3, they present difficult constitutional problems arising out of their violation of compulsory school attendance laws in refusing to send their children to high schools. In *United States v. Lee* (1982) the Burger Court was faced with a related problem arising under the Social Security Law. Lee, a member of the Old Order Amish, employed seven other members to work on his farm and his carpentry shop, but he refused, on ground of religious conscience, to pay the social security tax imposed upon employers.

The Amish have a religiously based obligation to provide their fellow members with the kind of assistance contemplated by the social security system but not to pay taxes to the government for that purpose. The government, while not challenging the sincerity of Lee's belief, contended that payment of social security taxes would not threaten the integrity of the religious belief or observance. Burger, in his opinion for himself and seven associates (John Paul Stevens issued his own concurring opinion), ruled that it was not within the functions of the Court or the competence of judges to decide whether the government or Lee stated the proper interpretation of the Amish faith. Nevertheless, said Burger, compulsory participation in the social security system did not violate Lee's rights under the Free Exercise Clause.

Not all burdens on religion, he continued, were unconstitutional; government may justify a limitation on religious liberty by showing that it is essential to accomplish an overriding governmental interest. Voluntary participation in the social security system would undermine its soundness and make it difficult if not impossible to administer. If, for example, he continued:

> a religious adherent believes war is a sin, and if a certain percentage of the federal budget can be identified as devoted to war-related activities, such individuals would have a similarly valid claim to be exempt from paying that percentage of the income tax. The tax system could not function if denominations were allowed to challenge the tax system because tax payments were spent in a manner that violates their religious belief. Because the broad public interest in maintaining a sound tax system is of such a high order, religious belief in conflict with the payment of taxes affords no basis for resisting the tax.

When, he concluded, followers of a particular sect enter into commercial activities as a matter of choice, the limits that they set on their own conduct cannot be imposed on a statutory program of social security. Accordingly, Lee was held subject to the tax to the same extent as all other employers.

CHAPTER 2

Aid to Religious Schools

AID: MANDATED, PERMISSIBLE, OR FORBIDDEN?

No decisions handed down by the Burger Court have divided the Catholic church from the non-Catholic community as those relating to abortion (treated more fully in Chapter 8) and aid to parochial schools and none have, until recently, so sorely disappointed the church. This does not mean that there are not a substantial number of American Catholics who disagree with their church on either or both of these issues and probably for the same reason. Catholics, no less than other Americans, are taxpayers, and financing parochial schools, to which most do not send children, and the upkeep, at least until they become self-supporting, of the unwanted children of poor women, can be achieved only by increasing taxes.

Yet, on the whole, with the exception of Jews with respect to Israel and to religious instruction or practices in the public schools, there are few political issues among the major religious groups in which there is a greater degree of cohesion between clergy and faithful than school aid and abortion. Concerning school aid, the subject of this chapter, what is probably the most realistic study of Catholic school enrollments (Andrew M. Greeley, William C. McReady, and Kathleen McCourt, *Catholic Schools in a Declining Church* [1976], p. 37) reports that ninety percent of American Catholics favor the continuation of Catholic schools. It can hardly be doubted that were tax-raised funds available to pay tuition costs, the percentage of Catholic parents electing to send their children to these schools would be substantially higher than it is today and their commitment to government aid would be even more widespread than it is now.

Catholics are not the only Americans who send their children to nonpublic religious schools, nor do only they urge government financing of those schools. Missouri Lutherans, Mormons, and Orthodox Jews, among others, take the same position. At the present time the rising number of Protestant fundamentalists who withdraw their children from public schools because they do not think them sufficiently Christian most often demand only exemption from taxation but, as the history of other religious groups indicates, it may be only a matter of time before they too will call for general, or at least substantial, government financial support for their schools. Finally, some protagonists of government aid are to be found among proprietors of nonreligious private schools catering to high-income families who have no difficulty meeting tuition costs. Thus, in the 1973 case of *Levitt v. Committee for Public Education and Religious Liberty (PEARL) (Levitt I)*, one of the aid-to-religious-schools cases, Horace Mann-Barnard School (nonsectarian), Long Island Lutheran School, Long Island Lutheran High School, St. Michael School (Catholic), and Yeshivah Rambam (Orthodox Jewish) were granted permission to intervene jointly in support of the challenged statute. It should be noted, however, that according to its president, the National Association of Independent Schools, a group of about one thousand private elementary and secondary schools, opposes tuition tax credits "as they have been proposed by the Reagan Administration" (*New York Times*, March 2, 1984).

There is no constitutional difficulty, at least none under the Establishment Clause, in tax aid to nonreligious private schools. For that reason, and the political reality that a measure so limited has practically no chance of being enacted, protagonists of aid to religious schools and legislators favoring such aid to schools uniformly use the terms "nonpublic" and "private" rather than "parochial," "religious," or "church-related," this notwithstanding the fact that probably as many as ninety-five percent of nonpublic schools are religious schools. (This apparently results in something like a small-sized tail wagging a very large dog.)

Another complicating aspect is to be found in the fact that too often parents are taking their children out of public schools or initially sending them to religious schools not so much that they fear God but that they fear blacks even more. (This helps to explain why Senator Jesse Helms from North Carolina, a state with a substantial Protestant majority, should so strongly favor aid to religious schools far beyond amounts necessary to finance the cost of transportation or secular textbooks. His strong opposition to busing as a means to effect racial integration in public schools undoubtedly embarrassed Catholic church leaders, who by a high percentage are liberal in their positions relating to racial, economic, and nuclear disarmament problems.)

Resorting to religion as a means of maintaining racial segregation is hardly new. In 1969, the United States Department of Justice did something that President Reagan would probably not now dream of allowing it to do; it brought suit for a judgment ordering racial integration in Waterbury, Connecticut. It charged among other things that "white children who reside in public school districts where substantial numbers of Negro and Puerto Rican children also reside have been transported by the City of Waterbury from such public school districts to all white or predominantly white independent non-public schools. Those schools, to a substantial extent, shared facilities with public schools which commonly are located adjacent to or near the respective independent non-public schools. This practice has resulted in certain public elementary schools becoming and remaining predominantly Negro and Puerto Rican." (The *New York Times* of March 5, 1984, reported that the Justice Department had gone to court not to enforce but to declare unlawful action by the City of Birmingham, Alabama, under a decree that the Justice Department itself had signed three years earlier to help blacks and women win promotions in the city's health and fire departments.)

In 1967, the United States Commission on Civil Rights reported that in St. Louis forty percent of the total white elementary school population attended nonpublic schools; in Boston it was forty-one percent and in Philadelphia more than sixty percent. In Detroit, according to a *New York Times* report of December 19, 1970, two-thirds of the children in the public schools were black, and similar statistics were applicable in other large cities. It is more than probable that the public-to-religious school exodus has increased since these statistics were gathered.

It is not within the purview of this book to consider and certainly not to pass judgment on the ethical or moral implications of parental transfer of children from public schools to religious schools in order to escape expected deteriorating teaching standards and even physical violence as the result of the influx of blacks and Hispanic-American pupils in public schools. The scope of this book extends only to the constitutionality and public policy of utilizing tax-raised funds to support the exodus of white pupils in search of a haven in religious schools.

The *Walz, Diffenderfer,* and *Bob Jones University* cases, discussed in the preceding chapter, all related to aid for religion through exemption from taxation. Helpful as it may be, the plea of the religious schools is that this is not enough. In earlier years birth rates among Catholics were considerably higher than among non-Catholics and teaching personnel consisted largely of sons and daughters who, given by the parents to the church, received no monetary compensation beyond their sustenance. Despite this, the cost of maintaining an educational system from kindergarten through medical and law school was, according to many church spokesmen, too heavy a burden to be borne by the Catholic community without government assistance. In more recent years, with the birth rate among Catholics not substantially higher, if higher at all, than among non-Catholics, many parochial schools cannot survive without employing lay teachers who have families and are dependent upon their salaries to maintain them.

Salaries, not only in Catholic but also in Jewish and Protestant evangelical schools, such as the two involved in the *Bob Jones University* case, have been uniformly lower than in public educational institutions at all levels—elementary, secondary, and college. As a result, faculties began to form unions for collective bargaining, only to be substantially frustrated by two Supreme Court decisions—*National Labor Relations Board (NLRB) v. Catholic Bishop of Chicago* (1979) and *NLRB v. Yeshiva University* (1980)—holding that teachers in religious schools were not within the scope of the National Labor Relations Act. These decisions did not affect the right of religious school faculties to strike for higher salaries, or forbid them from seeking employment in tax-supported institutions if religious schools could not offer substantially comparable salaries. The result was the intensification of church demands for governmental aid.

While salaries constitute the major school expense, they are by no means the only one. Costs of textbooks and other necessary educational school supplies, costs of maintaining the buildings and keeping them safe and sanitary through necessary repairs and cleaning, supplying some meals to pupils, furnishing medical and dental assistance, and transportation to and from the schools are expenditures that normally have to be met by either the schools or the parents of pupils attending them. The inevitable consequence of increasing costs threatening the survival of religious schools, coupled with growing Catholic political power manifested in part by the election of a Catholic to the presidency in 1960, resulted in the enactment by Congress of two aid laws. The first of these was the Higher Education Facilities Act of 1963 (to be considered later in this chapter), which provided funds for private colleges and universities; the second, two years later, was the Elementary and Secondary Education Act of 1965, providing similar relief for pre-college schools.

The case for state financing has been based on both constitutional command and simple justice. In regard to the former, the argument goes something like this: Every state has a compulsory school attendance law requiring parents to send their children at least to elementary school. In the case of *Pierce v. Society of Sisters* (1925) the Supreme Court ruled unconstitutional a law that required all schools to be public. If, said the

Court, a nonpublic school (secular or religious) provided the same basic elementary education as the public schools, the states had to accept the parents' choice. Otherwise, the parents would be denied the due process of law, since, the Court said, the "child is not the mere creature of the State; those who nurture him and direct his destiny have the right, coupled with the high duty, to recognize and prepare him for additional obligations."

On its face, this seems to mean no more than that parents have the right to send their children to nonpublic schools, including parochial schools such as those maintained by the Society of Sisters. This is fine for parents who can afford to pay tuition in those schools but it has no practical meaning for the majority who do not; these have no choice but to send their children to tuition-free public schools. Proponents of aid have consistently argued that this violates the First Amendment's guarantee of religious freedom (since religious conscience impels them to send their children to schools in which both religious and nonreligious subjects are taught) and the only way to avoid the violation is to make it economically feasible for the parents to enjoy their constitutional rights by providing financial aid.

It should be noted that acceptance of the position would not merely permit aid but require it. Moreover, except for deductions relating to the cost of teaching religious subjects, the Fourteenth Amendment guarantee of the equal protection of laws also requires rather than merely permits government financing of parochial schools to the same extent as public schools. These claims have on occasion been made to the Supreme Court but have, until now, been uniformly rejected. Indeed, the Supreme Court went even further. In *Luetkemeyer v. Kaufman* (1974) it affirmed, without opinion, a lower court decision holding it constitutional for a state to exclude parochial schools from its program of financing bus transportation. The lower court had based its decision on the right of states to maintain "a very high wall between church and state"—that is, one even higher than required by the Establishment Clause—and the Supreme Court accepted this as a valid ground for its exclusionary policy.

(The dissenting opinion by Byron R. White, joined by Burger, found the ruling to be inconsistent with the Court's opinion in *Everson*, which justified state-funded bus transportation to parochial schools on the ground that its secular purpose was to protect children from traffic dangers. As will be seen, it is probable that a later majority of the Court indicated unhappiness with the *Everson* decision and refused to extend it beyond its original limits. This may help explain its ruling in the *Luetkemeyer* case.)

Regarding general financing of parochial school operations, the principal ground for exclusion is predicated upon the premise that what is secular and what is religious are so intertwined in education that government financing of only the former is as a practical matter impossible, and the entanglement of religion and state is forbidden by the Establishment Clause. But this response, advocates of aid assert, is not logical, since the Supreme Court has ruled that disentanglement is feasible at the college level and government financing of teaching secular courses is therefore permissible. Under the Equal Protection Clause, moreover, permissibility would not be enough; full funding of instruction in secular subjects would be mandatory. The Court has not gone that far, although its decision in *Mueller v. Allen* (1983), discussed further in this chapter, might portend that it will.

In addition to that claimed constitutional right, the ethics of fairness, it is urged, require governmental funding. Public schools are financed through taxation imposed on parents who elect to send their children to nonpublic schools. They are thus subjected to double taxation: once by law and once by conscience. This, the argument goes, hardly conforms to the standard of simple justice.

There is apparent cogency to this double taxation argument, but it presents its own difficulties. Christian Scientists, Jehovah's Witnesses, and others, will not, for reasons of religious conscience, avail themselves of some or all of the services rendered in municipal hospitals or drink tax-financed fluoridated water. Notwithstanding this, they must pay taxes, part of which finance these services. Moreover, unmarried people and couples who are childless are not for that reason exempt from paying school taxes; nor are the Amish, whose faith forbids use of automobiles, exempt from paying taxes, part of which goes to maintain speedways; nor are Quakers exempt from paying taxes, a substantial portion of which goes to finance armaments. The reason for this, one applicable equally to education, lies in the assumption that the community as a whole is benefitted by these services and therefore everyone must pay for them so long as they are available to everyone.

These last three words indicate another difficulty with the double taxation argument. The *Pierce* decision, as it has been construed in later cases, stands for the proposition that parochial schools have the constitutional right to admit or refuse admission to applicants as they see fit. They can reject pupils who are not of the right religion or whose performance or intelligence quotas are below the parochial school's admission standards, and can return admitted pupils to the public schools if they do not perform satisfactorily or if they become discipline problems. Public schools do no have these options; they must admit all applicants regardless of race, religion, and educational competence and, with rare exceptions, keep them irrespective of their school behavior or unsatisfactory scholastic performance. Fairness would seem to dictate that parents whose children are excluded from schools should not be required to support them through taxation.

Finally, another aspect of fairness would seem to dictate exclusion of religious schools as recipients of tax-raised funds. Public schools are subject to public control. If the voters in a school district are dissatisfied with the policies or performance of a local school board, they have the power to vote them out at the next election but they have no such power over those who control and manage religious schools. Our forefathers fought the Revolutionary War because they deemed taxation without representation to be tyranny. To be taxed without having a voice in selecting those who are to use the resulting funds is not consistent with democratic principles.

These comments relate to tax support of religious schools but they are to some extent applicable to nonreligious private schools. There is no Establishment Clause barrier to allocation to the latter of funds raised by taxation of parents whose children are excluded from them for any reason or for no reason at all, nor does the general public participate in the selection of their management personnel. Simple justice would seem to dictate that all nonpublic schools should be treated alike; if some are denied tax-raised funds or if some are granted these funds, so should all others. As has been seen in the preceding chapter, President Reagan, in the first stage of the *Bob Jones University* case, agreed with this claim to the extent that it applied to tax exemptions but the Supreme Court did not. Established public policy, the Court held, does not merely authorize but requires that tax-exempt status be denied to colleges barring nonwhites from admission. So potent is this policy that it requires application to schools whose racial exclusionary rule is based upon sincerely held religious beliefs

It is obvious that if tax exemption violates public policy, out-and-out government financing certainly does. That public policy, however, has its limits. It obviously does not apply where nonadmittance is based exclusively on difference in religion rather than color, as where a parochial school will admit a black Catholic but not a black Protestant or Jew. Here, it is the First Amendment that defines what is the national public policy, and the balance of this chapter is devoted to an examination of how far this constitutionally mandated public policy extends.

ELEMENTARY AND SECONDARY SCHOOLS—PRE-LEMON

The major pre-Burger Supreme Court decision involving government aid to parochial schools was the 1947 bus transportation case of *Everson v. Board of Education*. That, however, was not the first time that the pre-Burger Court was faced by a challenge to the grant of tax-raised funds to aid religious institutions. As early as 1899 it rejected, in the case of *Bradfield v. Roberts*, a taxpayer's suit challenging the payment of federal funds for the construction of a hospital in the District of Columbia that was to be operated by a corporation formed by members of the Catholic Sisters of Charity. The Court held that, since the beneficiary of the grant was a corporation that was a nonreligious entity separate and apart from the Sisters who were its shareholders, there was no violation of the Establishment Clause.

Nine years later, in *Quick Bear v. Leupp*, the Court invoked exactly the opposite reasoning to achieve the same result of constitutionality. It ruled there that "treaty" money paid to Indians in compenstion for land taken from them but held in trust for them by the federal government could, at their designation, be disbursed to private religious schools to pay the cost of their children's education. The reason for this, said the Court, was that the Indians, not the government, were the real owners of the land. (In the *Bradfield* case it ruled that the corporation, and not the Sisters, was the real owner of the hospital.)

In *Cochran v. Louisiana State Board of Education*, the Court rejected a challenge to a law that included parochial schools in a program for free distribution of secular textbooks. The case was decided before the Court, in *Everson v. Board of Education*, ruled that not only the federal government but the states as well could make no law respecting an establishment of religion. Hence, the challenge was based upon the claim that the statute violated the provision in the Fourteenth Amendment forbidding states from depriving persons of property without due process of law. It was rejected on the ground that the beneficiaries of the statute were not the churches but the children who attended their schools (a concept later called the "child benefit" theory).

> One may scan the acts in vain [said the Court] to ascertain where any money is appropriated for the purchase of school books for the use of any church, private, sectarian or even public school. The appropriations were made for the specific purpose of purchasing school books for the use of the school children of the state, free of cost to them. It was for their benefit and the resulting benefit to the state that its appropriations were made. True,

these children attend some school, public or private, the latter, sectarian or non-sectarian, and that the books are to be furnished them for their use, free of cost, whichever they attend. The schools, however, are not the beneficiaries of these appropriations. They obtain nothing from them, nor are they relieved of a single obligation, because of them. The school children and the state alone are the beneficiaries. It is also true that the sectarian schools, which some of the children attend, instruct their pupils in religion, and books are used for that purpose, but one may search diligently the acts, though without result, in an effort to find anything to the effect that it is the purpose of the state to furnish religious books for the use of such children. . . . What the statutes contemplate is that the same books that are furnished children attending public schools shall be furnished children attending private schools. This is the only practical way of interpreting and executing the statutes, and this is what the state board of education is doing. Among these books, naturally, none is to be expected, adapted to religious instruction. The [Louisiana] Court also stated, although the point is not of importance in relation to the Federal question, that it was "only the use of the books that is granted to the children, or, in other words, the books are lent to them."

The last sentence requires some explanation. The Louisiana court, in upholding the statute, ruled that the law did not violate the state constitution because the books were not given to the pupils but only loaned to them. Chief Justice Charles E. Hughes, who wrote the *Cochran* opinion, said that the federal Constitution would even have allowed giving the books to the pupils.

In the *Everson* case the Court upheld the validity of a New Jersey law providing reimbursement to parents for money spent by them for bus transportation to either public or parochial schools. This, Black said in his opinion for the Court's majority, did not constitute financial support of the parochial schools, which of course would violate the Establishment Clause. Rather it was analogous to use of tax-raised funds to provide police and fire protection for the benefit of children attending the schools. True enough, many parents might be reluctant to send their children to parochial schools if transportation services were not available, but the First Amendment was not intended to make it more difficult for parents to send their children to parochial than to public schools. The amendment commands that the state be neutral, not that it be an adversary of religious parents. "State power," he concluded, "is no more to be used so as to handicap religions, than as to favor them."

The clear implication of this is that a law denying bus transportation for parochial school pupils while granting it to those attending public schools would violate at least three constitutional prohibitions: it would prefer nonbelievers in public schools over believers in parochial schools, thereby violating the neutrality mandate implicit in the Establishment Clause; it would make attendance at parochial schools economically impossible to children of low-income parents whose religious conscience impelled such attendance and, in clear violation of the Free Exercise Clause, would at the same time punish them for nonattendance; and, finally, funding only transportation to public schools would deny to parents of parochial school pupils the equal protection of the laws guaranteed by the Fourteenth Amendment.

Lest it be assumed that the *Everson* decision pleased only Catholic parents, it should be noted that it applied no less to Orthodox Jews, Missouri Lutherans, and later, other Protestant fundamentalists who by force of conscience sent their children to religious schools. And even more pleasing to protagonists of aid to parochial schools was the Court's 1968 decision in *Board of Education v. Allen*. There it ruled that the Establishment Clause was not violated by a New York law requiring public authorities to lend textbooks free of charge to students in all elementary and high schools, including those that were church related. On the authority of the *Everson* decision, White's opinion for the majority upheld the validity of the statute on the ground that its primary beneficiaries were not the schools but the children who attended them.

In his opinion White emphasized that the books were only loaned, not given to the pupils, this though in the *Cochran* case Hughes noted that since the books were secular, the federal Constitution would not have been violated even if the books were given to them.

Logic would appear to be on Hughes's side. If the beneficiaries of the law were the schools, it would not matter if the transaction was a gift or a loan; in either case the law would be unconstitutional, since loans constitute impermissible aid to religion. However, realistically it did not matter how the transaction might be characterized, whether gift or loan, since the books were kept in the possession of the schools until they were no longer usable, at which time new books were sent in. (One is reminded of the response by Shakespeare's Titus to Coriolanus, who had lost his horse in a wager and sought to buy it back: "No, I'll never sell nor give him; lend him to you I will, for half a hundred years.") If, on the other hand, the pupils were the beneficiaries of the transaction, whether gift like the nonreturnable bus rides in the *Everson* case, or only a loan, there would be no violation of the Establishment Clause.

While the issue before the Court related only to the loan of secular textbooks to pupils, White's accolade to private schools (almost all of which are church related) could hardly have been warmer.

. . . [P]rivate education [he said] has played and is playing a significant and valuable role in raising national levels of knowledge, competence and experience. Americans care about the quality of the secular education available to their children. They have considered high quality education to be an indispensable ingredient for achieving the kind of nation, and the kind of citizenry, that they have desired to create. Considering this attitude, the continued willingness to rely on private school systems, including parochial systems, strongly suggests that a wider segment of informed opinion, legislative and otherwise has found that those schools do an acceptable job of providing secular education to their students. . . .

Black (as well as Douglas and Abe Fortas) dissented. Yet if one took seriously his assertion in the *Everson* case that under the First and Fourteenth amendments state power could not be used to handicap religions any more than favor them, his opinion there could only mean that aid to religious schools was not merely permissible but mandatory, and that its refusal would violate the constitutional rights of parents who by reason of conscience send their children to religious schools. Despite this, the Court, without dissent by White, has consistently refused to hold that if textbooks or transportation services were made available to public school pupils they had to be equally available to those attending nonpublic schools.

An aftermath of the *Allen* decision was the formation of the New York Committee for Public Education and Religious Liberty (PEARL). White's praise of the parochial school system was to many legislatures an invitation to enact laws financing parochial school operations beyond merely the cost of secular textbooks. Understandably, the Catholic church with the support and cooperation of Orthodox Jewry exerted and continue to exert pressure upon reluctant legislators to enact such laws.

PEARL was formed to counteract these pressures in legislatures and courts. Its activities in the judicial arena are manifested by both instituting and conducting lawsuits challenging aid to parochial schools (and also intrusion of religion in public schools) and submitting *amicus curiae* briefs in cases brought by others.

PEARL's constituents are: American Ethical Union; Americans for Democratic Action; Americans for Public Schools; American Jewish Committee, New York Chapter; American Jewish Congress; A. Philip Randolph Institute; Association of Reform Rabbis of New York City and Vicinity; B'nai B'rith; Bronx Park Community; Citizens Union of the City of New York; City Club of New York; Community Church of New York; Community Service Society, Department of Public Affairs; Council of Churches of the City of New York; Episcopal Diocese of Long Island,

Department of Christian Social Relations; Humanist Society of Greater New York; Jewish Reconstructionist Foundation; Jewish War Veterans, New York Department; League for Industrial Democracy, New York City Chapter; National Council of Jewish Women; National Women's Conference of The American Ethical Union; New York Civil Liberties Union; New York Federation of Reform Synagogues; New York Jewish Labor Committee; New York Society for Ethical Culture; New York State Americans United for Separation of Church and State; New York State Council of Churches; State Congress of Parents and Teachers, New York City District; Union of American Hebrew Congregations, New York State Council; Unitarian-Universalist Ministers Association of Metropolitan New York; United Community Centers; United Federation of Teachers; United Parents Association; United Synagogue of America, New York Metropolitan Region; Women's City Club of New York; and Workmen's Circle, New York Division.

ELEMENTARY AND SECONDARY SCHOOLS—
FROM *LEMON* TO THE PRESENT

Such was the situation when in 1969 Burger was appointed Chief Justice. Five times the Court had faced the issue of government aid to religious institutions and five times aid won. Burger made the score six to zero when, in the *Walz* case, he wrote the Court's opinion upholding tax exemption accorded to these institutions. Ironically, however, it was Burger who also wrote the Court's 1971 joint opinion in *Lemon v. Kurtzman* and *Earley v. DiCenso* that brought to an end the shut-out record of those who championed aid to religious schools. It is a fair guess that, although he never admitted it, in his heart of hearts he later rued what he had done; his almost consistent dissents in later cases invalidating various measures aimed at aiding religious schools and his concurring votes in still later cases upholding them testify to this.

When handed down, the *Lemon-DiCenso* decision appeared to be a landmark in the history of church-state relations in the United States. The Rhode Island Salary Supplement Act, challenged in the *DiCenso* case, rested upon a legislative finding that the quality of education in "non-public" (meaning "religious") elementary schools had been jeopardized by the rapidly rising salaries needed to attract competent and dedicated teachers. Accordingly, the act authorized state officials to supplement the salaries of teachers of secular subjects in these schools by paying them fifteen percent of their current annual salary, provided that the average per pupil expenditure was below the average in public schools. (The obvious purpose of this provision was to exclude upper-income nonreligious preparatory schools.) The statute required eligible teachers to teach only courses offered in the public schools, to use only teaching materials used there, and to agree in writing not to teach a course in religion for as long as they received any salary supplements.

The Pennsylvania law in *Lemon v. Kurtzman* (1971) case authorized the state superintendent to "purchase" specified "secular educational services" from nonpublic schools under "contracts" providing for reimbursement by the state of the actual expenditures for teachers' salaries, textbooks, and instructional materials. Reimbursement was limited to courses in the "secular" subjects of mathematics, modern foreign languages, physical science, and physical education.

Evidence at the trial in the Rhode Island case showed that the church schools involved in the program were located close to parishes, thereby permitting convenient access for religious exercises since instruction in faith and morals was part of the schools' total educational process. The school buildings contained identifying religious symbols such as crosses, crucifixes, religious paintings, and statues either in the classrooms or hallways. Although only thirty minutes a day were devoted to direct religious instruction, approximately two-thirds of the teachers were nuns of various religious orders.

In the Pennsylvania case there was no trial record; the judge in the lower court simply dismissed the complaint because, in effect, he found the law to be so clearly constitutional that he considered it a waste of time and taxpayers' money to hold a trial. The Supreme Court waited until the last day of its 1970-1971 term before handing down its decision. Burger decided that one opinion should be written to cover both the *Lemon* and *DiCenso* cases, and appointed himself to write it.

The decision was a shock, as if the world of aid on the elementary and secondary school levels had come to an end not with a whimper but with a great big bang; or as if a pitcher who did not allow a run through the first half of the ninth inning (*Walz v. Tax Commission*) turned around and, batting for the other side, hit the home run (*Lemon-DiCenso*) that ended the game in the bottom of the ninth. What was surprising about the *Lemon* opinion was not White's partial dissent—his opinion in the *Allen* case made this almost inevitable—but rather that the Court's opinion should be written by the conservative Burger and concurred with by all the other members of the Court, including Rehnquist, the most conservative of them all. White's rather perplexing footnote 2 in his opinion has been considered in the Introduction to this book.

As has been noted, in the *Everson* case the Court had used the "aid" test, that is, a law violated the Establishment Clause if it aided religion. Beginning with the Sunday closing law case (*McGowan v. Maryland*) in 1961, the Court also suggested what later became known as the "purpose-effect" test, that is, a law violated the clause if its purpose was either to advance (or, later, to inhibit) religion, or if that was its primary effect. In the *Walz* decision, the Court added a third dimension to the purpose-effect test: a law violated the clause if it fostered excessive government entanglement with religion.

Burger found no constitutional difference between the Rhode Island law, which authorized payment to the parochial school teachers, and the Pennnsylvania statute under which the purchase price for the secular educational services was paid to the school; in both cases, the laws were challenged as being in violation of the "purpose-effect-entanglement" test and thus unconstitutional under the Establishment Clause.

Not so, said Burger, in regard to the purpose facet. There is no basis for the claim that the legislative intent was to advance religion. On the contrary, the statutes themselves clearly stated that they were intended to enhance the quality of *secular* education in all schools covered by compulsory attendance laws. There was, he continued, no need to decide whether either the Pennsylvania or Rhode Island law violated the effect aspect since both contravened the entanglement prohibition and hence were no less unconstitutional. What this means is that there is no need to put another bullet in a dead body, or to return to the baseball analogy, in a game in which the score is tied and the bases are full in the second half of the ninth inning, it makes no difference whether the batter hits a single (entanglement) or a triple (purpose-effect-entanglement).

If so, why did Burger bother to rule that the laws did not violate the purpose test? Perhaps it was an attempt to appease White, the author of the *Allen* decision, for Burger expressly cited it in support of his finding that there was no unconstitutionality in the purpose aspect. If that was what he intended, the effort was fruitless. White still filed a dissenting opinion even though none of his colleagues joined him in it. Nonetheless, in all succeeding cases involving aid to religious schools, the Court and all the justices thereof were able, on the authority of the *Lemon-DiCenso* opinion, to find a permissible secular purpose.

This was not so in cases other than those challenging financial aid to religious schools. In *Abington School District v. Schempp* (1963), for example, the Court held unconstitutional the daily reading of Bible verses and the Lord's Prayer in public schools, despite the school district's assertion of such secular purposes as "the promotion of moral values, the contradiction to the materialistic trends of our times, the perpetuation of our institutions and the teaching of literature."

The Rhode Island and Pennsylvania measures, said Burger in the *Lemon-DiCenso* opinion, failed the entanglement test because both required continuing state surveillance to assure that a teacher under religious control and discipline did not wander into the forbidden territory of teaching religion. The test was further violated by the provision in the statute requiring state officials to inspect school records in order to determine what part of the expenditures was attributable to secular as opposed to impermissible religious instruction.

What is meant, at least as pro-aid advocates saw it, was that religious school authorities were faced with a Hobson's choice of being damned if school officials were allowed to use state funds to finance religious instruction and equally damned if surveillance was necessary to assure that they did not. The answer may well be that this is exactly what was intended by the framers of the Establishment Clause, particularly James Madison, its principal draftsman. They did not want tax-raised funds to be used for religious instruction, nor did they want the government to intrude into the religious domain and pass judgment on how churches spend their own money. It was, Burger had said in the *Walz* case, this prevention of incursion into church affairs that justifies tax exemption and, conversely, also forbids subsidization.

Burger added another facet of entanglement in his *Lemon-DiCenso* opinion. Ordinarily, he said, political debate and division, however vigorous or even partisan, are normal and healthy manifestations of our democratic system of government, but political division along religious lines was one of the principal evils against which the First Amendment was intended to protect. Religious conflict is a threat to the normal political process and its avoidance is a factor to be considered in determining constitutional validity of government financing of religious schools. (Practically all the major Supreme Court decisions relating to abortion, aid to religious schools, religion in public schools, crèches and crosses on public property, and cultism, among others, testify to the accuracy of Burger's statement. Alas, Supreme Court decisions seeking to avoid such religious conflict have not proven successful.)

Burger concluded his opinion with an attempt to appease all protagonists of aid as he may have sought to appease White. Nothing in his opinion, he said, should be construed to disparage the role of church-related elementary and secondary schools in our national life. Their contributions were and are enormous and their economic plight in a period of rising costs and expanding need could not be ignored. Nonetheless, the

Constitution decrees that religion must be a private matter for the family and the institutions of private choice and, while some involvement and entanglement were inevitable, lines must be drawn (obviously, though he did not expressly say so) by the Court.

On the last day of its term in June 1973 the Court decided three cases involving aid to religious schools at the elementary and secondary levels. (*Hunt v. McNair*, also decided on that day, involved aid at the college level and will be discussed later in this chapter.) In two of them, *Levitt v. Committee for Public Education and Religious Liberty* and *Sloan v. Lemon*, Burger and Rehnquist remained loyal to the majority that decided the *Lemon-DiCenso* cases; in the third and most important of them, *Committee for Public Education and Religious Liberty v. Nyquist*, they broke off and joined White to form a minority for the next decade until it became a majority when Lewis F. Powell deserted and Reagan appointed Sandra Day O'Connor to the bench to replace Stewart.

In the *Nyquist* case the Court handed down a decision holding invalid under the Establishment Clause a New York law providing financial assistance to nonpublic (in almost all cases, religious) elementary and secondary schools. The purpose of the law, enacted by the New York legislature a year after the *Lemon-DiCenso* decision was handed down, was to provide financial aid to parents with middle or low incomes who sent their children to nonpublic schools. Somehow or other seven of these parents were able to retain one of the highest priced law firms in the nation (Davis, Polk and Wardell) to intervene in the suit against the state commissioner of education and, through Porter R. Chandler, a senior partner, to defend the constitutionality of the law. (The firm was also involved in the *Levitt* case, where it did not represent parents but the Catholic schools themselves.)

The challenged statute set forth three financial aid programs for these parents and the schools their children attended. The first provided for direct money grants to the school to be used for the maintenance and repair of the buildings, such as furnishing heat, light, water, janitorial, and other services necessary for the upkeep of the school buildings. The second provided partial tuition reimbursement to parents in the lowest income category (i.e., earning less than five thousand dollars of taxable income and therefore not required to pay taxes), and the third granted partial relief in the form of tax benefits to parents who earned up to twenty-five thousand dollars and did pay taxes.

The Court, in Powell's opinion for the majority, held all three parts of the law to be unconstitutional, notwithstanding the declaration in the statute that the assistance granted was "clearly secular, neutral and non-ideological" (did anyone expect it to say that it was not?), an assertion usually made in lawyers' briefs and courts' decisions rather than in the statutes themselves.

In its opinion the Court adopted, and thereafter often cited, a profile of sectarian nonpublic schools first suggested by counsel for the Committee for Public Education and Religious Liberty in its complaint. These schools were ones that (1) imposed religious restrictions on admissions; (2) required attendance of pupils at religious activities; (3) required obedience by students to the doctrines and dogmas of a particular faith; (4) required pupils to attend instruction in the theology or doctrine of a particular faith; (5) were an integral part of the religious mission of the church sponsoring it; (6) had as a substantial purpose the inculcation of religious values; (7) imposed religious restrictions on faculty appointments; and (8) imposed religious restrictions on what or how the faculty taught. (The brief argued that the presence of any one of these factors required an adjudication of unconstitutionality.)

As was to be expected, the Court had no difficulty in finding that the challenged statute had the requisite secular legislative purpose. It did, however, rule that it violated both the effect and entanglement aspects of the test for constitutionality, although most of its opinion dealt with the former. With respect to the "maintenance and repair" provision, the Court noted that no attempt was made to restrict payments to expenditures related to the upkeep of facilities used exclusively for secular purposes nor, it added, could it do so within the context of religiously oriented institutions. Thus nothing in the statute barred qualifying schools from paying out of state funds the salaries of employees who maintained the school chapel or the cost of repairing, heating, and lighting classrooms in which religion was taught.

The tuition reimbursement plan likewise failed the "effect" test even though the grants were to be made to parents rather than to the schools. In the absence of practicable means to guarantee that the state aid would be used exclusively for secular purposes, it did not matter whether the funds were paid directly to the schools or indirectly to them through payments to the parents. Nor, said the Court, did it matter that the monies were paid before a school year began and were thus a subsidy, or afterwards when it could be labelled a reimbursement; the substantive impact was the same in both cases.

Finally, the Court said, the "effect" mandate was violated by whatever name the income tax benefit was labelled, whether a tax "credit," a "modification," or a "deduction." However called, it was not constitutionally different from the tuition grants accorded to low-income parents.

To support their claim, the parents had placed their strongest reliance upon the *Walz* decision but, said Powell, not only did that case fail to support their position, but it compelled an opposite conclusion. Among other reasons, he said, was the fact that the *Walz* decision was based on the premise that nonexemption would effect entanglement between church and state, whereas the challenged aid law tended to increase rather than eliminate it. Burger, who as author of the *Walz* opinion should have known what it meant or at least was intended to mean, did not agree; to him the opinion led to a determination of constitutionality.

A footnote, numbered 49, in the *Nyquist* opinion was later to haunt William J. Brennan, Thurgood Marshall, Harry A. Blackmun, and John Paul Stevens, all of whom concurred with Powell's opinion. It read:

> Since the program here does not have the elements of a genuine tax deduction, such as for charitable contributions, we do not have before us, and do not decide whether that form of tax benefit is constitutionally acceptable under the "neutrality" test in *Walz*.

As we shall see, that question was answered ten years later in Rehnquist's majority opinion in *Mueller v. Allen*, but in a way that did not make these four justices happy.

The *Nyquist* decision was based on the "effect" aspect and it was not necessary, said Powell, to decide the entanglement issue upon which the *Lemon* decision had been based. Nevertheless, he could not resist the temptation to cite the part of Burger's opinion that brought political entanglement into the constitutionality test. Political strife over religion, said Powell, was an evil the entanglement ban sought to prevent not only in a *Lemon* but also in a *Nyquist* type situation.

Rehnquist, with the concurrence of White and Burger, dissented on the ground that the *Walz* opinion required a directly opposite result.

> Here [said Rehnquist] the effect of the tax benefit is trebly attenuated as compared with the outright exemption considered in *Walz*. There the result was a complete forgiveness of taxes, while here the result is merely a reduction in taxes. There the ultimate benefit was available to an actual house of worship, while here even the ultimate benefit redounds only to a religiously sponsored school. There the churches themselves received the direct reduction in the tax bill, while here it is only the parents of the children who are sent to religiously sponsored schools who receive the direct benefit.

Sloan v. Lemon involved a Pennsylvania statute providing funds to reimburse parents for a portion of tuition expenses incurred in sending their children to nonpublic schools. Again over the dissents of Burger, White, and Rehnquist, the Court, in an opinion by Powell, ruled the statute unconstitutional for the same reasons that it invalidated the New York law in the *Nyquist* case.

(Although not mentioned, the Pennsylvania law did have one redeeming feature not possessed by the New York law: the money to fund the program was derived not from the state's general treasury but from a portion of the revenues from the state's tax on cigarette sales. It must be assumed that Lemon, who brought the suit, was a cigarette smoker; otherwise he would not have been affected by the law and would thus have no standing to sue. It is possible—though, alas, not probable—that had the Court upheld the law it would have increased the price of cigarettes and might have accomplished what warnings against smoking being injurious to one's health could not, that is, to impel Lemon and all other smokers to kick the habit [and thus add to their life expectancy]. Not that this would bring the constitutional controversy to an end, since it is almost a certainty that the church would have been able to persuade the legislature to find another source for the funds, perhaps a tax on talcum powder or children's cereal, products which could not be injurious to their health.)

At issue in the *Levitt* case was an appropriation by the New York legislature of twenty-eight million dollars to reimburse nonpublic elementary and secondary schools for expenses incurred in conducting tests and examinations and reporting the results to the state educational authorities. The tests, involving only secular subjects, were of two types: those that were state-prepared for use in all schools and the other traditional teacher-prepared tests, which were the type most often used in the majority of public and nonpublic schools.

For performing these services the schools were allotted twenty-seven dollars for each elementary school pupil and forty-five dollars for each student in secondary schools. Apparently these figures were reached as the result of common everyday political lobbying by the religious groups. The governor and legislative leaders decided that twenty-eight million dollars could be spared from the annual budget to meet the demands of the religious groups. Representatives of the budget and education departments and the governor's legal staff were then called in to figure out how this sum could be divided among the nonpublic schools, and the twenty-seven and forty-five dollar figures were reached as reasonable amounts. It did not matter whether a pupil was in the first or sixth grade, or whether a particular teacher gave tests one or one hundred times a semester. The unacknowledged reality was that the purpose and primary effect of the legislation was to appropriate twenty-eight million dollars for the support of religious schools.

In an opinion by Burger, from which White but not Rehnquist dissented, the Court declared the law unconstitutional. Testing, Burger said, was an integral part of the total teaching process and there was no practicable way of assuring that even with the best of good faith a teacher would be able to avoid using tests to further the religious purposes of the school in which he or she teaches.

Viewed objectively, it is difficult to quarrel with this conclusion. It is a rare teacher in a Catholic school who would give a passing grade for an answer in an examination that denied the divinity of Jesus, one in a Jewish school that asserted his divinity, or one in a fundamentalist Protestant school that rejected creationism. Yet, as will be seen later, the Court, in *Committee for Public Education and Religious Liberty v. Regan*, was to hold such an outcome entirely constitutional.

In 1975, two years after the *Nyquist* ruling, the Court decided the Pennsylvania case of *Meek v. Pittenger*. The Pennsylvania law challenged in the *Meek* case was patterned closely after the Elementary and Secondary Education Act of 1965 and its purpose was to supplement the funds available to the state under that law. The historic background of the federal statute and its constitutionality are presented in the next section of this chapter. Here it is sufficient to note that the purpose of the Pennsylvania law was to supplement the funds available to the state under the federal act.

The Pennsylvania law encompassed three categories of state-financed benefits: auxiliary (the federal act used the term "special") services, loans of textbooks, and loans of instructional materials and equipment useful to the education of nonpublic school children. These auxiliary services included counseling, testing, psychological services, speech and hearing therapy, and related remedial services for educationally disadvantaged pupils, services that were to be provided to the same extent that they were provided for public school pupils. The textbooks loaned were those acceptable for use in the public schools and the instructional materials, which included periodicals, photographs, maps, charts, recordings, and films, also had to be those acceptable for use in public schools.

In regard to the loans of textbooks, the Court in the *Meek* case felt that it was bound by the *Allen* decision and, over the dissents of Douglas, Brennan, and Marshall, upheld constitutionality. A reading of the majority opinion, written by Potter Stewart, leaves little doubt that had there been no *Allen* decision, the majority would have ruled that this part of the law was unconstitutional. However, Stewart's opinion, over the dissent of Burger, White, and Rehnquist, made it quite clear that the majority was not prepared to extend the *Allen* precedent beyond the loan of textbooks. The provision relating to the lending of secular instructional materials and equipment, Stewart said, inescapably resulted in the direct and substantial advancement of religion, thus constituting an impermissible establishment of religion.

Also unconstitutional, but this time because of excessive entanglement of church and state, was the law's major provision, the one that related to auxiliary services. It was immaterial, said Stewart, that these services were performed not by employees of the nonpublic schools but by teachers and counselors from the public school system, since this did not substantially eliminate the need for continuing surveillance to make certain that the teachers remained religiously neutral. This was so because the services were performed in schools where education was an integral and dominant part of the sectarian mission and where an atmosphere dedicated to the advancement of religious belief was constantly maintained. Such continuing surveillance in itself resulted in excessive entanglement.

Forbidden entanglement, he said, was not limited to the teaching of particular courses which, like history, current events, or civics, are specially vulnerable to religiously oriented instruction. "The likelihood of inadvertent fostering of religion," the Court said, "may be less in a remedial arithmetic class than in a medieval history seminar, but a diminishing probability of impermissible conduct is not sufficient."

The validity of this conclusion is supported by the following extracts from an article by Professor George La Noue entitled, "Religious Schools and 'Secular' Subjects," that appeared in the Summer 1962 issue of the *Harvard Educational Review.* The first two sets of extracts are from textbooks used in Catholic schools; the third from one published for Protestant schools:

How much money must I have to buy these four books? *Poems About the Christ Child,* $1.85; *Story of Our Lady,* $2.25; *Saint Joseph,* $1.05; *Saint Theresa,* $2.00.

The children of St. Francis School ransomed 125 pagan babies last year. This year they hope to increase this number by 20%. If they succeed, how many babies will they ransom this year?

David sells subscriptions to the *Catholic Digest* on a commission basis of 20%. If the subscription is $2.50 a year what is David's commission on each sale?

China has a population of approximately 600,000,000. Through the efforts of missionaries 3,000,000 have been converted to Catholicism. What percentage of the people of China have been converted?

In Africa, Father Murray, a Holy Ghost father, was given a triangular piece of ground upon which to build his church. What was the area of this ground if it had a base of 80 feet and an altitude of 120 feet?

* * *

Jim made the way of the Cross. He likes the sixth station very much. What Roman numeral was written above it?

In millions of homes Our Lady's challenge has been accepted, but she wants billions throughout the world to join the Family Rosary for Peace. Do you know how to write in figures large numbers such as those just mentioned?

* * *

Why is it important to learn mathematics? Responses should relate to the idea that mathematics reveals God.

Why should a student's work be neat, accurate, and honest? Responses should relate to the idea that mathematics is a useful tool for work and service and must be done according to God's standards.

What should be the basis on which you would establish a business? Responses should relate to Christian ethics, stewardship, and usefulness.

As pointed out by the Supreme Court in its opinion in the *Meek* case, the plaintiffs did not challenge the constitutionality of a law that authorized providing secular auxiliary services by public school teachers in publicly owned or leased neutral buildings. The Establishment Clause, the plaintiffs argued, forbids entanglement of church and state, not of state and state.

Though not mentioned by the Court, the plaintiffs had argued that such a law would be valid only if pupils of all or no religions were assigned to the same classes irrespective of religious faith or of nonfaith. Two years later, in the case of *Wolman v. Walter*, this argument was presented to the Court but was rejected by it. "The fact that a unit on a neutral site on occasion may serve only sectarian schools" does not render it unconstitutional, the Court said.

There can be little argument on this score if the separation by religion took place only "on occasion." The difficulty lies in the fact that it takes place regularly, in many cases throughout all the years of elementary school instruction. One of the great benefits of public education lies in the fact that it brings together pupils of all faiths, races, and economic status not "on occasion" but every school day throughout the school year. *Pierce v. Society of Sisters* guarantees the right of parents to withhold this benefit from their children but it does not require that the state subsidize the exercise of that right. So the Court ruled in *Bob Jones University*, and that case involved only tax exemption. It should certainly be no less valid where direct subsidization is the contested issue.

As already noted, the Pennsylvania law was taken in many respects almost word for word from the Elementary and Secondary Education Act of 1965 and the relevant regulations issued by the United States Department of Education. Their constitutionality has until now not been passed upon by the Supreme Court, although there are now a number of cases challenging the federal act and regulations in the lower courts, and one of them, *Aguilar v. Felton* (1984), has already been accepted for argument by the Supreme Court.

Were it certain that the Supreme Court would follow and apply its own precedents, particularly but by no means exclusively *Meek v. Pittenger*, it could then be predicted that the federal law would be invalidated except to the extent that it was applied to medical, dental, and health or nutritional services (such as milk and cookies or full breakfasts and lunches) and to costs of bus transportation (but only from home to school and back) and loaned textbooks (but not other educational supplementary teaching materials). Today, however, this prediction cannot be made with any reasonable degree of certainty. A summary of the Court's post-*Meek* decisions until the present writing, and particularly *Mueller v. Allen* (to be discussed shortly), manifests consistent unfriendliness to church-state suits against aid to religious schools. The first evidence of this turn of events can in some part be found in *Wolman v. Walter*, decided two years after the *Meek* decision was handed down.

Enactment of the Ohio statutes challenged in the *Wolman* case followed the usual pattern: enact a law, appropriate monies to carry it out until the Supreme Court declares it unconstitutional, then enact a new one that hopefully avoids the provisions upon which the Court based its opinion, and continue paying under the new law. If that too is adjudged unacceptable, try again with a newer one—a strategy that can be employed as long as the ingenuity of statutory-drafting lawyers lasts. The

Pennsylvania law invalidated in *Lemon v. Kurtzman* was followed by the one voided in *Sloan v. Lemon*, and when this suffered the same fate, the legislature tried again with the statute later to be adjudged unconstitutional in *Meek v. Pittenger*. In New York the pattern was *Levitt v. Committee for Public Education and Religious Liberty*, followed by *Committee for Public Education and Religious Liberty v. Nyquist*, which in turn was followed in 1980 by *Committee for Public Education and Religious Liberty v. Regan*.

By itself there is nothing wrong with this procedure and it is certainly not limited to church-state litigation. "If at first you don't succeed, try, try, again" has long been a respected maxim taught to our children from the time they are taught to hold a rattle in their hands. There is, however, one critical aspect that makes church-state litigation different. A law violates the Establishment Clause if its purpose is to advance religion and, in determining whether that purpose is present, it would seem to be entirely appropriate to consider the history of the challenged statute. This, as will be seen in the next chapter, was the pattern resorted to in *Epperson v. Arkansas* and *Stone v. Graham*.

In the *Wolman* case the second paragraph of the Court's opinion expressly states that the challenged law was enacted after the *Meek* decision was handed down and was obviously "an attempt to conform to the teachings of that decision," that is, to find a way to use tax-raised funds to aid religious schools. If that does not constitute a purpose to advance religion, it is difficult to find one that does. To say that the purpose of an act is not to advance religion but to do so in a constitutional way is a contradiction in terms, since there is no constitutional way to advance religion.

However, the Court quickly rejected the purpose challenge and devoted itself to examining constitutionality under the effect and entanglement criteria. Shifting majorities reached the following conclusions:

1. The loan of textbooks was upheld in the *Allen* case, and a majority of the Court found no reason to overrule that decision.

2. An appropriation of funds to finance speech, hearing, and diagnostic services on nonpublic school premises is not constitutionally different from one to finance concededly permissible financing of physician, nursing, dental, and optometric services offered on religious school premises, and is therefore equally constitutional. Diagnostic services, unlike those relating to teaching and counseling, have little or no educational content and the limited contact that the diagnostician has with the child does not provide the same opportunity for transmitting sectarian views as does the teacher- or counselor-student relationship, so they too are valid.

3. Constitutional too was the section authorizing expenditures to

finance guidance and remedial services offered but only if they were offered on sites not physically or educationally identified with the non-public schools and only if they were administered by public employees. The services could be offered in mobile units parked close to but not on school property. (As previously noted, under *Meek v. Pittenger*, providing the services within the classrooms would have been unconstitutional.)

4. The section authorizing the loan not only of books but of "book substitutes" was upheld in the *Allen* and *Meek* decisions, and the Court found no reason to overrule those decisions.

5. Somewhat surprisingly the Court majority refused to extend the *Everson* holding so as to allow funding of field trips during the school day to visit "governmental, industrial, cultural and scientific centers designed to enrich the secular studies of students." "The field trips," said Blackmun speaking for a majority of five, "are an integral part of the educational experience, and where the teacher works within and for a sectarian institution, an unacceptable risk of fostering of religion is an inevitable byproduct." This then was invalid.

In the early days of the Supreme Court, John Marshall, through the force of his personality and the laziness of some justices, assigned to himself the writing of about half of the Court's opinions for the greater part of his long term as Chief Justice, and thus was usually able to achieve unanimity. By the time the *Wolman* case was decided, unanimous opinions, at least in the arena covered in this book, were a rarity, if they existed at all. The *Wolman* decision marked the peak or nadir, depending on how you look at it, of individual opinions, either concurring with or dissenting from the majority or plurality (i.e., if five justices vote to affirm or reverse but give different reasons for their votes, or vote differently on individual parts of the same statute). Even though you can with difficulty tell the players without a scorecard, the following chart of votes in the *Wolman* case may be helpful. ("C" marks a vote for constitutionality; "U" for unconstitutionality.) As can be seen, there was not a single issue in the case in which unanimity was achieved.

Committee for Public Education and Religious Liberty v. Regan (1980) indicates the Court's unwillingness to extend the ban on aid to religious schools beyond the limits already set by previous cases. It marks the beginning of a new era in which, because of Powell's shift from left to right, accommodation rather than separation becomes the paramount concern in deciding church-state cases.

Immediately after the Court in the *Levitt* case invalidated a New York law appropriating public funds to reimburse nonpublic schools for performing mandated services in relation to the administration, grading, and

THE JUSTICES' VOTES IN THE WOLMAN CASE

	Books	Testing and Scoring	Diagnostic Services	Therapeutic and Remedial Services	Instructional Material and Equipment	Field Trips
Burger	C	C	C	C	C	C
Brennan	U	U	U	U	U	U
Stewart	C	C	C	C	U	U
White	C	C	C	C	C	C
Marshall	U	U	U	U	U	U
Blackmun	C	C	C	C	U	U
Powell	C	C	C	C	C	C
Rehnquist	C	C	C	C	C	C
Stevens	U	U	C	U	C	U

C = a vote for constitutionality
U = a vote for unconstitutionality

reporting of both state-prepared and teacher-prepared examinations, the legislature passed a new law seeking to achieve the same goals to the extent that a majority of the Court would accept them. The law directed payments to cover the costs of complying with state requirements respecting pupil attendance records, the administration of state-prepared tests, and the reporting of the information and results of both to state educational authorities.

Burger assigned the writing of the majority five to four opinion upholding the law to White, who had never reconciled himself to the post-*Allen* decisions striking down aid-to-religion laws. In what at that time appeared to be wishful thinking, White suggested that the Court, in the *Wolman* opinion (notwithstanding its ban on transportation other than between home and school), might have been "silently disavowing" *Meek v. Pittenger* and presumably all the prior post-*Allen* decisions on which it was based. In any case, said White, the *Wolman* decision required the Court to uphold the second New York statute with respect to all its provisions. With what might have been malice aforethought, White went out of his way to note that it was Blackmun, a consistent supporter of *Lemon v. Kurtzman* and all its progeny, who wrote the majority opinion in the *Wolman* case (or more correctly, in that part of the decision in which there was a majority opinion).

The tests financed in the new law, said White, were state-prepared and objectively graded, and encompassed purely secular subjects, such as reading, mathematics, biology, chemistry, earth science, and social studies, none with religious subject matter. (It is unlikely that all sides in the evolution controversy would entirely agree with the inclusion of biology and earth science.) True enough, said White, some of the comprehensive tests might include an essay question or two, but the chance that grading the answers to state-drafted questions in secular subjects could or would be used to gauge a student's grasp of religious ideas was "minimal." (To a pupil whose answer to a question relating to the origin of life or the age of the universe might not agree with the beliefs of the instructor, the grading consequences might hardly be only minimal.)

In his dissenting opinion for himself, Brennan, and Marshall, Blackmun disputed White's contention that his opinion in *Wolman* justified the *Regan* decision. On the contrary, he said, White's opinion reflects "a long step backwards" in the inevitable controversy that emerges when a state legislature continues to provide public aid to parochial schools. In his separate dissenting opinion, Stevens expressed agreement with Blackmun's demonstration that White was wrong in asserting that the decision was compelled by prior precedents, including the *Wolman* case. At the same time, however, he expressed dissatisfaction with the purpose-effect-entanglement test, and recommended a return to the no-aid principle first announced in the *Everson* case, presumably assuming that the outcome would be different if that test were used. (Realistically, tests do not make decisions; judges do.)

The next episode in the Burger Court's campaign to nullify, to the fullest extent possible, the meaningfulness of all rulings from *Lemon-DiCenso* through *Meek v. Pittenger* and part of *Wolman v. Walter* appeared in its 1982 decision in *Valley Forge Christian College v. Americans United for Separation of Church and State.* Since, as can be seen by its title, the case relates to aid at the college level, and will therefore be considered in detail later in this chapter, it is mentioned here only to note the progress of the campaign.

Up till the time this was written, the ruling in *Mueller v. Allen* has been the most serious assault upon the principles stated in the Court's decisions from *Lemon-DiCenso* on. There are a number of indications that the justices were fully aware of the significance of their decision in that case. First, it was handed down on June 29, 1983, just one day before the last day of the 1982–83 term. (The Court reserved the last decision day for *Marsh v. Chambers*, the legislative prayer case considered later in this book.) Second, Burger selected Rehnquist, the majority's most able and articulate member, to write the Court's opinion. Third, unlike practically all the church-state cases relating to aid to religious schools, all the members of the Court, those in the majority and the four who dissented, resisted the temptation of writing separate opinions and instead joined either in the majority opinion written by Rehnquist or the dissenting opinion by Marshall.

It may reasonably be assumed that Burger did not intend that government should finance the abandonment by whites of the public school systems; after all, it was he who wrote the Court's opinion in the *Bob Jones University* case. Nevertheless, it was Rehnquist, the only dissenter in that case, whom Burger chose to write for the majority in the *Mueller* case, an opinion that was an implicit invitation to legislatures to finance such abandonment, with the inevitable result of leaving public schools to those pupils, disproportionately black, who are too poor to enjoy the tax benefits nominally available to them by the Court's pro-aid decisions.

The Minnesota statute challenged in the *Mueller* case permitted state income taxpayers to claim as a deduction from reportable gross income expenses incurred for "tuition, textbooks and transportation" in attending elementary or secondary schools. The key word is obviously "tuition," since there is no serious problem regarding transportation and textbooks.

Upholding constitutionality, Rehnquist indicated that there was not much need to justify a determination that the statute had a secular purpose. By educating a substantial number of students, he said, the nonpublic schools relieve public schools of a great burden, to the benefit of all taxpayers. Moreover, the nonpublic schools afford wholesome competition with public schools. And, finally, the state had a legitimate secular purpose in facilitating education of the highest quality for all children within its boundaries, whatever school the parents choose for them.

(Even Marshall agreed that the Minnesota law could be said to serve a secular purpose, although he did so by a somewhat different approach. The statute, he said, could be said to serve the legitimate purpose of promoting pluralism and diversity among public and nonpublic schools, presumably by enabling pupils in families of low income [but not so low that they pay no income tax] to enter nonpublic schools. Inasmuch as the Court in every case involving aid to religious schools from *Lemon v. Kurtzman* on found a constitutionally acceptable purpose, Marshall might have decided that further efforts along these lines would constitute an exercise in futility, this though, of all ethnic groups, blacks suffer most from government funding of parochial schools.)

Rehnquist recognized that the primary effect question was a more difficult one but he managed to overcome it to the satisfaction of four of his colleagues. The tax deduction, he noted, was one among many available under Minnesota law, including, for example, those relating to medical expenses and charitable contributions. More important, the deduction was available for educational expenses incurred by *"all"* (his emphasis) parents, including those whose children attend public schools and those whose children attend nonsectarian private schools or sectarian private schools. A program, he said, "that neutrally provides state assistance to a broad spectrum of citizens is not readily subject to challenge under the Establishment Clause."

Rehnquist did not let the *Nyquist* decision trouble him too much; he disposed of it by a footnote upon a footnote. "Indeed," he said in footnote 6, "the question whether a program having the elements of a 'genuine tax deduction' would be constitutionally acceptable was expressly reserved in *Nyquist*," and he cited footnote 49 in that case in support of his assertion. That footnote, set forth earlier in this chapter but repeated here for convenience, reads:

Since the program here does not have the elements of a genuine tax deduction, such as for charitable contributions, we do not have before us, and do not decide whether that form of tax benefit is constitutionally acceptable under the "neutrality" test in *Walz*.

Were it not for footnote 49 it would have been difficult (although probably not too much so) for Rehnquist to assert that the issue of deductions had not been passed upon in that case. The Court's opinion there noted that the *amicus curiae* brief of the New York Solicitor General (who presumably should know) "referred throughout to the New York law as one authorizing tax 'deductions,'" and stated that determination of unconstitutionality did not in any event turn upon the label given to the granted benefit. This could only mean that the statute was unconstitutional whether the conferred benefits were called tax "credits," "deductions," or any other synonym.

There is, nevertheless, nothing ambiguous in footnote 49, and what would seem irrefutable proof that Rehnquist was correct in his analysis of the *Nyquist* decision can be found in the fact that its author, Powell, concurred without any qualification in *Mueller v. Allen.*

The flaw in Rehnquist's reasoning lies not in the wording of Powell's opinion in the *Nyquist* case but in the reality that the *Mueller* decision was not written upon what philosophers refer to as a *tabula rasa*, or clean slate. Six years after the *Nyquist* case was decided the Supreme Court did not merely deny a petition for certiorari, but affirmed a Court of Appeals decision in the case of *Public Funds for Public Schools v. Byrne*, which ruled unconstitutional a New Jersey statute conferring a tax *"deduction"* privilege for dependents attending nonpublic schools. That Rehnquist was fully aware of what the Court of Appeals decided is evidenced by the fact that he (along with Burger and White) had dissented from the affirmance, but Powell, the author of footnote 49 in the *Nyquist* opinion, *had not.*

Rehnquist made no mention of the *Byrne* decision, but Marshall, in his dissenting opinion, did. Moreover, he noted that under Supreme Court practice an affirmance constituted a "decision on the merits" binding upon the Court until the Court overruled it, which the Court had not done.

Rehnquist must have had a heavenly influence not only upon Powell, but also upon some other members of the Court, specifically Burger, White, and, later, O'Connor. He dismissed in one paragraph Burger's contribution of entanglement as a critical factor in determining constitutionality and disposed in a footnote of what he called a "rather elusive inquiry" relating to "divisive political potential" as an element in making the determination. This he did notwithstanding the fact that Burger devoted three full pages of his opinion in *Lemon v. Kurtzman* to that issue and Powell quoted from it in support of the holding in the *Nyquist* case. Hereafter, Rehnquist said, like a teacher speaking to backward pupils, the term "political divisiveness" must "be confined to cases where direct financial subsidies are paid to parochial schools or to teachers in parochial schools" but not to those in which tax or other financial benefits are given to parents. (It is doubtful that many political scientists or social psychologists would recognize any significant difference between the permissible and forbidden uses.)

Even White, Rehnquist's mentor in effecting his conversion after the *Lemon* decision, was not entirely spared. He was the author of the *Allen* decision that upheld a New York law authorizing the loan to pupils attending nonpublic schools of textbooks that had been selected for use in public schools. As Marshall noted in his dissent in the *Mueller* case, the textbooks permitted in the *Allen* decision were the very textbooks that had been purchased by the state for use by public schools.

> In contrast [Marshall said] the Minnesota statute does not limit the tax deduction to those books which the State has approved for use in public schools. Rather, it permits a deduction for books that are chosen by the parochial schools themselves. Indeed, under the Minnesota statutory scheme, textbooks chosen by parochial schools but not used by public schools are likely to be precisely the ones purchased by parents for their children's use.

This chapter earlier quoted from George La Noue's article setting forth extracts from textbooks used in some religious schools that indicated how teaching, in the language of the Minnesota statute, "only those subjects legally and commonly taught in public elementary and secondary schools" could nevertheless affect or strengthen religious beliefs. True enough, the Minnesota law excluded books "used in the teaching of religious tenets, doctrines and worship," but the examples given by La Noue came exclusively from the teaching of so secular a subject as arithmetic.

As will be seen in the next chapter, in *Epperson v. Arkansas* the Court ruled unconstitutional a statute forbidding the teaching of evolution in the public schools on the ground that its purpose was to advance religion. White concurred in that opinion. Rehnquist's opinion in the *Mueller* case would permit tax deductions for biology textbooks that not only omit mention of evolution but include creationism as a scientific reality. No matter how broadly White's opinion in the *Allen* case is interpreted, it is doubtful that he intended to defend government subsidization, even through tax deductions, of books such as these. Yet he too concurred without reservations in Rehnquist's opinion in *Mueller v. Allen*.

FEDERAL AID TO RELIGIOUS SCHOOLS

The cases decided in this chapter relate to state laws providing funds to finance the operations of religious schools at the elementary and secondary levels. This is quite natural, since education is primarily a function of the state rather than the federal government. While equality of access to schools meeting a high standard of excellence would appear to be an important goal in a nation committed to the self-evident truth that all men are created equal, wealth and income are unfortunately not distributed equally among all the states. Alabama and Mississippi cannot meet the high standards prevailing in California and New York.

Moreover, even within the states equality of standards do not prevail, since traditionally school taxes are in large measure imposed by local rather than state legislative bodies. Obviously, counties in which land is owned by individual farmers rather than by large corporations are not able to meet the standards set in high-income school districts. Nor are counties in which a large proportion of the population are low-income blacks likely to provide schooling available in upper- or middle-income counties.

To help resolve these problems, Congress enacted the Higher Education Facilities Act of 1963 and, two years later, the Elementary and Secondary Education Act of 1965. The former will be considered later in this chapter; the latter is our concern here.

Both President John Kennedy and President Lyndon Johnson were of the view that inclusion of parochial schools as beneficiaries of government programs for school financing would violate the Establishment Clause. Catholic spokesmen, on the other hand, argued that a measure could be drafted that would be held constitutional, and the political influence of the Catholic church was sufficiently strong to block any measure that did not include parochial schools to the same proportionate extent as public schools. However, to make constitutionality doubly sure, the measure in the proposed act would not refer expressly to parochial or religious schools but would use the term "private" schools. It did not matter that nonreligious private schools usually cater to high-income parents who have no need for government funding but were not likely to reject it if it were offered. Nor did it matter that measured by enrollment more than ninety percent of nonpublic school pupils attend religious schools.

Because of the political reality that noninclusion of these schools in the measure would doom any chance of adoption by Congress, the following paragraph was written into Title I of the statute:

> To the extent consistent with the number of educationally deprived children in the school district of the local educational agency who are enrolled in

private elementary and secondary schools, such agency shall make provision for including special educational services and arrangements (such as dual enrollment, educational radio and television, and mobile educational services and equipment) in which such children can participate . . . . Expenditures for educational services and arrangements pursuant to this section for educationally deprived children in private schools shall be equal [taking into account the number of children to be served and the special educational needs of such children] to expenditures for children enrolled in the public schools of the local educational agency.

Not long after the law became effective, a suit challenging its constitutionality was instituted in the Federal District Court for the Southern District of New York. The suit, *Flast v. Cohen,* was sponsored by a number of organizations committed to church-state separation in the area of education, and the plaintiffs, although officials of these organizations, sued as individual taxpayers.

The District Court dismissed the complaint on the ground the plaintiffs had no standing (meaning capacity) to sue. It relied upon the 1923 case of *Frothingham v. Mellon* in which the Supreme Court held that, since a taxpayer's interest in challenging an appropriation of federal funds to administer a law seeking to combat maternal and infant mortality was shared by millions of others, and its effect upon an individual taxpayer minute, the federal courts should not accept jurisdiction of a suit by a taxpayer. The Court's concern, as stated in its decision, was that if one taxpayer were allowed to bring a suit, so could every other in any case involving expenditure of federal funds. If Frothingham could not sue the Secretary of the Treasury, the District Court held, neither could Flast sue the Secretary of Health, Education and Welfare, and accordingly it dismissed the complaint.

The Supreme Court, in an opinion by Chief Justice Earl Warren, did not agree. It did not completely accept Douglas's view that it should expressly overrule the *Frothingham* decision. (Had it done so it would have had to rule differently in the *Valley Forge Christian College* case discussed later in this chapter.) Instead, it held that an action could be brought if it challenged an act of Congress exercising its taxing and spending power conferred in Article I, Section 8, of the Constitution. Since that was the case in the *Flast* suit, the Court's decision allowed the suit to be continued to its culmination.

The decision was handed down on the same day that the ruling in *Board of Education v. Allen* was announced. White's language in that opinion seemed to justify all government aid to parochial schools, and one of its consequences was the formation of the New York Committee for Public Education and Religious Liberty (New York PEARL), which decided not to pursue the case until a more favorable time.

In the interim between the *Flast* decision and the case of *National Coalition for Public Education and Religious Liberty (National PEARL) v. Hufstedter and Anker,* to be considered shortly, the Court, in the case of *Wheeler v. Barrera* (1974), was faced with a challenge relating to the constitutionality of Title I as applicable to religious schools. Unlike *Flast v. Cohen,* however, the suit was brought not by a person suing as a taxpayer but by a parent of a child attending a parochial school. Its basis was the claim that refusal by the State of Missouri to utilize Title I funds to finance assignment of public school teachers to conduct special programs for educationally deprived children within parochial schools violated the statute. The state's defense was that use of the funds to do so would violate the Missouri constitution.

Ordinarily the rule is that, where there is a conflict between a state constitution and a federal statute, the federal statute prevails. (Otherwise, acts of Congress aimed at eliminating racial discrimination and segregation would be meaningless.) However, the federal courts must, if possible, construe the statute in a way that avoids the need to pass upon the issue of constitutionality. In the *Wheeler* case, Blackmun's opinion for the majority stated that Title I did not require *identical* but rather *comparable* services in the nonpublic schools. Accordingly, the case was remanded to the Federal District Court to determine whether comparable services that did not require on-premise instruction were practicable. Only if the answer was no would it be necessary to pass upon the question of constitutionality.

Only the arch-separationist Douglas dissented. To him, the First Amendment barred financing any program serving students in parochial schools, whether during regular school hours, after school hours, or weekend hours, and it did not matter whether the act supported sectarian schools directly or indirectly. The Court should therefore make that ruling without further ado.

The National PEARL suit was brought against the Secretary of the United States Department of Education and the head of the New York City Board of Education. It challenged a 1960 Board of Education resolution, approved by the United States Department of Health, Education and Welfare, that public school teachers, paid out of Title I funds, would go from one nonpublic school to another to provide remedial reading, remedial arithmetic, speech therapy, and guidance counseling during the school day. The resolution was adopted after the Catholic church authorities refused to participate in a program that would provide the services on publicly owned premises or even in a bus stationed close to but not on parochial school premises. To obtain cooperation the board felt that it had no choice but to alter its resolution so as to require in-school instruction. The constitutionality of this resolution was challenged in a suit instituted by the National PEARL in February 1976. The participating organizations of National PEARL are: American Association of School Administrators, American Civil Liberties Union (ACLU), ACLU National Capital Area, ACLU of Connecticut, American Ethical Union, American Humanist Association, American Jewish Congress, Americans United for Separation of Church and State, Anti-Defamation League of B'nai B'rith, Baptist Joint Committee on Public Affairs, Board of Church and Society of the United Methodist Church, Central Conference of American Rabbis, Illinois PEARL, Minnesota Civil Liberties Union, Missouri Baptist Christian Life Commission, Missouri PEARL, New York PEARL, Monroe County (New York) PEARL, Nassau-Suffolk PEARL, Michigan Council Against Parochiaid, National Association of Catholic Laity, National Council of Jewish Women, National Education Association, National Women's Conference of The American Ethical Union, Preserve Our Public Schools, Public Funds for Public Schools of New Jersey, New York State United Teachers, Ohio Free Schools Association, Union of American Hebrew Congregations, and the Unitarian Universalist Association.

This was after the Supreme Court had handed down its decision in *Meek v. Pittenger,* and was based on the premise that the *Meek* decision required a determination that the federal program was unconstitutional. Supporting this position was a 1973 Federal Court decision, *Public Funds for Public Schools v. Marburger,* ruling unconstitutional a New Jersey law providing for use of Title I funds to finance a program under which public school teachers would furnish remedial reading and mathematics services for nonpublic school pupils. Without issuing any opinion, the Supreme Court in 1974 affirmed the ruling.

The National PEARL suit, entitled *National Coalition for Public Education and Religious Liberty v. Hufstedter and Anker* (the former was Secretary of the United States Department of Education, the latter head of the New York City Board of Education) was tried on May 19, 1979, more than three years after the suit was started. The trial took only one day but the trial court did not hand down its decision against PEARL until almost a year later.

At the trial the plaintiffs' attorney called only one witness, Dr. John Ellis, the official in the Department of Education in charge of administering the Title I program. In response to a series of questions Ellis answered each in the affirmative. Summarized, the questions were:

Whether the Secretary of Health, Education and Welfare and the Commissioner of Education had construed and applied and continued to construe and apply the Elementary and Secondary Education Act of 1965 as not excluding the use of Title I funds to finance the assignment of teachers to perform educational services during school hours within schools that for religious reasons segregated the pupils as to sex; imposed religious restrictions on admissions; required attendance of pupils at religious activities; required obedience by students to the doctrines and dogmas of a particular faith; required pupils to attend instruction in the theology or doctrines of a particular faith; were an integral part of the religious mission of the church sponsoring it; had as a substantial purpose the inculcation of religious values; imposed religious restrictions on faculty appointments; imposed religious restrictions on what the faculty might teach; maintained, operated, and conducted instruction in a religious atmosphere which pervaded the school; was located on property proximate to a parish church in order to facilitate access to the church for certain religious exercises; had religious symbols such as crucifixes, paintings, and statues in the parish school buildings; made adjustment in daily class schedules to accommodate liturgical observances and recognition of religious holidays; included in its faculty religious members (such as priests and nuns) whose religious vocations were promoted and encouraged by the parish schools; had majorities of lay teachers in the parish schools who were practicing members of a particular religion and whose religious character, along with that of other teachers, was a critical factor assessed in choosing them for employment in the parish schools; imposed discipline and dismissal upon teachers who did not achieve or maintain a certain standard of a particular faith or a proper standard of morality consistent with its religious tenets; determined whether discipline or dismissal of a teacher was appropriate in keeping with the religious mission of the schools; engrained and transmitted a particular faith to the student in the parish schools not only by instruction but also by the very presence of teachers who exhibited and displayed firm religious beliefs consistent with that faith; considered the curriculum and the religious and moral conduct of faculty members as crucial to the inculcation of religious values in the students and the realization by the parish schools of the religious mission of a particular church; and required that religious truths and values pervade each subject instructed in the schools.

At the trial, the following colloquy took place upon objection by the attorney for intervenors to the questions put to Dr. Ellis:

Mr. Pfeffer: Up to this point, what I am taking, including this, comes from the relevant decision from the United States Supreme Court, and I am using the exact language used by the United States Supreme Court in these cases.

Mr. Williams: That doesn't make it a comprehensible question, though, your Honor.

The Court: You may be taking something out of context, with that thought.

Mr. Pfeffer: I'm certain Mr. Williams and his associates in their briefs would point out very strongly I am taking something out of context. The answer, your Honor, is what I am doing in performance of my obligations, is to ascertain whether the Government of the United States is complying with what plaintiffs deem to be the relevant and binding decisions of the United States Supreme Court, and therefore lest I misword or misinterpret or misconstrue what the Supreme Court said, I am using the exact language of the Supreme Court of the United States.

The trial court allowed the testimony.

As can be seen from the above, the defendants' case was presented, not, as would be expected, by the two Assistant United States Attorneys handling it but, with their consent, by the noted trial attorney Edward Bennett Williams, who intervened in the suit on behalf of several parents of children attending parochial schools. The witnesses Williams called to the stand were the director of the Title I program in New York City and several public school teachers and supervisors assigned to provide Title I instruction in the nonpublic schools. All testified that what they taught in the nonpublic schools was identical with what they taught in the public schools and in no way did their teaching have any religious content.

In its decision upholding the New York program, the District Court determined that the evidence produced at the trial indicated that advancement of religion was not the purpose or effect of the Title I program in New York City, nor did it result in excessive government entanglement with religion. An effort by plaintiffs' counsel to appeal the decision to the Supreme Court failed because the notice of appeal was not filed within the sixty-day period required by law.

This ended the *National PEARL* case, but not the controversy nor access to the courts. The case was brought in the Federal Court for the Southern District of New York, which constitutes the boroughs of Manhattan and the Bronx but not the other boroughs or the counties of Nassau and Suffolk, all of which are in the Eastern District. Under

American judicial procedure, the decisions of one federal district court need not be followed by other district courts. Because of this fact, it is permissible for a suit challenging the constitutionality of a federal law to be brought in one district while, or even after, an identical suit has been brought or decided in another district.

In August of 1978, two and a half years after the *National PEARL* suit had been started, there was still no indication as to when that case would come to trial. New York PEARL then decided that a parallel suit should be brought in the Eastern District by New York PEARL members who were not plaintiffs in the *National PEARL* suit. The suit, entitled *Felton v. Secretary, United States Department of Education,* was instituted by New York PEARL's secretary, Stanley Geller, who, together with his law partner, had successfully prosecuted the landmark public school prayer case of *Engel v. Vitale* and its counsel. (During the course of the proceedings in the case, PEARL's counsel suffered a serious illness requiring his withdrawal as co-counsel.)

No sooner had the *Felton* case been started than the government obtained a court order postponing any further action in the case until the *National PEARL* case was decided. When this happened, in 1980, the *Felton* case was resumed. The judge in that case, however, agreed with the decision in the *National PEARL* case and ruled against the plaintiffs, who immediately appealed to the Court of Appeals for the Second Circuit.

The jurisdiction of that court includes all of New York City, but the Court of Appeals elected not to accept the *National PEARL* decision as correct. Instead it ruled, without dissent, that the District Court was wrong in its decision in the *National PEARL* case and that the decision in the *Meek* case had to be accepted as binding precedent to be followed until it was overruled by the Supreme Court.

Specifically, it ruled that tax-raised funds could be used to accord remedial instruction or related counseling services to students in religious schools only if the instruction and services were accorded by publicly employed teachers and took place off the premises of the religious schools. Whatever the forms of state aid to religious elementary and secondary schools, the Court said, they must not create a risk sufficiently significant to require policing to assure that public school personnel will not act, even unwittingly, to foster religion. The Court stated in its opinion that a "fair" case could be made that the government's financing constituted a direct and substantial advancement of religious activity, as was the case in the *Meek* decision. It preferred, however, to rest its decision on the entanglement prohibition in the Establishment Clause.

At the present writing the defendants have instituted an appeal from the decision to the Supreme Court.* How the Court will decide the case cannot easily be predicted. The probabilities are that its decision, whichever way it goes, will be a five to four ruling. The tenor of the Court's most recent decisions point to a reversal, but Powell's concurrence in the *Meek* decision might compel him to vote for affirmance, although it had no such effect in the *Mueller* case.

AID IN HIGHER EDUCATION

Decision day in 1971 was not what at that time seemed to many proponents of aid to be a total disaster. Simultaneously with the *Lemon-DiCenso* decision the Court handed down its ruling in *Tilton v. Richardson,* with an opinion also by Burger, upholding the validity of a provision in the Higher Education Facilities Act of 1963 that authorized federal construction grants for colleges and universities, including those that were church related. The act provided that the grants were not allowable if their purpose was to finance any facility used for sectarian instruction or religious worship, or if its purpose was to finance any part of a divinity school. (The Court did strike out a provision in the statute that permitted religious use of government-financed buildings after a twenty-year period.) Thus, under the Court's holding, a grant to construct a chemistry laboratory or a gymnasium in a church-related college other than a divinity school would be valid even though it could not constitutionally be made if the facility were in an elementary or secondary church-related school.

There are three reasons, Burger said, for distinguishing between colleges on the one hand and elementary and secondary schools on the other. First, religious indoctrination is not a substantial purpose or activity of church-related colleges; second, the record in the case showed that classrooms and other facilities were themselves religiously neutral, with correspondingly less need for government surveillance; and, third, the government aid in the case was in the form of a one-time, single-purpose construction grant with only minimal need for inspection, and hence less danger of government entanglement with religion.

A reasonable argument could be made to support Burger's distinguishing between higher and lower educational institutions. As noted in his opinion, by the time students reach college age they are mature (mature enough, it might be added, to be drafted for military service). Their re-

---

*Since this was written, the Supreme Court has agreed to review the decision.

ligious commitments are generally fixed so that they can reasonably be expected to withstand efforts by instructors to sway them from the faith of their fathers as "he or she receives the same at mother's knee or father's side," so eloquently if not elegantly expressed by the New York Regents, who promulgated the prayer challenged in *Engel v. Vitale*.

There is, nevertheless, considerable difficulty with this reasoning. In the first place, the assumption of lesser vulnerability to religious-influencing at the college level is by no means indisputable. As discussed in Chapter 7, a substantial percentage of converts to "cults" are of college age; even if that were not so, the Establishment Clause forbids government financing of unsuccessful no less than successful efforts to inculcate religious commitments.

Moreover, does it make much difference whether faculty members in a governmentally supported college seek to inculcate religious values in the nonfinanced social sciences building rather than the financed physical science building on the same campus? If inculcation is not the purpose of the entire enterprise, why undertake it at all? It hardly makes sense to predicate constitutionality on the fact that the nonsectarian Dr. Jekyll controls and manages the science building but the Reverend Mr. Hyde is in charge of the building in which philosophy or history is taught. Even if the funds received from the government go into a special bank account marked for nonsectarian use only, this simple act would free for religious use monies otherwise needed to finance the nonsectarian budget.

An analogous situation dealing with sexual rather than religious separation of funds was presented to the Supreme Court in the case of *Grove City College v. Bell*, decided in February 1984. Involved was an interpretation of a 1972 amendment to Title IX of the Civil Rights Act of 1964 forbidding sexual discrimination in schools that receive federal financial assistance. Pre-Reagan administrations consistently interpreted this as barring federal financial assistance if any of the institution's programs (e.g., athletics) discriminated against women. But, as in the *Bob Jones University* case, the Reagan administration changed its mind and urged that the 1972 amendment applied only to the particular department or program that was federally financed, thus leaving others to discriminate on the basis of sex without losing federal financial assistance. In its decision the Supreme Court agreed with this interpretation.

On the authority of the *Tilton* decision the Court, in *Hunt v. McNair* (1973), upheld the validity of a South Carolina law authorizing a transaction under which the state issued bonds to finance capital improvements on the campus of the Baptist College of Charleston. The members of the College Board of Trustees were elected by the South Carolina Baptist

Convention, the approval of the convention was required for certain financial transactions, and the charter of the college could be amended only by the convention. In compliance with the restrictions prescribed in the *Tilton* case, the South Carolina statute provided that the monies raised would not be used to finance any building used for sectarian instruction or religious worship, or in connection with any part of the program of a divinity school.

As in the *Tilton* case, the Court found that the college involved in the suit was not "pervasively sectarian," that neither the purpose nor the primary effect of the statute was to advance religion, and that (since the benefitted institution was a college rather than an elementary or secondary school) the degree of entanglement of church and state would be within the limits of constitutional permissibility. Like *Tilton,* the *Hunt* case involved a one-purpose grant; the monies were to be applied to finance only secular improvements such as the completion of dining hall facilities.

Several interesting, whether or not particularly significant, aspects are relevant here. As in the *Diffenderfer* case, discussed in Chapter 1, the benefitted religion in *Hunt v. McNair* was Southern Baptist, which might seem surprising in view of the fact that of all the Christian faiths none is more committed to church-state separation than the Baptist religion. Second, both *Tilton v. Richardson* and *Hunt v. McNair* were decided on the last day of the Court's term for the particular year, just before the justices pack up their belongings and go back to their respective homes, not to return to court until a new term begins about October 1. Finally, in each of the latter two cases, the decision was accompanied by a ruling that invalidated statutes enacted to aid religious schools at the elementary and secondary levels, *Lemon v. Kurtzman* and *Committee for Public Education and Religious Liberty v. Nyquist,* respectively, as if the justices were like legislators who seek to appease two competing interest groups by giving something to each.

The next Supreme Court decision relating to institutions of higher learning came in the 1976 case of *Roemer v. Board of Works of Maryland.* Here again a majority of the Court found no violation of the Constitution in a law which included four Catholic colleges among the beneficiaries of state aid. In the *Tilton* and *Hunt* cases the Court had emphasized that the subsidies were "one-time single purpose construction grants and thus avoid excessive entanglement because they entailed no continual financial relationships, no annual audits and no government analysis of an institution's expenditures." In the *Roemer* case, however, the state aid was in the form of annual subsidies that could be repeated indefinitely. This, the majority held, did not matter; nor was it material that the colleges had complete freedom in determining how the state funds were to be used so long as it was not for sectarian purposes, or that the students were required to take religion or theology courses taught by Catholic clerics, or that at least some classes were begun with prayer, or that the annual grant was to be fifteen percent of the state's appropriation for each full-time student in the state's college system rather than a specific sum to finance a particular project.

Notwithstanding all this and much more, a majority of the Court found that neither the purpose nor primary effect of the grants were to advance religion, nor did they result in excessive entanglement. To an objective observer, one not influenced by either pro- or anti-religious predilections, the reasoning underlying the *Roemer* opinion and to a somewhat lesser but nevertheless substantial extent the *Tilton* and *Hunt* decisions, if taken seriously, approach sheer nonsense. Nothing in this decision prevents a sectarian college from transferring to the chapel account the amount budgeted for building a new gymnasium and simultaneously seeking federal funds to finance the construction of a gymnasium, and in all of them the Court held that this did not matter. The net result is to require church-related colleges that might seek government funds to engage the services not only of a competent lawyer but of a public accountant as well.

The only rational explanation is a realistic one. Blackmun, who wrote the *Roemer* opinion, and Burger and Powell, who joined in it, could not be persuaded to do what White, with Rehnquist's concurrence, urged them to do, that is, abandon Burger's three-prong entanglement test and remove all Establishment Clause restrictions on aid to colleges. The net result was a compromise that went too far for Brennan, Marshall, Stewart, and Stevens; not far enough for White and Rehnquist; but just right for Burger, Blackmun, and Powell.

As of this writing, the most recent decision on aid for church-related colleges was in *Valley Forge Christian College v. Americans United for Separation of Church and State* (1982). This was an action brought by Americans United for Separation of Church and State together with several of its officers who sued as taxpayers. The tenor of the majority opinion by Rehnquist reflects an unhappiness with the Court's initial 1968 decision in *Flast v. Cohen*, which recognized the standing or right of individual taxpayers to bring suit challenging grants to religious schools. Were it in Rehnquist's power to nullify all decisions from *Lemon v. Kurtzman* on and to return to the pre-1968 decisions that did not allow taxpayers to challenge an act of Congress on constitutional grounds, there is little doubt that he would have exercised that power. Recognizing that as a practical reality this was not possible (no matter how much he might now have rued it, White had concurred in the *Flast v. Cohen* decision), the majority in *Valley Forge* went as far as it could to limit the damage originally done.

The controversy arose out of a provision in the 1949 Federal Property and Administration Services Act that authorized the Secretary of the Department of Health, Education and Welfare to dispose of "surplus" government owned properties by selling or leasing them to nonprofit, tax-exempt educational institutions. One would assume that selling or leasing implied some payment by the buyer or renter but the Secretary did not interpret it that way and authorized the transfer for free of a seventy-seven acre tract of land valued at 1.3 million dollars. The beneficiary, earlier known as the Northeast Bible College, operated under the supervision of a religious order known as the Assemblies of God, and had been organized "to offer systematic training on the collegiate level to men and women for Christian Service as either ministers or laymen."

It is difficult to see how the Court could uphold the constitutionality of this grant even under the most tolerant interpretation of the Establishment Clause as applied to institutions of higher education. Valley Forge Christian College was a divinity school, so that under the *Tilton, Hunt,* and *Roemer* decisions it would not matter that the building was to be used to teach only secular subjects, and in any event, the agreement of transfer did not require that use be so limited.

The Court majority (in which O'Connor replaced Stewart but Blackmun returned to his natural habitat with Brennan, Marshall, and Stevens) avoided the problem of constitutionality by holding that the plaintiffs had no standing to bring the action because they were not challenging an act of *Congress* but a decision of the *Department of Health, Education and Welfare.* Nor was the conveyance an exercise of a power conferred by the Taxing and Spending Clause in Article I, Section 8, of the Constitution, but rather by Article IV, Section 3, of the same Constitution, which authorizes Congress "to dispose of property belonging to the United States." Since Congress had the power to make a gift of the property to any educational institution, Rehnquist said for the majority, the plaintiffs as taxpayers suffered no monetary injury by reason of the fact that the department chose a religious rather than a secular institution to be the beneficiary, and if they suffered no injury it follows as day the night they had no standing to sue.

If this appears to be a mere legalistic technicality, it is no more so than the fiction, translated into reality by the *Flast* ruling, that someone whose tax bill amounts to ten dollars annually really suffers a constitutionally recognized wrong entitling him to sue for the complete nullification of a duly enacted legislative measure appropriating funds to finance religious education. Champions of aid would, if they could, overrule the *Flast* ruling. Opponents, on the other hand, would extend it to overrule the *Valley Forge* decision, asserting to support their demand Madison's statement in the Virginia Memorial and Remonstrance that "the same authority that can force a citizen to contribute three pence only of his property for the support of any one establishment, may force him to conform to any other establishment whatsoever."

Briefly summarized, this chapter traces the rise and (since the *Nyquist* decision has not expressly been overruled, almost though not quite completely) the fall of constitutional restrictions upon financial aid to church-related educational institutions. The chief no-aid champion was Brennan, and the leader on the opposing side was first White but later Rehnquist. The turning point in the struggle was Powell's desertion of the no-aid forces and his enlistment, after the *Meek* and *Wolman* decisions, in the yes-aid army.

Religion in Public Schools

COMPULSORY SCHOOL ATTENDANCE

There is now no question that states may require parents to provide their children with a basic secular education, either at public or private schools, including those religiously affiliated. Nor is there any doubt that they have the power to extend the obligation beyond the elementary school level, so long as it provides tuition-free schools for that purpose. In *Wisconsin v. Yoder* (1972), however, the Burger Court was called upon to decide for how long in a child's life that obligation lasts.

The defendants in the case were Old Order Amish, whose religious conviction, based upon the Biblical injunction from the Epistle of Paul to the Romans "be not conformed to this world," forbade them to send their children to school after they had completed elementary schooling, not-withstanding a statute requiring attendance until the age of sixteen. In an opinion by Burger, the Court held that enforcement of the statute against the Amish parents would violate the Free Exercise Clause of the First Amendment. The Amish, he noted, did not object to elementary educa-tion through the first eight grades as a general proposition because they agreed that their children must have basic skills in the "three R's" in order to read the Bible, to be good farmers and citizens, and to be able to deal with non-Amish people when necessary in the course of daily affairs. They viewed such a basic education as acceptable because it did not significantly expose their children to worldly values or interfere with their development in the Amish community during the crucial adolescent period. According to Amish belief, higher learning tended to develop values they rejected as influences that alienate man from God.

There was no doubt, Burger said, as to the power of a state, having high responsibility for the education of children, to impose reasonable regulations for the control and duration of basic education. Yet, high as it might be, a state's interest in universal education must be balanced against the rights protected by the Free Exercise Clause and the traditional interests of parents with respect to the religious upbringing of their children. The Amish were not opposed to education beyond the eighth grade level; their long-established program of informal vocational education on the farm attested to that. What they did not accept was the assumption that education means only conventional classroom instruction. The essence of all that had been said and written on the subject, Burger concluded, was that only interests of the highest order not otherwise served could overbalance legitimate claims to the free exercise of religion. An additional one or two years of formal high school attendance in place of the long-established Amish program of informal education at home would do little to serve those interests and were certainly not high enough to outweigh First Amendment values.

Douglas dissented in part from the Court's judgment, and this not because Burger went too far in protecting religious freedom (it would have been more than merely surprising if that were the complaint of the Court's most doctrinaire defender of free exercise), but because it did not go far enough. One of the Amish pupils appeared at the trial and testified that her only reason for not going to school was that her religion forbade it, and as to her he had no quarrel with the majority opinion. But, by not requiring testimony from the other Amish pupils, the Court ignored their free exercise rights. Children, he said, were persons "within the meaning of the Bill of Rights, which was not for adults only." If the other Amish pupils were to testify that their religious conscience would not be violated by two additional years in public schools, the Court would have to decide between conflicting rights and, while it might reach the same conclusion, the judgment would have been reached in conformity with due process of law. (Unanswered by him was the question of what the effect on the family's life would be if the Court ruled against the parents and in favor of the children as the children themselves judged their best interests to be.)

The Amish did not challenge a state's power to require parents to send their children to some elementary school, religious or secular, which provides a state-prescribed minimum curriculum and engages state-certified teachers, even though their religious conscience forbade them to do so. As long ago as 1951 the Supreme Court (although over the dissents of Black and Douglas) dismissed for want of a substantial federal question an appeal in the case of *Donner v. New York* and *Auster v. Weberman*. In these companion cases, the lower courts ruled that the Free Exercise Clause did not protect the right of ultra-Hasidic parents to send their children to a probably unique *yeshivah* (Orthodox Jewish all-day school) in which no secular subjects were taught because all knowledge was to be found in the Torah and Talmudic writings.

Now pending before the Supreme Court is a petition for certiorari in the case of *North Platte Baptist Church v. State of Nebraska*. Involved in it is a challenge to the state's compelling attendance law on the ground that it violates the Free Exercise Clause. The case involves extreme Christian fundamentalists rather than Hasidic Jews but the basic issue is the same. In 1981, the Supreme Court dismissed for lack of a substantial federal issue an appeal in the case of *Douglas v. Faith Baptist Church of Louisville, Nebraska*. The appeal, as that in the *North Platte* case, was from a state court ruling that the Free Exercise Clause was not violated in requiring parents to send their children either to public schools or to state-certified schools that complied with the law mandating a state-prescribed minimum curriculum to be taught by state-licensed teachers.

Many, if not most, of these "Christian" schools (as the Catholic "parochial" schools and the Orthodox Jewish "yeshivahs") complied with these requirements, but some, like the Faith Baptist Church, did not. Also among the nonconformers were the North Platte Baptist Church and the North Platte Christian Church, both situated in Nebraska.

In a suit instituted against them to require compliance with the statute, the Nebraska high court ruled that the *Faith Baptist Church* decision was conclusive and ordered the churches to abide by it. However, in the interim between the Nebraska court's ruling and the decision of the church to seek review by the United States Supreme Court, the legislature amended the statute so that compliance would not violate the conscience of Christian church parents. The amendment came as a result of a report to the governor by a panel appointed by him to seek a solution to the problem of conscience faced by nonconforming Christian schools. The report and its recommendation for legislative action manifest a sincere and thoughtful effort to resolve the problem in a way that would satisfy the purposes of the state's school attendance law without violating the conscience of Christian school parents.

The report noted that the problem of Christian school regulation was a comparatively recent one (probably because the revival of fundamentalist religion was a recent phenomenon). Some states have sought to meet it by mandatory teacher certification regulations but, unlike Nebraska, some of these do not go to court to force them. Other states expressly exempt church-related schools from some or all state regulations, but most do not.

The resolution suggested in the report was to offer parents a choice.

They could send their children to licensed nonpublic schools or, if by reason of religious conscience they elect not to do so, could exercise the option of submitting the children to periodic state-formulated tests to assure that they were meeting the general statutory standards of educational achievement applicable equally to public and nonpublic schools.

Since the governor and legislature accepted the recommendations and enacted them into law, the school defendants in *State of Nebraska v. North Platte Baptist Church* seem to have gotten everything they wanted. Because of this the controversy may have become moot, and the Supreme Court may dismiss the appeal for that reason.

Whether a state can refuse to accept home instruction by parents or tutors for children who have no physical incapacity that prevents school attendance has not definitively been decided by the Supreme Court. More relevant to the subject of this book is the question of constitutionality when the parents' refusal to send their child to any school (public, secular private, or parochial) in the community in which they live is based on a bona fide religious commitment.

In the *Bob Jones University* case the Court ruled even religiously mandated racial discrimination in education to be contrary to public policy, at least to the extent of justifying denial of tax exemption privileges. A reasonable argument can be made that the same concept of public policy, and a recognition of the government's power to exercise a parental duty when—even for religious reasons—the natural parents refuse to do so, can justify laws compelling not merely school but public school attendance. Only in a public school can a child be assured of an opportunity to learn to live some part of the day with persons of all religions, races, and social and economic classes, as he will have to do throughout his adult life. The state (that is, the community at large) also benefits from this compulsory mixing, since it could mitigate the interracial and interreligious conflicts that plague a pluralistic society.

Nevertheless, the Supreme Court's 1925 decision in the companion cases of *Pierce v. Society of Sisters* and *Pierce v. Hall Military Academy* recognized the constitutional rights of parents to send their children to nonpublic schools restricted to pupils of a particular religion, race, or social or economic standing. The *Bob Jones University* case recognizes the public policy interest only to the extent that it justifies withdrawal of tax exemption for schools that violate it, but it could conceivably go further to impose penal sanctions to protect it.

RELIGIOUS INSTRUCTION IN PUBLIC SCHOOLS

Viewed in the light of its history, the issue of religion in the public schools has brought together a rather unusual set of alliances, one that has joined Protestant fundamentalists (most prominently the Moral Majority of Jerry Falwell), Roman Catholics, and political conservatives (led by Ronald Reagan and Jesse Helms) on one side and, on the other, liberal Protestants represented by the National Council of Churches, Jews, atheists, and secular humanists. It was not always so. For a century before the case of *McCollum v. Board of Education of Champaign, Illinois*, was decided in 1948, practically the sole opponent to religious instruction and prayer recitation in the public schools was the Catholic church. American Protestantism generally (that is, not limited to Southern fundamentalism) warmly supported these practices, at least if provision were made for non-Protestant pupils by either offering parallel prayer or instruction practices, or excusal if that were not practicable.

The *McCollum* case presented a challenge to a system of religious instruction, called in-school released time, under which teachers not paid out of public funds entered the public schools to provide religious instruction to pupils whose parents consented to it. These pupils were divided into two groups and, since the majority were Protestant, they remained in their classrooms to receive the instruction while Catholics received theirs in other rooms made available for that purpose.

It should be noted that in theory a separate room was available to the Jewish pupils as well but there were not enough of them to make participation in the program practicable, assuming their parents wanted them to participate, with the result that they remained in the classroom in which the Protestant instruction was given. The following is an extract from the trial testimony in the *McCollum* case. (The unwilling witness was a Sunday school teacher who conducted a Protestant pupils' class.)

The Witness *(continuing)*: I do not think I spoke ever of the Jews as [Christ's] enemies; that was several years ago and I do not remember.

Q. Will you tell us just what you did teach with reference to who his enemies were?

. . .

A. I think if you read the Bible you will know them.

Q. I want to know what you teach. Don't you teach that the Jews were the enemies of Christ?

A. They were hostile to Jesus in many ways.

. . .

Q. Did you teach the children that the Jews were afraid of Jesus?
A. Some of them were.
Q. How about the others?
A. Some of them were not.

. . .

Q. Have you during the last three years at any time been teaching that the Jews had anything to do with the crucifixion of Jesus Christ?
The Witness *(continuing)*: Individual Jews did participate. I did not tell the children so, I did not mention it. In connection with the crucifixion of Christ, in my teaching during the last three years I mentioned that Jews were present at his trial and perhaps testified. I do not teach those doctrinal things. I just teach the Bible story and the paper you talk about, I have not used since several years ago. I have had such an outline. I have taught that some of the Jews accepted Jesus and that some of them rejected him. I do not teach the pupils that the Jews were accepted or rejected but I may have stated that, but remember that those things are explained. If you use an outline an explanation is given to pupils. An outline does not include everything.

Line 13 on page 3 of the exhibit says, "The Jews rejected Jesus." It does not mean as a people. It means individuals.

This testimony came from a witness who obviously had a strong interest in maintaining the practice challenged in the suit. It is difficult to believe that it relates fully and with complete accuracy how religion was taught in the public schools of Champaign, nor does it even mention the feelings of Jewish pupils who for all practical purposes were compelled to be present while the instruction was given. It is enough, however, to explain at least in part why ever since the *McCollum* case came to the Supreme Court American Jewry, rabbinic and congregational, has consistently opposed religious instruction and prayer in the public schools.

With only Stanley Reed dissenting, the Court ruled the Champaign released time practice to be a violation of the Establishment Clause. Its opinion relied upon the ruling in the *Everson* case that under the Establishment Clause neither a state nor the federal government could pass laws aiding one, some, or all religions but must maintain a status of neutrality among religions and between religion and nonreligion.

The *Everson* decision had been warmly praised by Catholic church spokesmen and bitterly assailed by Protestants, so much so that it immediately led to the establishment of Protestants and Other Americans United for Separation of Church and State (later, Americans United for Separation of Church and State). What, however, that decision had rendered asunder, the *McCollum* decision in large part joined together. It was not surprising that leading spokesmen in both camps attacked the decision (although, as we shall see, not nearly as vehemently as in the *Engel v. Vitale* prayer case in 1962). The reason for this coalition lay in the fact that both Protestant and Catholic teachers availed themselves of the opportunity to furnish religious instruction in separate public school classrooms in Champaign.

OFF-SCHOOL PREMISES RELEASED TIME

Four years after the *McCollum* decision was handed down, the Court decided the case of *Zorach v. Clauson*. Over the dissents of Black (who wrote the *McCollum* opinion), Felix Frankfurter, and Robert H. Jackson, it upheld the constitutionality of New York's released time system under which those pupils whose parents consented were excused for an hour each week to participate in religious instruction off public school premises, while the nonparticipating pupils remained in class. The majority opinion, written by Douglas, rejected as "obtuse" the argument that "free exercise of religion" was an issue in the case, since no pupil was forced to go to the religious classroom and no religious exercise or instruction was brought into the classroom. Government, he said, may not finance religious groups or undertake religious instruction or blend secular and sectarian education or use secular institutions to force one or some religion on any person. But to invalidate the released time program would bring the concept of church-state separation to an unjustifiable extreme. It would render unconstitutional granting a Catholic student permission to leave the school to attend mass on a Holy Day of Obligation, or allowing a Jewish student to be absent on Yom Kippur, or excusing a Protestant student to attend a family baptismal ceremony. Such hostility to religion could not and should not be read into the Bill of Rights.

In itself, the victory won by proponents of released time religious education was hardly of momentous proportions. The hope that they had when the project was initiated in Gary, Indiana, in 1913 was that it would enable large numbers of public school pupils to receive some degree of religious instruction that they would otherwise not have received. For those who did not attend Sunday schools, it would be the only source for such instruction; for those who did, it would be a valuable addition. The program had been conceived by Protestant churchmen and, as indicated by the Champaign system, the great majority of the affected pupils were Protestants.

It did not work out that way. Today the great majority of participating pupils, in the large cities as much as ninety percent, are Catholics. And all together the percentage of pupils of both faiths (Jewish participation is rare) enrolled in the program is a small fraction of the total school enrollment.

Considerably more important than the statistical benefits resulting from the decision has been the language used by Douglas to justify the decision.

We are a religious people, [he said] whose institutions presuppose a Supreme Being. We guarantee the freedom to worship as one chooses. We make room for as wide a variety of beliefs and creeds as the spiritual needs of man deem necessary. We sponsor an attitude on the part of government that shows no partiality to any one group and that lets each flourish according to the zeal of its adherents and the appeal of its dogma. When the state encourages religious instruction or cooperates with religious authorities by adjusting the schedule of public events to sectarian needs, it follows the best of our traditions. For it then respects the religious nature of our people and accommodates the public service to their spiritual needs. To hold that it may not would be to find in the Constitution a requirement that the government show a callous indifference to religious groups. That would be preferring those who believe in no religion over those who do believe.

That the *Zorach* opinion may have been an effort at appeasing the assailants of the *McCollum* ruling is broadly hinted in Black's dissenting opinion.

I am aware [he wrote] that our *McCollum* decision has been subjected to a most searching examination throughout the country. Probably few opinions from this Court in recent years have attracted more attention or stirred wider debate. Our insistence on a "wall of separation between Church and State which must be kept high and impregnable" has seemed to some a correct exposition of the philosophy and a true interpretation of the language of the First Amendment to which we should strictly adhere. With equal conviction and sincerity, others have thought the *McCollum* decision fundamentally wrong and have pledged continuous warfare against it.

In his own dissent Frankfurter expressed "the hope that in future variations of the problem which are bound to come here, these [*McCollum*] principles may again be honored in the observance." (As will shortly be seen, this hope became a reality a decade later, but for how long is far from certain.) Also worthy of note is the dissenting opinion of Jackson, who though a master of writing style did not hesitate to mix a metaphor now and then. He called Douglas's majority opinion an exercise in "passionate dialectics" and expressed regret that the *McCollum* decision has "passed like a storm in a teacup." (Only in *Alice in Wonderland* could that come to pass.) Concluding with a bow to those committed to what political scientists call legal realism, he predicted that in time the Court's judgment would be "more interesting to students of psychology and of the judicial process than to students of constitutional law."

If there was any redeeming aspect that strict separationists could find in the situation, it must have been in the fact that Douglas was later to become the greatest separationist of them all, as indicated by his lonely dissent in the *Walz* tax exemption case discussed in Chapter 1 of this book.

Nor have the not-so-strict separationists become reconciled to the *McCollum* decision or expressed willingness to accept the *Zorach* ruling as completely satisfactory. *America*, the nation's leading Catholic journal, in an editorial in its March 24, 1984, issue acknowledged that Protestant Bible instruction and prayer recitation were factors that led to the creation of the Catholic school system and that a return to such practices would destroy the ecumenical good will that had grown in the country since the Second Vatican Council. While approving a moment of silence, it doubted that an amendment to the Constitution was necessary to achieve it, since it was quite possible that, judging from the Court's recent decisions, it could find the moment of silence to be constitutionally acceptable.

A better way of dealing with this problem [of secularity in public education] than any prayer amendment [the editorial concluded] would be an amendment reversing the Supreme Court decision in *McCollum* (1948), which forbade the use of public school classrooms for voluntary religious instruction by ministers, priests and rabbis during school hours. The Supreme Court in *Zorach* (1948), allowed released-time instruction off campus, but not on school property. Released time off the premises has proven logistically difficult or impossible in many situations. Time is consumed in transporting the children to an off-campus location. Even if a home is available within walking distance of the school, adults must be available to supervise the trip. If children, at their parents' discretion and expense, could be instructed in their faith on the school property, this would be much more beneficial to the children than a token moment of prayer at the beginning of school.

SHARED TIME INSTRUCTION

Now before the Supreme Court is the case of *School District of Grand Rapids, Michigan v. Ball.* This is an appeal from a decision ruling unconstitutional a system sometimes called shared time and sometimes dual enrollment. Involved in it is a contract under which a public school district leases space in a parochial school for the teaching by the parochial school staff of secular courses that are available solely to students enrolled in the school. In 1974 a Federal District Court, in the case of *Americans United for Separation of Church and State v. Board of Education of Beechwood, Kentucky,* held such a program to be unconstitutional because its effect was to advance religion and it fostered excessive government administrative entanglement with religion. The Beechwood school board elected not to appeal that decision but the Grand Rapids board chose otherwise after a similar judgment was handed down in the Michigan federal court.

At the trial Sister Marie Heyda, author of the book *Catholic Central and West Catholic High Schools,* candidly testified that the following sentence in her book stated the purpose of education in Catholic schools:

> Certainly *religion* and the *values of the spiritual life must always* be an integral part of the atmosphere of the Catholic high school for in the modern age *they are the only reason for its being.* (Emphasis supplied by the trial court.)

The *St. Jude School Parent Handbook* contained this typical statement of the elements of Catholic education:

> A God oriented environment which *permeates* the total educational program.

* * *

> Opportunities to pray, worship and celebrate as members of a Christian community.

> A Christian atmosphere which guides and encourages participation in the church's commitment to social justice.

> A continuous development of knowledge of the Catholic faith, its traditions, teaching and theology. (Emphasis supplied by the trial court.)

Each of the Catholic schools in Grand Rapids was governed by its own board of education, normally composed of the pastor and some lay members elected by constituents of the parish with which the school was associated.

Besides the Catholic schools, five elementary and one secondary Protestant school participated in the program. Theirs was operated by the Grand Rapids Christian School Association, an association composed of parents and others who supported Christian education. Membership in the association was restricted to those who subscribed to a doctrinal basis. The basis, contained within the association's bylaws, provided:

> Section 1.3 Basis. The supreme standard of the Association shall be the scriptures of the Old and New Testament, herein confessed to be the infallible Word of God, as these are interpreted in the historic Reformed confessions: The Belgic Confession; Heidelberg Catechism, and Canons of Dort.

* * *

> In a school which seeks to provide a Christian education it is not sufficient that the teaching of Christianity be a separate subject in the curriculum, but *the Word of God must be an all-pervading force in the educational program.* (Emphasis supplied by the trial court.)

* * *

The purposes of Lutheran education were set forth as follows:

> 1. Leading the child to faith in the Lord Jesus Christ, and keeping him/her in that faith to eternal life in heaven.
> 2. Helping the child in Christian growth in all relationships of life, such as the family, the Church, the State, the relationship of friendship, of employment and labor, of art and culture.

* * *

> The Holy Bible influences all lessons and activities in our Christian Day School. Through Scripture the Holy Spirit works to increase the child's understanding of himself, his purpose, his destiny, and his Lord.

From this testimony and other trial evidence, the trial judge concluded that "there was no basis to form a conclusion that there was any purpose or intent [on the part of the Michigan legislature] to advance religion unconstitutionally." That the Court of Appeals affirmed this conclusion is hardly surprising; as has been indicated earlier, beginning with the *Lemon* decision, the Supreme Court has consistently refused to find an impermissible purpose of advancing religion in suits that challenge aid to religious schools.

Nevertheless, there is a bit of naiveté in using the word "unconstitutionally." It is more than probable that the legislators' purpose was to enact the challenged statute, period. But even if that were not so, and even though there is a presumption in law that legislators intend to act constitutionally, the language used in the opinion carried the presumption (or fiction) of constitutional purpose just a little too far.

Beyond exonerating purpose, the judge would not go. When, he said (and the Court of Appeals agreed), courses are offered within the "abdomen" of a sectarian school to students brought together for a religious mission, there was a distinctly impermissible constitutional effect.

By entering into legalistic agreements with the public schools, the judge continued, the religious schools gained more than access to facilities. The agreements conferred substantial financial benefits upon the religious institutions by employing and paying from tax funds the numerous instructors who taught subjects in the leased classrooms. Without any change in the character of the student body or infusion of any students from other schools, the programs undeniably rendered direct benefits, both financial and otherwise, to the sectarian institutions. Such an effect, said the judge, was clearly irreconcilable with the dictates of the Establishment Clause.

The Court of Appeals also affirmed the trial judge's decision that the monitoring arrangements required to avoid religious effect constituted impermissible entanglement of church and state. It ruled that prior Supreme Court decisions upholding constitutionality differed from the Grand Rapids pattern in four significant respects. First, the Grand Rapids programs were primarily programs of assistance to elementary schools; second, they gave substantial financial aid to education in parochial school buildings; third, the parochial schools had religious indoctrination as a primary school purpose; and, fourth, the impact upon taxpayers and the parochial schools was direct.

Finally, the Court of Appeals noted Rehnquist's majority opinion in *Mueller v. Allen* but found the Grand Rapids case to be different in two respects. First, the Minnesota law had made some deductions (for books, school supplies, transportation, etc.) generally available to parents of all school children and, second, the aid was given to the parents involved and not to the parochial schools.

The majority opinion presented two dire predictions:

We recognize, of course, the increasing impact of Supreme Court majority approval of public funding for religiously neutral supplies and services which are provided to all schools, including parochial schools. If, however, what has been adopted by the Grand Rapids School Board were to be added to the list of such approvals, the separation of church and state will be effectively ended in the field of public education. Legislatures in many states are notoriously vulnerable to pressures from religious constituencies. Under such pressures legislatures can be expected to allocate increasing . . . funds to the point where the great majority of parochial school costs will be carried by taxpayers. The only costs not covered may in time be those specifically allocated to religious services or classes in religious instruction. Constant secular inspection and surveillance of all activities not specifically labeled religious would be required to maintain even a fiction of separation. Such a result would end public education as a major aspect of the American goal of equality of opportunity.

The third judge on the Court of Appeals dissented on several grounds: that, notwithstanding *Flast v. Cohen*, taxpayers had no standing to bring the Grand Rapids suit; that "no evidence of record [supported] a finding that any teacher ever advanced religious views during the 6-year period at issue. Rather, [it was] replete with myriad affidavits and testimony of program instructors attesting to the contrary; and finally, that the suit did not challenge the constitutionality of the Michigan law, but only how it was applied."

EVOLUTION

In 1925 not merely the United States but much of the world was fascinated by the trial of John Scopes, a biology teacher in Dayton, Tennessee, for violating a law forbidding the teaching of anything contrary to "the story of the Divine Creation of man, as related in the Bible." Scopes was found guilty and fined one hundred dollars but the state's highest court reversed the decision on the ground that the jury, not the judge, should have imposed the fine.

The statutory penalty included discharge of the offending teacher and disqualification from any other teaching position in the state, but this was irrelevant since Scopes had resigned from his position and had moved to another state. In any event, the Court said that it saw "nothing to be gained by prolonging this bizarre case," and directed that it be dropped "in the interests of the peace and dignity of the State."

Epperson v. Arkansas (1968) involved a challenge to the constitution-ality of a statute enacted shortly after the *State v. Scopes* trial. The statute forbade the teaching in state-supported schools and universities of "the theory or doctrine that mankind ascended or descended from a lower order of animals." In an opinion by Abe Fortas, the Court adjudged the Arkansas law to be unconstitutional because its purpose was to advance fundamentalist religion, which commands a literal interpretation of cre-ationism as set forth in the Bible. This was so, said Fortas, nothwith-standing the fact that the Arkansas statute did not mention the Bible, as did the Tennessee law in the *Scopes* case.

(The *amicus curiae* brief submitted on behalf of the American Civil Liberties Union and the American Jewish Congress presented the argu-ment, accepted by the Court though not urged in the brief of Miss Epperson's attorney, that the decision in the *Everson* and *Torcaso* cases required a determination that Miss Epperson's discharge violated the Establishment Clause of the First Amendment.)

In support of his conclusion that the purpose of the law was to advance religion, Fortas cited an advertisement in the Arkansas *Gazette* reading:

THE BIBLE OR ATHEISM, WHICH?

All atheists oppose religion. If you agree with atheism vote against Act No. 1. If you agree with the Bible vote for Act No. 1.

Shall conscientious church members be forced to pay taxes to support teachers to teach evolution which will undermine the faith of their children? The *Gazette* said Russian Bolshevists laughed at Tennessee. True, and that sort will laugh at Arkansas. Who cares? Vote for Act No. 1.

In separate opinions, Black and John Marshall Harlan agreed that the law as enforced in the *Epperson* case was unconstitutional but expressed the view that the Court should not have taken the case in the first place, since the challenged Act No. 1 had become a dead letter law; that is, though on the books, it was never enforced. Black noted that the Little Rock school where Susan Epperson taught had adopted for use a biology textbook which devoted an entire chapter to evolution and, like Scopes, she had moved to another state. Fortas himself conceded that it "is possible that the statute is presently more of a curiosity than a vital fact of life" in the three states (Arkansas, Mississippi, and Tennessee) that had enacted it. Nevertheless, he said, once the suit was brought to declare the law unconstitutional, the Court had no choice but to decide it.

In 1972 Mississippi, the third state with an anti-evolution law, repealed it, thus allowing evolution to be taught. It thereby took off the back of public education an imaginary monkey that was never there in the first place.

Or so it seemed. The then unrecognized factor in the evolution controversy was the rise of fundamentalism as a potent political force in the late seventies and the eighties, a movement that has been strongest in the South and in the Bible Belt. But lest one assume that only fundamentalists residing below the Mason-Dixon line believe that God created man in his present form at one particular time in the last ten thousand years, it should be noted that a Gallup poll reported in the *New York Times* in August 1982 indicated that fully forty-four percent of the persons interviewed, nearly a quarter of whom were college graduates, shared this belief, and that southerners and midwesterners were only slightly more likely to accept creationism than those living elsewhere. (It might be noted parenthetically that a woman on the staff of the Methodist Commission on Christian Unity and Interreligious Concerns called the phrasing of the questions offensive because they referred not to the creation of humankind or of man and woman, but only to the "creation of man.")

Fundamentalist efforts after the *Epperson* decision were first aimed at persuading the courts to bar the teaching of evolution in the public schools on the ground that evolution itself was a religion. They recognized that, whatever were the chances of a constitutional amendment to return prayer to the public schools, there was little hope for an amendment bringing back Genesis. Nor could they count on the Supreme Court to overrule itself and uphold statutes forbidding the teaching of evolution in the schools. (Notwithstanding the Court's 1984 decision in *Lynch v. Donnelly,* allowing public financing of a nativity scene or crèche in an annual Christmas display, it is very doubtful that a majority could be persuaded to overrule the *Epperson* decision.) For want of any other remedy, the fundamentalists decided to appeal to the American ethic of fair play predicated upon the equal time concept in radio and television broadcasting. Accordingly, in both legislatures and courts they have urged that if Darwinism is taught in a particular school, so too should Genesis. Evolution, they assert, is the religion of "Secular Humanism" and, if that may be taught in the public schools, the clause in the Fourteenth Amendment guaranteeing the equal protection of the laws requires that equal time be accorded to the teaching of creationism.

It would seem that if "Secular Humanism," whatever that may mean, is a religion, then the appropriate judicial remedy is an injunction against it being taught in the public schools rather than giving equal time to conventional religious instruction, for that would compound the wrong rather than eliminate it.

Exactly what is meant by the term "Secular Humanism" has never been judicially determined. It could mean different things to different people. Darwinism could hardly be a synonym of atheism for Darwin himself believed in God. The last sentence in *Origin of Species* reads: "There is grandeur in this view of life, with its several powers, having been originally breathed by the Creator into a few forms or into one; and to that, whilst this planet has gone cycling on according to the fixed law of gravity, from so simple a beginning endless forms most beautiful and most wonderful have been, and are being evolved."

But even if Darwinism were the equivalent of atheism there would be no need for a law forbidding its being taught in public schools. In the *Everson* case, Black (who was responsible for bringing the term "neutral" into constitutional jurisprudence relating to the Establishment Clause) ruled that the First Amendment "requires the state to be neutral in its relations with groups of religious believers and nonbelievers," a requirement that forbids inculcating atheism in pupils. If, on the other hand, "Secular Humanism" is a religion, its constitutional effect goes beyond the evolution controversy. In briefs defending or even demanding aid to parochial schools the argument has been asserted—but never accepted by the Court—that government financing of "Secular Humanism" in public schools requires similar treatment to schools that teach other religions such as Christianity and Judaism.

The term "Secular Humanism" came into church-state controversies in the case of *Torcaso v. Watkins,* decided in 1961. There the Court, in an opinion by Black, ruled unconstitutional a state law under which an applicant was denied the right to be appointed to the office of notary public because of his refusal to sign an oath that he believed in the existence of God. The brief of Torcaso's attorney made the following statement:

It is frequently assumed that all religions are founded upon a belief in the existence of a personal "God" no matter how that term is defined. This is not so. So great a religion as the Buddhist religion with over 150 millions throughout the world including the United States . . . is not founded upon a belief in the existence of God.

Footnote 11 of Black's opinion (footnotes can get one into a lot of trouble, as indicated with respect to Footnote 49 in the *Nyquist* case) reads as follows:

Among religions in this country which do not teach what would generally be considered a belief in the existence of God is Buddhism, Taoism, Ethical Culture, Secular Humanism and others.

Judicial efforts to achieve the goal of teaching creationism have so far been unsuccessful, and this notwithstanding Reagan's endorsement. In *Wright v. Houston Independent School District* (1972) a Federal District Court in Texas threw out a case seeking an injunction against the use of textbooks presenting the theory of evolution on the ground that their use violated the Free Exercise and Establishment clauses of the First Amendment and the Equal Protection Clause of the Fourteenth Amendment. The Court rejected the assertion that teaching evolution supported a "religion of secularism," and that equal time must therefore be accorded to non-Darwinian teachings. To do the latter, said the Court, could oblige teachers to provide equal time for an exposition of the Mormon belief in the inequality of the races and for indoctrination in the Christian Science view of health and disease. Since the Texas law provided for excusal, the Court said, there was no violation of the Constitution. The United States Court of Appeals affirmed the decision and the plaintiff decided to go no further.

Other suits proved equally fruitless. In *Daniel v. Waters* (1975) another Court of Appeals held unconstitutional a Tennessee statute requiring that any textbook expressing an opinion about the origin of man must state that it was only a theory and must also set forth the Biblical account of creation but, as to the latter, the "theory" statement did not need to be printed—an exception not easily justifiable under the Equal Protection Clause. To be on the safe side, the legislators included a disclaimer stating that the "teaching of all occult or satanical beliefs of human origin is expressly excluded from this Act." The Court of Appeals rejected the "Secular Humanism" argument in affirming the lower court's decision dismissing the complaint.

In *Crowley v. Smithsonian Institute* (1980) the Court of Appeals in the District of Columbia affirmed a decision dismissing a suit for an injunction against an exhibit at the Museum of Natural History that contained references to evolution. There, too, the plaintiff complained that the exhibit promoted the religion of "Secular Humanism" and therefore was unconstitutional unless equal funds were provided for exhibits supporting Genesis.

However, the most recent efforts towards achieving the goal of Genesis-in-or-Darwin-out involve an elaborately constructed "Balanced Treatment for Creation-Science and Evolution-Science Act." As of now, the Balanced Treatment Bill has been introduced in quite a number of states but has been enacted only in two, Arkansas and Louisiana. This carefully drafted legislation seeking to achieve the goal of equal treatment avoids terms like "God," "Lord," "Supreme Being," "Bible," or "Genesis." Instead it uses the neutral term "creation-science" as differentiated from "evolution-science" and ·its stated purpose is to protect academic freedom, as indicated by its title, "Balanced Treatment for Creation-Science and Evolution-Science Act." "Creation-science" is defined as "the scientific evidences for creation and inferences from those scientific evidences."

Fairness requires noting that present-day American anti-evolutionists were not the first to wed Biblical literalism to science; more than a century earlier Mary Baker Eddy established a faith which she named Christian Science. New or old, however, literalist religion and modern science are contradictory: one is founded upon faith and the other rejects it. For this reason it would seem impossible to comply with the requirement in the Balanced Treatment Act that "existing library acquisition funds shall be used to purchase *nonreligious* library books as are necessary to give a balanced treatment to the creation-science model and the evolution-science model." (Emphasis added.)

Apparently to assure that it too satisfied American concepts of fairness, exemplified in the Bill of Rights and the Fourteenth Amendment, and hopefully to avoid nullification under the *Epperson* ruling, the Balanced Treatment Act mandates teaching of creation-science only if evolution-science is taught. It is nevertheless difficult to reconcile this requirement with the claim of nonreligiosity. Legislatures do not usually require equality of treatment in other areas of learning, such as mathematics or foreign languages. One can sympathize with nonfundamentalist students who, after graduation from a high school which has elected to teach neither evolution nor creationism, are faced with a college entrance examination anywhere but in Arkansas and Louisiana.

Despite the careful drafting of the Arkansas act, it was ruled unconstitutional by the United States District Court in the case of *McLean v. Arkansas Board of Education* (1982). The act, the Court held, violated the Establishment Clause in three ways: it lacked a secular legislative purpose; its effect was the advancement of religion in public schools; and its unavoidable consequence was impermissible entanglement with religion.

For undisclosed reasons, the anti-evolutionists decided not to appeal the court's decision but to rely instead upon successful defense of a Louisiana lawsuit, entitled *Aquillard v. Treen.* That suit, still pending in the Federal District Court in New Orleans, challenges a statute which follows the Arkansas law word for word. It was instituted by a number of parents, teachers, and taxpayers together with a minority member of the state legislature; a number of clergymen, Protestant (mostly), Catholic, and Jewish; teachers' federations; and the National Coalition for Public Education and Religious Liberty (National PEARL).

The complaint in the suit asserts that the statute violates the Establishment Clause, deprives teachers of their right to academic freedom, and is unconstitutionally vague. With respect to the first ground, which relates to the subject treated in this book, the complaint claims that the Creationism Act lacks a secular purpose, has a principal and primary effect of advancing religion, fosters excessive government entanglement with religion, and creates potential for political devisiveness along religious lines. The determined commitment on both sides makes it highly probable that the case will reach the Burger Court. If so, it may safely be presumed that Reagan, who has expressed his agreement with the anti-evolutionists, will see to it that the Court receives the benefit of an *amicus curiae* brief from the United States Solicitor General.

What the anti-evolutionists have as yet been unable to accomplish in the courts, they may well be winning in the marketplace. According to a report in the February 24, 1984, issue of *Publishers Weekly,* two textbook publishers have been giving decreasing attention to evolution during the past ten years. This has been occurring gradually after the Texas Board of Education decided that presentations of evolution had to state that it was theory, not fact, and had to give equal weight to other theories of origin. Because Texas buys more textbooks than any other state and accounts for ten percent of all biology textbook sales, its Board of Education's adoption requirements have great influence on what is made available to the rest of the country. Whether this is a case of bad textbooks driving out the good or *vice versa* depends on how you look at things. (The board recently decided that it was not necessary for textbooks to mention Darwin and the theory of evolution to be eligible for adoption in Texas.)

TEN COMMANDMENTS

Unlike *Epperson v. Arkansas,* in which there was no dissent as to the outcome although there was some disagreement as to how it should have been reached, *Stone v. Graham* (1980) was decided by a five to four vote with respect to both the outcome and the reasoning that supported it. Challenged in this suit was a Kentucky law directing the state superintendent of schools to ensure that a durable permanent copy of the Ten Commandments be displayed on the wall in every elementary and secondary school classroom in the state. The copy was to be sixteen inches wide and twenty inches high, and in small print below the last commandment there was to appear a notation concerning the purpose of the display. This was to read: "The secular application of the Ten Commandments is clearly seen in its adoption as the fundamental legal code of Western Civilization and the Common Law of the United States." The statute also provided that the necessary funds were to be obtained by voluntary contributions specified for that purpose.

The majority of the Court, in a *per curium* opinion—one not signed by any justice—ruled the law to be a violation of the First Amendment because it had no secular purpose. There was therefore no need to consider whether its effect was to advance religion or whether it fostered government entanglement with religion. The statement in the statute relating to the "secular application of the Ten Commandments" was held not to be binding upon the Court. "The preeminent purpose for posting the Ten Commandments on schoolroom walls," the Court said, "is plainly religious in nature, [since] the Ten Commandments are undoubtedly a sacred text in the Jewish and Christian faiths." They do not concern themselves only with secular matters such as honoring one's parents, murder, adultery, stealing, bearing false witness, and covetousness but also with the religious duties of worshiping the Lord God alone, avoiding idolatry, not using the Lord's name in vain, and observing the Sabbath.

It is immaterial, the Court concluded, that the Bible verses were merely to be posted on the wall rather than to be read aloud as in the prayer case of *Engel v. Vitale* and the Bible reading case of *Abington School District v. Schempp* (both considered later in this chapter), inasmuch as it is not a defense that religious practices are minor encroachments on the First Amendment.

(The Court could have, but for some reason did not, cite the case of *Tudor v. Board of Education* (1954) in support of its ruling. There New Jersey's highest court, in a decision which the United States Supreme Court, under the title, *Gideon International v. Tudor,* refused to review, ruled that the practice of allowing volunteers to distribute free copies of the Gideon Bible within public school classrooms and corridors violated the First Amendment. Realistically, the violation of the Establishment Clause in the *Tudor* case was less egregious than that in *Stone v. Graham.* In the former case, distribution took but a few minutes in the school day and acceptance of the Bible was entirely voluntary; in the latter case, exposure to the Ten Commandments continued from the moment classes began until the pupils were dismissed at the end of the school day. Moreover, there was no escape from this exposure, since it was hardly practicable for the pupils to keep their eyes closed during the whole school day or seek refuge in the lavatories. This point is hardly frivolous, since the Kentucky legislators did not deem perpetual exposure meaningless, otherwise they would not have enacted the offending statutes.)

It would seem that even if the school authorities' purpose had not been religious, other aspects of the Establishment Clause would point to a judgment of unconstitutionality. School children, certainly at the elementary level, assume that everything they learn in school is true. It follows from this that posting the Ten Commandments would advance those religions, Protestant, Catholic, and Jewish, that believe the commandments to be the words of God. In addition, entanglement would be an almost certain consequence, since it could hardly be expected that the children would not ask questions regarding the meaning of the commandments and their relation to God.

The joint *amicus curiae* brief submitted by the Synagogue Council and the National Jewish Community Relations Advisory Council sets forth as an appendix the following chart indicating the differences among the faiths as to the placement of each of the commandments. No matter which version was chosen, the unavoidable result would be the preference of the chosen faith over the other two, a consequence forbidden by both the Establishment and Equal Protection clauses of the Constitution.

PRAYER IN PUBLIC SCHOOLS—THE COURT'S DECISIONS

On the whole, discontinuance of public school religious instruction mandated by the *McCollum* decision was effected with comparative ease. A century earlier, Catholicism had established its parochial school system so as to realize its doctrine that all instruction including, as indicated in the preceding chapter, that in arithmetic (at least in its earliest stage) must be impregnated with religion. In recent years, fundamentalist Protestants, though lacking the financial resources of the Catholic church, have begun to follow the Catholics, and so too have Orthodox Jews, in establishing parallel school systems.

It is, however, not necessary to set up a separate school system in order to open the school day with prayer. Parents can, of course, have their children pray each morning before they go to school; all Orthodox Jewish parents do that. But many, perhaps too many, find it easier to "leave the praying to them," "them" being the public school teachers, no matter what the Supreme Court might say. What the Court, in *Engel v. Vitale,* said was "no," but it said it on June 25th, the last day of the

THE TEN COMMANDMENTS

Jewish Version	Roman Catholic Version	Protestant & Greek Orthodox Version
Introduction: None	Introduction: I am the Lord thy God, who brought you out of the land of Egypt, out of the house of bondage.	Introduction: I am the Lord your God, who brought you out of the land of Egypt, out of the house of bondage.
First: I am the Lord thy God, who brought thee out of the land of Egypt, out of the house of bondage.	First: Thou shalt have no other gods before me.	First: Thou shalt have no other gods before me.
Second: Thou shalt have no other gods before me.	Second: Thou shalt not take the name of the Lord thy God in vain.	Second: Thou shalt not make unto thee any graven image.
Third: Thou shalt not take the name of thy Lord God in vain.	Third: Remember the Sabbath day to keep it holy.	Third: Thou shalt not take the name of the Lord thy God in vain.
Fourth: Remember the Sabbath to keep it holy.	Fourth: Honor thy father and mother.	Fourth: Remember the Sabbath day to keep it holy.
Fifth: Honor thy father and mother.	Fifth: Thou shalt not kill.	Fifth: Honor thy father and mother.
Sixth: Thou shalt not kill.	Sixth: Thou shalt not commit adultery.	Sixth: Thou shalt not kill.
Seventh: Thou shalt not commit adultery.	Seventh: Thou shalt not steal.	Seventh: Thou shalt not commit adultery.
Eighth: Thou shalt not steal.	Eighth: Thou shalt not bear false witness.	Eighth: Thou shalt not steal.
Ninth: Thou shalt not bear false witness.	Ninth: Thou shalt not covet they neighbor's house.	Ninth: Thou shalt not bear false witness.
Tenth: Thou shalt not covet thy neighbor's house. Thou shalt not covet they neighbor's wife.	Tenth: Thou shalt not covet thy neighbor's wife.	Tenth: Thou shalt not covet thy neighbor's house. Thou shalt not covet thy neighbor's wife.

Court's 1961-62 term, thereby establishing an oft-repeated practice of announcing controversial church-state decisions just before the justices leave Washington not to return until October.

There was a practical reason for this. The *McCollum* decision forbidding religious instruction in the public schools was announced in March in the middle of the school semester. It applied not only to the schools in Champaign but to schools throughout the nation, and undoubtedly imposed considerable problems for school administrators whose duty it was to implement the decision. (*Zorach v. Clauson*, decided in April, caused no such problem, since it sustained rather than upset current practice.) The *McCollum* case experience may have led the Court to withhold announcing the *Engel* decision until the last day or close to the last day of the public school semester before the summer recess.

There may, however, have been another practical explanation for instituting a last-day-of-term practice. As has been noted, Black, in his dissenting opinion in the *Zorach* case, noted the "wide debate" (euphemism for acrimonious attacks upon the Court) that had followed the *McCollum* decision.

It is, therefore, a plausible guess that June 25th was chosen as the day on which to announce the *Engel* decision for another reason as well. On that day or a few days later the public school terms ended and classes would not begin again until September. Chief Justice Earl Warren might have hoped that passions would have cooled off by then and the decision accepted if not welcomed. If so, hope was vanquished by reality, as will shortly be related. First, however, the background of the case and the substance of the Court's decision, from which only Stewart dissented, must be set forth.

Upon recommendation of the Board of Regents, New York's highest educational body, a number of public school districts instituted the practice of having those pupils who did not object to doing so recite a prayer each morning. What the Regents were aiming for was a purely "non-sectarian" prayer, one that could be recited by all God-fearing pupils, Protestant, Catholic, or Jewish. (Since participating in recitation of the prayer was entirely voluntary, atheists, if there were any among the schools' parents, supposedly had no reason to object.) To make sure of this, the Regents formulated their own prayer and submitted it to leading clergymen of the three faiths for their approval. After receiving it, they submitted their proposal to all school boards in the state.

The Regents' Prayer, as it popularly became known, consisted of the following twenty-two words:

Almighty God, we acknowledge our dependence upon Thee, and we beg
thy blessings upon us, our parents, our teachers and our country.

The attempt to satisfy all Protestants, including the fundamentalists
who from the beginning were the chief defenders of public school prayer,
did not succeed. The Regents' effort at nonsectarianism evoked a protest
from the leaders of the Lutheran Church of Our Redeemer in Peekskill,
New York. According to a report in the *Peekskill Evening Star* of January
16, 1961, they protested that the name of Jesus had "deliberately been
omitted to mollify non-Christian elements," and that the Regents' prayer
was "a denial of Christ and His prescription for a proper prayer."

The effort to avoid invalidation of the nonsectarian prayer proposal
under the First Amendment proved equally futile. "It is no part of the
business of government," Black said in his opinion for the majority, "to
compose official prayers for any group of the American people to recite
as part of a religious program carried on by government." The Regents'
action was unconstitutional and neither the fact that the prayer might be
denominationally neutral nor that its observance on the part of pupils
might be voluntary could serve to free it from the limitations of the
Establishment Clause. Black noted "the unfortunate fact of history that
when some of the very groups which had most strenuously opposed the
established Church of England found themselves sufficiently in control of
colonial government in this country to write their own prayers into law,
they passed laws making their own religion the official religion of the
respective colonies."

He might have noted but did not that in England Catholics had numerically been the chief victims of governmental persecution (to some extent
even after the 1689 Act of Toleration). In reply to an Irish town which
offered to surrender if the inhabitants would be permitted liberty of
conscience, Oliver Cromwell wrote:

For that which you mention concerning liberty of conscience, I meddle not
with any man's conscience. But if by liberty you mean a liberty to exercise
the mass, I judge it best to use plain dealing, and to let you know, where
Parliament of England have power, that will not be allowed of.

REACTION TO THE DECISION

Southern statesmen were practically unanimous in their reaction to the
decision. Representative George W. Andrews of Alabama found a rela-

tionship between race, religion, and the Supreme Court. "They," he said, referring to the latter, "put the Negroes in the schools, and now they've driven God out." West Virginia Senator Robert C. Byrd broadly intimated that the evil was Communism imported from the Soviet Union. "Can it be," he asked rhetorically, "that we, too, are ready to embrace the foul concept of atheism? Somebody is tampering with America's soul. I leave it to you who that somebody is." And, according to a report in the *Washington Post* issue of July 7, 1962, Senator Sam Ervin of North Carolina asserted that "The Supreme Court has made God unconstitutional." It must be added, however, that not long thereafter Ervin changed his views and strongly opposed public school prayers. His present position is stated in an article he wrote for the Summer 1983 issue of *Free Inquiry*. It reads:

> Many sincere persons charge that the school-prayer cases show the Supreme Court to be hostile to religion. This charge is untrue and unjust. In these cases the Supreme Court was faithful to its judicial duty. It enforced the First Amendment, which commands government to maintain strict neutrality respecting religion, neither aiding nor opposing it.

In the United States, as in England, Catholics were numerically the chief victims of laws and/or regulations that either mandated or allowed school-sponsored religion in the public schools. Prior to the *McCollum* suit, all state lawsuits challenging instruction or prayer recitation were brought by Catholics. Nevertheless, the decision in that case was condemned by authoritative Catholic voices, although there had been no active Catholic involvement in the suit itself. Not so in *Engel v. Vitale*; some Catholic parents of public school children formally intervened in the suit in defense of the regulation and were represented by Porter Chandler, who as has been noted, was then the most prominent lawyer active in suits challenging aid to parochial schools. It was therefore not surprising that authoritative Catholic voices should join those of Evangelical Protestant and Southern political leaders in condemning the decision and the Court that promulgated it.

Thus Cardinal Spellman declared, "I am shocked and frightened that the Supreme Court has declared unconstitutional a simple and voluntary declaration of belief in God by public school children. The decision strikes at the very heart of the Godly tradition in which America's children have so long been raised." Other priests and prelates echoed this sentiment and so did Catholic periodicals throughout the nation.

The editors of *America* identified the real villains. In an editorial entitled "To Our Jewish Friends," which appeared shortly after the decision was handed down, they said that since the decision "there have been disturbing hints of heightened anti-Semitic feeling" and that "all necessary steps should be taken to prevent an outbreak of anti-Semitism." It then continued, ". . . we should recognize that full responsibility for the decision in *Engel v. Vitale* is not to be pinned on the Jewish community. Along with that well-publicized Jewish spokesman, Leo Pfeffer, and such organizations as the American Jewish Congress, responsibility for the concerted opposition to the New York prayer—and to other forms of religious practice in the public schools and public life—belongs to the American Civil Liberties Union, the Ethical Culture Society, the Humanist associations, some Unitarians, many atheists and certain other groups with doctrinaire views on the meaning and application of the principle of separation of Church and State."

The editorial charged further that "one long-range objective" of this "sector of the Jewish Community" is to "create a 'climate of opinion' in which the [Supreme] Court can more readily continue to make decisions in consonance with the principle of separation of church and state as that principle has been interpreted in absolutistic terms by Leo Pfeffer, by the American Jewish Congress, and by the Supreme Court in the *McCollum* case of 1948."

> It would be most unfortunate [the editorial continued] if the entire Jewish community were to be blamed for the unrelenting pressure tactics of a small but overly vocal segment within it . . . . Conceivably with help from some important Jewish groups, the recitation of the Lord's Prayer, as well as the reading of passages from the Bible in the public schools, can and may, in the near future be declared unconstitutional. We wonder, therefore, whether it is not time for provident leaders of American Judaism to ask their more militant colleagues whether what is gained through the courts by some victories is worth the breakdown of community relations which will inevitably follow them. What will have been accomplished if our Jewish friends win all the legal immunities they seek, but thereby paint themselves into a corner of social and cultural alienation? The time has come for these fellow citizens to decide among themselves what they conceive to be the final objective of the Jewish community in the United States—in a word, what bargain they are willing to strike as one of the minorities in a pluralistic society. When victories produce only a harvest of fear and distrust, will it all have been worth-while?

The *Christian Century*, the nation's leading Protestant periodical, reacted sharply. In an editorial entitled, "Is *America* Trying to Bully the Jews?" it called the *America* editorial "a thinly veiled threat" whose purpose "seems to be to frighten Jews into deserting Protestants and other Americans who support the Supreme Court's ruling." The editorial then continued:

> Along with "certain other groups with doctrinaire views on the meaning and application of the principle of separation of church and state," the American Jewish Congress and its general counsel, Leo Pfeffer, are cited by *America* as responsible for the court's decision . . . . Do the editors of *America* mean to imply that the only way Jews will be able to forestall anti-Semitic attacks is to maintain silence on issues involving the constitutional liberties of all citizens, including Jews? If so, they are guilty of an attempt to bully a segment of our population as part of a general assault on the liberties of all Americans . . . . We hope and believe that the American Jewish Congress and its distinguished counsel will persist in using all legal means to uphold liberties which they will continue to share with all Americans so long as the repressive spirit that informs the *America* editorial is resisted with courage.

This, however, did not daunt the editors at *America*. Two weeks after the initial editorial appeared, they published a second editorial on the subject. In this editorial, entitled "The Main Issue," they said:

> This fall the Supreme Court will rule on a number of cases relative to religious practices in the schools. If, as they are now bending every effort to do, Leo Pfeffer and his fellow campaigners succeed in winning Supreme Court decisions that strike down the Lord's Prayer and Bible reading in school classrooms, there will be once again—as there was at the time of the Engel decision, only more so—an intensely unfavorable public reaction. When and if such decisions are handed down, then unless it has been made clear that Dr. Pfeffer and the American Jewish Congress do not speak for the whole of American Jewry, Jews in general will be unfairly blamed for what in fact will have been accomplished by a mere handful of militants, allied with an assortment of humanist groups, ethical culturists, Unitarians, secularists and atheists.

It should not, however, be assumed that *The Christian Century* was the only non-Jewish voice raised in support of the decision. There was no absence of reputable organizations and prominent individuals who defended it, among them a number of liberal Protestant ministers. Most prominent of these was The Reverend Dr. Martin Luther King, revered black leader, who called it "a sound and good decision reaffirming something that is basic in our Constitution, namely separation of church and state."

King is the only American whose birthdate, except for George Washington's, was later to become a national holiday through an act of Congress, reluctantly signed into law by President Reagan. This he did over the initial protest of Helms, who echoed Byrd's apprehension of Communist influence. Byrd's reluctance to identify by name the "who" that was tampering with America's soul twenty years ago was not shared by Helms. He unsuccessfully urged that final action on the measure to make King's birthday a national holiday be postponed pending investigation of the possibility that he may have been a Communist, as indicated in the files of J. Edgar Hoover's Federal Bureau of Investigation.

A group of Protestant leaders, including the dean of Harvard Divinity School, joined in a statement supporting the *Engel* decision. Support also came from the United Church of Christ and from the Joint Baptist Committee on Public Affairs, the latter representing churches whose combined memberships totaled some twenty-seven million parishioners. The reaction of American Jewry was naturally wholly favorable to the decision.

As was to be expected, however, Protestant Evangelicals shared the Catholic reaction. Typical was the voice of Dr. Billy Graham who, at least until his return from a visit to the Soviet Union two decades later, was probably the nation's most respected and revered clergyman. The decision, he said, was "another step towards the secularization of the United States . . . . The framers of our Constitution meant we were to have freedom of religion, not freedom from religion."

If there were any who hoped that the Supreme Court could be frightened into overruling the *Engel* decision and allow public school prayers, they were soon to be sadly disappointed. A year after that decision, the Court handed down its decision in the combined case of *Abington School District v. Schempp* and *Murray v. Curlett* (considered more fully in the next section). The Court reaffirmed the *Engel* ruling and extended it to encompass recitation of the Lord's Prayer.

Protagonists of prayer and (after the *Schempp-Murray* decision) Bible reading in the public schools did not give up. After the *Engel* decision was handed down a kindergarten teacher in DeKalb County, Illinois, with or without advice of counsel, sought to avoid unconstitutionality by removing God from prayer. Prior to the decision it was the practice in the Elwood Public School in that county for the children in the kindergarten to recite a simple four-line prayer, later to become nationally known as the "cookie prayer." It read:

> We thank you for the flowers so sweet,
> We thank you for the food we eat,

We thank you for the birds that sing,
We thank you, God, for everything.

After the *Engel* and *Schempp* decisions came down, the teacher or school principal sought to secularize the prayer and make it constitutionally permissible by making it Godless. The secularized prayer read:

We thank you for the flowers so sweet,
We thank you for the food we eat,
We thank you for the birds that sing,
We thank you for everything.

To avoid invalidation as religious instruction forbidden by the *McCollum* ruling, it became common practice for principals to warn their teachers not to answer any questions put to them by their pupils that could call for what might be adjudged religious instruction but to advise the pupils that they should seek the answers from their parents or clergymen. It could therefore be assumed that the Elwood school teacher was aware of this mandate and, if asked by any pupils to identify the "you" to whom the cookie prayer was addressed, would advise the pupil to ask his or her parent or clergyman. If so, it was all for naught; in *DeKalb School District v. DeSpain* the Supreme Court, in 1968, refused to upset a lower court decision ruling the practice unconstitutional.

Another approach assumed that the fatal flaw in the *Engel* and *Schempp* cases lay in the school or teacher sponsorship of the prayer programs even though the specific prayers were selected by the students. If the initiative for the prayer recitation came from the students themselves, it was felt that the program would be permissible or even required. Thus, in *Stein v. Olshinsky,* a group of God-fearing parents in a New York City school brought a suit in the federal court against school officials who would not allow pupils to engage in self-initiated prayer recitation during school hours. The court was not persuaded; it dismissed their complaint and the Supreme Court (in 1965) refused to review the case.

All the cases from *Engel* to *Stein v. Olshinsky* relating to prayer at the elementary and secondary school level were decided by the Warren Court but, as of now, the pro-prayer advocates fared no better after Burger became Chief Justice.

Stein v. Olshinsky had held only that parents could not compel schools to permit pupil-initiated prayers; it did not hold that the school authorities might not on their own sanction them. So the school committee in Leyden, Massachusetts, adopted a resolution permitting student-initiated religious exercises, in which those students and teachers who wished to do so could participate. In *State Commissioner of Education v. School Committee,* the state's highest court declared this unconstitutional; the school committee sought to appeal to the Supreme Court, but once more the Court (in 1971) rejected the appeal.

Another tack was tried in Netcong, New Jersey. The local school board instituted a program "for the free exercise of religion" that provided a period prior to the formal opening of classes, during which students who wished to join in the exercise could meditate after listening to the chaplain's opening prayer or to appropriate "remarks" in the United States Senate or House, read from the Congressional Record. The state board of education ordered the Netcong school board to terminate the program and, upon its refusal, went into the state courts and obtained an injunction. The Netcong school board appealed to the Burger Court which, in *Board of Education of Netcong v. State Board of Education,* rejected the appeal in 1971.

Such, too, was the fate of *Brandon v. Board of Education of the Guilderland Central School District,* which reached and was rejected by the Supreme Court ten years later. That case challenged the refusal by the principal of Guilderland High School in New York to allow several students, organized as a group under the name Students for Voluntary Prayers, to conduct communal prayer meetings in a classroom for a half hour each school day before classes started. The group did not seek supervision or faculty involvement (obviously to avoid entanglement of church and state), and asserted that its activities were voluntary and would not conflict with other school functions.

Both the Federal District Court and the Court of Appeals ruled that granting the request would have the impermissible effect of advancing religion and would result in excessive entanglement, the latter because faculty surveillance would be needed to assure that the meetings were truly voluntary. Without issuing a written opinion, the Supreme Court refused to accept the appeal.

It would seem unlikely that the Burger Court will yield to the apparently unceasing effort urging it to overrule the *Engel* and *Schempp* rulings. In 1982 the Court, in the case of *Treen v. Karen B.,* was faced with an appeal from a decision invalidating a Louisiana statute providing for morning prayer in the public schools during school hours, authorizing teachers to conduct the prayer observance, to select among student volunteers and say a prayer if no student wished to pray, and requiring the teachers to monitor the prayer so as to enforce the statutory one-minute time limitation and assure that all participation was purely voluntary. Without any dissent, the Court did more than reject the appeal, it affirmed the decision, thus making it a ruling of the Supreme Court. This action was taken *after* the Court had handed down its decision in the case of *Widmar v. Vincent,* shortly to be discussed. (The title of the *Karen B.* case is significant. The plaintiff's family name is not given, a practice common in prosecutions for sex offenses against children. The lower court's permission to follow this practice testifies to the fears some parents still experience in bringing suits challenging religious practices in the public schools.)

As of the present writing the latest action of the Supreme Court in the arena of public school prayers was in the case of *Lubbock Independent School District v. Lubbock Civil Liberties Union* (1983). There it refused to review a Court of Appeals decision invalidating, under all three aspects of the purpose-effect-entanglement test, a statement of policy that read:

> The School Board permits students to gather at school with supervision either before or after regular hours on the same basis as determined by the school administration to meet for any educational, moral, religious or ethical purposes so long as attendance at such meetings is voluntary.

With respect to purpose, the Court followed the holdings in *Stone v. Graham* and *Treen v. Karen B.* and found that the preeminent purpose of the school board's rule was to promote meetings of a religious nature. It held, too, that the primary effect of the policy was the advancement of religion by placing the state's imprimatur upon religious activity. As in the *Brandon* case, it held that the symbolic inference of secular endorsement of religious activities resulted in the impermissible advancement of religion. Moreover, as the Supreme Court had done in *Engel v. Vitale,* it ruled it entirely irrelevant in determining effect that participation in prayer was purely voluntary and the prayer itself might have been denominationally neutral. Nor could the *Brandon* and *Karen B.* cases be distinguished on the ground that the religious activities there were held after the school buses had arrived, while the religious meetings in *Lubbock* took place before or after the school buses had run. The pupils were in school because the state's compulsory machinery drew the student to school and this provided an audience for the religious activities.

The entanglement ban, said the Court, was violated in that, in compliance with Texas law, the school district was required to exercise supervision over the students. In addition, the surveillance that was required to guarantee that participation in the prayer meetings was entirely voluntary itself constituted impermissible entanglement.

The Court of Appeals concluded its consideration of constitutionality under the First Amendment by rejecting the school board's claim that refusing to provide facilities for prayer would violate the students' rights under both the free exercise and free speech guarantees of the amendment. As to the former, the Court said:

> . . . A school is obligated to provide facilities only if its failure to do so would effectively foreclose a person's practice of religion. Here there is no problem with students being foreclosed from practicing religion. The students attend school only several hours a day, five days a week, nine months during the year. The other hours are effectively open for their attendance at religious activities at places other than state supported schools.

Finally, said the Court in response to the free speech clause, "a high school [was] not a 'public forum' where religious views can be freely aired . . . ." Again quoting from the *Brandon* decision, it said:

> . . . The expression of religious points of view, and even the performance of religious rituals, is permissible in parks and streets when subject to reasonable time, place, and manner regulations. The facilities of a university have also been identified as a "public forum," where religious speech and association cannot be prohibited. A high school classroom, however, is different. While students have First Amendment rights to political speech in public schools, sensitive Establishment Clause considerations limit their right to air religious doctrines.

CAMPAIGNS FOR CONSTITUTIONAL AMENDMENTS

Almost as soon as the *Engel* decision was announced, members of the Senate and House, mostly but not exclusively from the South, rushed to introduce amendments to the Constitution that would nullify it. A year later, when the Court in the *Schempp-Murray* cases decided that devotional Bible reading was likewise unconstitutional, some of the proposed amendments were extended to encompass that as well. In response, a counterstatement signed by more than four hundred constitutional law professors and legal practitioners was presented to Congress. Its significance merits its full presentation here. Under the title "Our Most Precious Heritage," it reads:

> Our Bill of Rights is America's most precious heritage. For a century and three-quarters it has spread the mantle of protection over persons of all faiths and creeds, political, cultural and religious.
>   Under our system, special responsibility for the interpretation and application of the Bill of Rights rests with the Supreme Court. In discharging

this responsibility the Court has from time to time handed down decisions which have aroused considerable controversy. Some of the decisions have been subjected to strong criticism and even condemnation. There have, no doubt, been decisions which have been deemed by a majority of the American people, at least in their immediate reaction, to have been unwise, either in the conclusion reached by the Court or in the manner by which that conclusion was reached.

It may be that the Court's 1962 and 1963 decisions against state-sponsored prayer and devotional Bible reading in the public schools belong in this category. If so, it is much too early to judge whether it will be the popular judgment or the Court's that will be vindicated by time. But whichever the case, we are convinced that it would be far wiser for our nation to accept the decisions than to amend the Bill of Rights in order to nullify them.

We recognize that the Constitution provides for its own amendment, and that no provision of it, including the Bill of Rights, is immune to repeal or alteration at the will of the people expressed through the medium of constitutional amendment. Yet, it is relevant to recall in this respect the concluding paragraph of Thomas Jefferson's great Virginia Statute for Establishing Religious Freedom: "And though we well know that this as-sembly, elected by the people for the ordinary purposes of legislation only, have no power to restrain the acts of succeeding assemblies, constituted with powers equal to our own, and that therefore to declare this act to be irrevocable would be of no effect in law, yet we are free to declare, and do declare, that the rights hereby asserted are of the natural rights of mankind, and that if any act shall be hereafter passed to repeal the present, or to narrow its operation, such act will be an infringement of natural right."

American liberties have been secure in large measure because they have been guaranteed by a Bill of Rights which the American people have until now deemed practically unamendable. If now, for the first time, an amend-ment to "narrow its operation" is adopted, a precedent will have been established which may prove too easy to follow when other controversial decisions interpreting the Bill of Rights are handed down. In the past, the Court has construed the provisions against infringement of the free exercise of religion and of speech and assembly, of securing the privilege against self-incrimination, or requiring fair trial procedures, in a manner deemed by many at the time to be unduly restrictive of the proper powers of government. It is certain that it will do so again in the future. If the first clause of the Bill of Rights, forbidding laws respecting an establishment of religion should prove so easily susceptible to impairment by amendment, none of the succeeding clauses will be secure.

A grave responsibility rests upon the Congress in taking this "first experi-ment on our liberties." Whatever disagreement some may have with the Bible-Prayer decisions, we believe strongly that they do not justify this experiment. Accordingly, we urge that Congress approve no measures to amend the First Amendment in order to overrule these decisions.

Those who signed "Our Most Precious Heritage" placed their reliance upon the conscience of the people and their representatives in Congress (or at least on negative votes by one-third plus one of either House). Not that there was a lack of effort to achieve amendment. Barely had the *Engel* decision been announced when Senator James Eastland of Mississippi proposed an amendment stating that nothing in the Constitution should be read as prohibiting prayers in the public schools. However, he quickly and quietly abandoned the venture when he found that, notwithstanding their vocal assault upon the Court, not a single Catholic prelate was willing to appear at a hearing held in November 1962 to consider the proposed amendment.

It should not be assumed from this that the Catholic church necessarily opposed or at least remained opposed to amending the Constitution to overcome the *Engel* decision. Indeed, in 1973, the United State's Catholic Conference, the highest authority within the church on political matters, proposed the following amendment to the Constitution (as can be seen, the proposal sought to nullify not only the *Engel* and *Schempp* decisions but the *McCollum* decision as well):

Section 1. Nothing in this constitution shall be construed to (i) forbid prayer in public places or in institutions of the several states or to the United States, including schools; (ii) forbid religious instruction in public places or in institutions of the several states or of the United States, including schools, if such instruction is provided under private auspices, whether or not religious.

Section 2. The right of the people to participate or not to participate in prayer or religious instruction shall never be infringed by the several states or the United States.

Neither Eastland's withdrawal nor the church's earlier hands-off position deterred further efforts towards a constitutional amendment. In every session of Congress proposals seeking to overrule the *Engel* and *Schempp* decisions were introduced. Typical was that of New York Congressman Frank Becker, who shortly after the *Schempp* decision was handed down undertook a one-man crusade to assure that the effort would succeed. First, he prevailed upon the many congressmen who had introduced separate measures to join in introducing a single proposal. After a co-operative measure was introduced and referred to the House Judiciary

Committee, he began rounding up signatures to a petition for its discharge so that it might be voted on by the entire House. Ironically, Becker himself had in the past always refused to sign discharge petitions, including those for civil rights bills aimed at achieving equality for blacks and other racial minorities. The reason for the difference, he explained, was that all other discharge petitions "dealt with material things and material benefits. This one deals only with the spiritual. The urgency of this matter leaves no alternative if we are to prevent the advocates of a godless society to accomplish in the United States that which the communists have accomplished in Soviet Russia." (Becker, like Helms later, did not share Senator Byrd's reticence in identifying Soviet Russia as what President Reagan was later to call the "evil empire.")

The proposed amendment (H. J. Res. 693, 88th Congress) agreed to by the various congressmen read as follows:

Section 1. Nothing in this Constitution shall be deemed to prohibit the offering, reading from or listening to prayers or Bible Scriptures, if participation therein is on a voluntary basis, in any governmental or public school, institution, or place.

Section 2. Nothing in this Constitution shall be deemed to prohibit making reference to belief in, reliance upon, or invoking the aid of God or a Supreme Being, in any governmental or public document, proceeding, activity, ceremony, school, institution, or place or upon any coinage, currency, or obligation of the United States.

Section 3. Nothing in this Article shall constitute an establishment of religion.

Becker was unable to achieve enactment of his measure but, with respect to "public institutions," the Burger Court was to do for him in substantial part what Congress would not. As we shall see later, in *Widmar v. Vincent* it refused to extend the *Engel* and *Schempp* bans to encompass state colleges; in *Marsh v. Chambers* it ruled that no constitutional amendment was needed to authorize opening legislative sessions with prayer or even using tax-raised funds to pay the clergymen who deliver the prayers; and in *Lynch v. Donnelly* (1984) it held constitutional the presence of a nativity scene or crèche in a municipally sponsored display. In these three cases the Court did not find itself handicapped by the absence of Section 3 of Becker's amendment, nor did it need legal advice as to whether the amendment violated the Establishment Clause. Even if Becker was wrong in stating that the amendment did not constitute an establishment of religion, that would not matter (except possibly for public relations purposes), since it is generally the purpose of amendments to change what is in, or what the Supreme Court says is in, the Constitution; else what's an amendment for?

Becker's efforts failed, but that was hardly the end of the matter. Proposed amendments, in substantially the same language, were introduced by Senator Everett Dirkson of Illinois and, after his death in 1969, by his son-in-law, Howard Baker of Tennessee. These and others got nowhere. Baker's name (like Ervin's) was shortly to achieve nationwide fame by reason of his active role in the Watergate affair, which made him remove public school prayer to the back burner, not to be brought forward until Reagan became president.

Reagan's endorsement of a constitutional amendment was consistent with his policy of returning powers and responsibilities to the states, free as far as possible of national interference, including that of the Supreme Court. Perhaps more important, however, was his need to pay back the debt owed to far right conservatives as well as religious fundamentalists. While the Catholic church was considerably more interested in measures that forbade abortions and those that provided government aid to parochial schools, it had never revoked its 1973 proposal for overruling the *Engel* decision by constitutional amendment and presumably would therefore applaud Reagan's efforts. However, Reagan, who in his 1983 State of the Union message declared that "God should never have been expelled from America's classrooms," was not satisfied with the wording of the many prior efforts to return prayer to the public schools and accordingly decided to draft his own. The following is what came from his pen and was introduced in the Senate by Strom Thurman of South Carolina on May 18, 1982:

> Nothing in this Constitution should be construed to prohibit individual or group prayer in public schools or other public institutions. No person shall be required by the United States or any State to participate in prayer.

If the second sentence was intended to placate Jewish voters, who though not in agreement among themselves on aid to religious schools agreed in opposing school prayer, it failed in effecting that end. Few of even the staunchest of Jewish Republicans accepted it as adequate protection for Jewish children, and the history of public school religion attested to the validity of their fears of pressure from teachers and fellow pupils. It should be noted, too, that Reagan's proposed amendment was not limited to "nonsectarian" prayer; nothing in it excluded prayers addressed to Jesus Christ or the Holy Trinity. It was a frequent practice before the *Engel* decision, and even later in schools that disregarded it, for a teacher to formulate his or her own prayer or invite pupils to do so and it was quite probably that in more than a few instances a formulated prayer would make reference to the crucifixion and the role Jews played in it.

Nor, at that time, were the liberal National Council of Churches or the generally conservative constituents of the Baptist Joint Committee on Public Affairs persuaded to change their position against public school sponsored prayers. But perhaps most interesting was the reponse of *America*, the Jesuit weekly that twenty years earlier had so virulently attacked defenders of the *Engel* decision. Its issue of September 25, 1982, carried an article by its associate editor, John W. Donahue, S. J., entitled "Prayer in the Schools: The Unanswered Question." Its penultimate paragraph read:

> Since the President made his announcement in the Rose Garden last May, there has been fairly general agreement among commentators that school prayer will rarely be voluntary because classrooms are rarely protected against coercion. But if the wisdom of the school prayer is doubtful the wisdom of cranking up the enormous mechanism of a constitutional amendment to make such prayer possible is even more so.

Although not directly related to the substance of this book, notice should also be taken of the remarkable leftward trend of *America* in issues relating to both domestic and foreign affairs. An article by another Jesuit, Francis Chamberlain, entitled "Six Unanswered Questions About Latin America," in the February 25, 1984, issue, sharply criticized Reagan's policies in respect to foreign affairs. He condemned our government's anti-Marxist military involvement in support of anti-democratic governments such as those in El Salvador, Guatemala, Brazil, Uruguay, and Paraguay and disagreed with the administration's assumption that all Marxists are controlled by Moscow.

Other articles and editorials in *America* have been critical of our nation's policies with respect to American-Soviet relations and, above all, nuclear disarmament. Three Catholic publications expressing pro-disarmament views, *America, Commonweal,* and *National Catholic Reporter,* rank high among liberal publications in the United States in sharp contrast to the strong anti-disarmament position of *Commentary,* a publication of the American Jewish Committee.

Reagan's proposal for a constitutional amendment got no further in

1982 and 1983 than any of those that preceded it and he found it necessary to repeat his plea in his 1984 State of the Union message:

> And while I'm on the subject [he said]—each day, your members observe a 200-year-old tradition meant to signify America as one nation under God. I must ask: If you can begin your day with a member of the clergy standing right here to lead you in prayer, then why can't freedom to acknowledge God be enjoyed again [i.e., as before the *Engel* decision] by children in every schoolroom across the land?

As was to be expected, Reagan's proposal was warmly endorsed by Helms, the Moral Majority, and other fundamentalists. Nevertheless, that it had to be repeated in two State of the Union messages indicated, to Helms at least, that prudence dictated recognition of the possibility that the necessary two-thirds vote in both houses of Congress and in three-fourths of the states would not soon be forthcoming. For this reason he did not abandon his own plan to get around the impasse. It was quite simple and required only majority votes in each house of Congress and the almost certain approval by Reagan. It provided that no federal court, up to and including the Supreme Court, should have jurisdiction in any case arising out of a statute relating to "voluntary" prayers in public schools and buildings.

There were, however, two obvious faults in the proposal. In the first place, it did not and could not guarantee that the states' highest courts would ignore the *Engel* and *Schempp* decisions in determining constitutionality under the First Amendment to the Constitution. State court judges, like all other public officials, take an oath that they will uphold the Constitution and most of them would probably understand this to mean the Constitution as construed by the nation's highest court.

The second fault is even more serious, for it goes to the heart of Helms's proposal. It does not relate to the constitutionality of school prayer recitation but rather seeks to set up a barrier to determination of that question by the United States Supreme Court. The reasoning in support of the proposed statute goes something like this: Article I, Section 3, of the Constitution states that "the judicial power of the United States shall be vested in one Supreme Court and in such inferior courts as the Congress may from time to time ordain and establish." If Congress has the power to "ordain and establish" lower federal courts, it obviously has the power to disestablish them in their entirety and, if so, it clearly has the power to disestablish them partially by limiting their jurisdiction, so long as other forums, i.e., state courts, are available. This reasoning would not apply to the Supreme Court, since it is not ordained or established by Congress but by the Constitution itself, Article III of which states that the "judicial power of the United States shall be vested in one Supreme Court." However, the same article also declares that the Supreme Court "shall have appellate jurisdiction, both as to law and fact, with such exceptions, and under such regulations as the Congress shall make," and there is nothing in that provision which forbids Congress from making an "exception" in cases challenging public school prayer.

The real trouble with this argument is that it proves too much. Helms's device is not patentable and there is no reason why it could not be resorted to for other purposes by a determined president and a pliant Congress. They could, for example, deprive the federal courts of jurisdiction in cases involving racial segregation in the public schools, or challenging as unconstitutional state laws imposing the death penalty in prosecutions of blacks for raping whites but not *vice versa,* or laws forbidding press criticisms of federal and/or state officials (the Sedition Act of 1798 sought to do just that), or laws forbidding employment or promotion of women to any position higher than that of teachers in public schools, or laws providing that in any election for government office a vote in favor of the incumbent shall be deemed the equivalent of three votes for other candidates. The net result is that the Bill of Rights and the Fourteenth Amendment are expunged from the Constitution insofar as Supreme Court review is concerned.

In June of 1980 the pre-Reagan Department of Justice, in response to a question presented to it by the House Chairman on the Judiciary, expressed the opinion that the "Helms Amendment" was "unconstitutional because it impinges on the essential role of the Supreme Court to pass on the constitutionality of State acts and thereby to maintain the unity and supremacy of the Constitution." There is little doubt that were the question put to Reagan's Department of Justice it would come out with a response of constitutionality; its on-again-off-again and once-more-on-again acrobatics in the *Bob Jones University* case attests to that.

Reagan was not convinced that amendment was unattainable. At his urging, Howard Baker returned to the fray and took the lead in a campaign to obtain the necessary two-thirds vote in the Senate as the first step towards returning prayer to the public schools by constitutional amendment. On the assumption that the proposed prayer amendment as worded by the president was not likely to receive the necessary two-thirds vote in the Senate, the wording, with his consent, was changed to read:

Nothing in this Constitution shall be construed to prohibit individual or group prayer in public schools or other institutions. Neither the United

States nor any State shall compose the words of prayers to be said in the public schools.

So worded, the amendment would allow recitation of a patently Christological prayer such as the Lord's Prayer forbidden in the *Schempp-Murray* decision, since that prayer was not "composed by the United States or any State." (Enterprising publishers, following the lead of those who deleted evolution from public school textbooks, could do well by publishing for public school use books of "Prayers Not Composed By The United States Or Any State.") Moreover, the proposed amendment did not on its face limit permissibility to voluntary prayers, inasmuch as it did not include the provision in the Reagan-drafted prayer that "No person shall be required by the United States or any State to participate in prayer."

Strong opposition to the proposed amendment came from a variety of sources, Christian, Jewish, and secular. The statement "Our Most Precious Heritage," updated to include silent prayer and signed by more than three hundred constitutional lawyers and law professors, was again presented to both houses of Congress. When the vote was taken on March 20, 1984, the project received fifty-six aye votes, eleven short of the necessary two-thirds.

To some of the president's supporters the defeat of the measure was all to the good, for it provided Reagan with excellent material for his reelection campaign. Not only did it solidify his popularity with the fundamentalists in the South but, in view of the polls indicating that an overwhelming majority of Americans favor return of prayer to the public schools, the president's valiant if unsuccessful campaign should win favor even among Democrats.

Yet the outcome was not as desirable as it could have been. In the first place, the major opponent of the proposed amendment was not a Democrat, but Lowell Weicker, Republican senator from Connecticut. Moreover, he was joined in opposition by seventeen other Republicans, including the revered Barry Goldwater of Arizona, a former Republican candidate for the presidency. Added to this was the fact that there were nineteen Democrats (all but four from below the Mason-Dixon line) who voted for the amendment, one more than the number of Republicans who voted against it.

Two postscripts are in order here. The first relates to an Associated Press item in the *New York Times* of March 8, 1984, reporting that Reagan's press secretary had explained that the reason for the president's rare attendance at church services was his dislike of "inconveniencing parishioners." House Speaker Thomas O'Neill's response, published in the next day's issue of the *Times* was: "There's a man who doesn't go to church and he talks about prayer. They ought to put a chapel at Camp David so he can go" (a comment suggestive of the maxim that if Mohammed won't come to the mountain, let the mountain come to Mohammed).

The second refers to the following story in the *New York Times* of March 24, 1984:

> One of the soft-sell tactics President Reagan used to try to lobby the Senate for passage of a constitutional amendment to permit officially sanctioned prayer in public schools was to recall his boyhood in Illinois's public schools.
>
> Mr. Reagan met with a group of senators at the White House to tell them that as a child he had had no problems listening to a variety of prayers in school.
>
> The years, of course, temper and sometimes alter memories. Court records show that on June 29, 1910, the Supreme Court of Illinois, in *People ex rel Ring et al. v. Board of Education of Dist. 24*, issued a decision banning mandatory school prayer. The decision was handed down nearly eight months before Mr. Reagan was born Feb. 6, 1911, in Tampico, Ill.
>
> The decision said, in part, that "religion is taught and should be taught in the churches" and imposing prayer in which a student felt he could not take part "subjects him to a religious stigma and places him at a disadvantage in the school, which the law never contemplated."
>
> Anson Franklin, the deputy White House secretary, said that although mandatory prayer was outlawed in Illinois, there were special occasions when a public school class prayed as a group, for instance praying for soldiers wounded in World War I. Such prayer was not obligatory, he said, but students were given the right to pray if they wished.

But the defeat of the proposed constitutional amendment was not the last chapter in the struggle to bring prayer back into the public schools. Finally recognizing that, notwithstanding his prior optimism, a constitutional amendment to return prayer to public schools was not attainable within the foreseeable future, Reagan decided to settle for something less. That something less was the introduction into the Senate of a measure known as the Equal Access Act.

The act makes it unlawful for any federally financed public *secondary* school that has a "limited open forum" to deny, on the basis of religious, political, philosophical, or other speech content, equal access or fair opportunity to any students seeking to conduct a meeting on school premises. The term "open forum" is defined as an opportunity for non-curriculum-related student groups to meet on school premises during noninstructional time.

The meeting, the measure continues, must be voluntary and student initiated; there may be no school sponsorship; school or government agents may be present at religious meetings only in a nonparticipatory capacity; the meeting may not substantially interfere with the orderly conduct of school activities; and nonschool persons may not control or even regularly attend meetings of the group.

The law also forbids any governmental body, federal or state, to influence the form or content of prayer or other religious activity; to require any person to participate in the activities; to expend public funds beyond the incidental cost of providing space; to compel any school employee to attend if it would be contrary to his or her religious beliefs; to sanction meetings that are otherwise unlawful; to limit the rights of groups that are not of a specified numerical size; and, finally, to abridge the constitutional rights of any person.

Reagan had no difficulty in obtaining acceptance by the Senate with its Republican majority. The Democrat controlled House, however, refused to go along until after its convention. Walter Mondale and the other party leaders could then not avoid recognizing the reality that refusing to go along would probably be fatal to any chance of Democrats winning the election because of their refusal to defend "religious speech." Hence they made a turnabout and the measure received a substantial majority in the House.

Happily, or unhappily, Reagan approved the measure. He had not concealed his intention to make the Democrats' obstinancy a major issue in the campaign. He could and did attack them for refusing to enact his tax credit proposal, blandly ignoring the fact that the measure had been defeated in the Republican controlled Senate. Enactment of the prayer measure deprived him of this weapon.

As it was, Reagan had achieved what might almost be considered to be a political miracle: enactment of a measure in the bitterly controversial arena of prayer in the public schools, which was not only approved by substantial majorities in both houses of Congress but, with only one significant exception, was favored by practically all of the nation's prominent religious organizations from the fundamental right (National Association of Evangelicals) to the liberal left (Friends Committee on National Legislation) and everything in between (National Council of Churches, United States Catholic Conference, Baptist Joint Committee on Public Affairs, and the General Conference of Seventh Day Adventists, among others).

Americans United for Separation of Church and State also endorsed the measure, although what the measure obviously sought to do was the direct opposite of separating church and state. This, however, was not the first time that Americans United and the United States Catholic Conference were on the same side of a controversial issue; as noted in Chapter 1, both defended the tax exemption challenged in the *Walz* case.

Only the obdurate Jews would not go along, thus making Reagan's achievement just short of miraculous. (Well, almost only. Some Lutheran spokesmen also were dissatisfied with the measure, but not for the same reason. As has been noted earlier, they found the Regents' prayer unacceptable because it did not go far enough in bringing Christ, but only Christ, back into the schools.) Even the Orthodox wing of American Jewry, which joined the Catholic Conference on such issues as aid to religious schools and abortion, would not go along. The organizations representing all branches of Judaism on both the rabbinic and congregational levels and all the Jewish civil rights organizations, among others the American Jewish Congress, the American Jewish Committee, and the Anti-Defamation League of B'nai B'rith, vigorously opposed the measure, but to no avail.

While Jewish opposition to the measure was not surprising, the same cannot be said of the American Civil Liberties Union's position of neutrality. It certainly could not join the protagonists of the measure but it must have been aware of what was almost a certainty—that its opposition would not induce the House of Representatives, or the president, to abandon the measure. The American Civil Liberties Union, and in all probability some of the liberal religious organizations that urged enactment, were willing to accept as a compromise the exclusion of a provision urged by the fundamentalists and offered by Congressman Bonker that would exclude from benefits otherwise available under the Elementary and Secondary Education Act school districts that refused to allow prayer in the public schools. Moreover, the nonconformist organizations were not content with noninclusion of the Bonker proposal but insisted upon and prevailed in persuading Reagan to include an express provision that refusal to allow prayer in the public schools would not justify withholding federal financial assistance.

This, however, was not all that the American Civil Liberties Union and other civil libertarians demanded and received for neutrality or even endorsement. As reported in the *New York Times* issue of July 27, 1984, Barry W. Lynn, an American Civil Liberties Union lawyer in Washington, explained: "To the extent that the bill protects and clarifies secular free speech rights it's a good bill. I suspect that if two years from now we find American troops in Nicaragua, it would be a real good tool for students who want to organize groups against that." Lynn said he expected that many of those who voted to strike a blow for school prayer "will climb the walls" at some of the bill's effects.

The same story reports that Representative Barney Frank, a liberal Democrat from Massachusetts who supported the bill, said: "In some ways, this is the best empowerment of teen-agers that's come along. People should understand what this means, which is that 15-year-olds have some decisions to make that adults can't interfere with. It means the young Troskyites can meet, it means the gay rights activists can meet. I think it's wonderful, but I'm surprised at some of my allies." (Lynn and Frank could also have included cults, the Ku Klux Klan, and the American Nazi Party as other happily surprised beneficiaries of the measure.)

The American Civil Liberties Union's neutrality might have been based upon an expectation of the almost certainty of a lawsuit and, if tested by prior decisions, a highly probable expectation of judicial nullification under the Establishment Clause. But the American Civil Liberties Union may have been overly optimistic on this score. According to a report in the July 27, 1984, issue of the *New York Times*, Harvard Law School's Laurence Tribe expressed confidence that the Supreme Court would uphold the measure. He endorsed it in Senate hearings on it and may have taken part in drafting it. Nevertheless, measured by the Supreme Court's decisions in previous cases, the law seemed vulnerable to Establishment Clause attack under both the effect and entanglement criteria. Utilization of public school premises, coupled with the cost of lighting and heating them, and of compensating the instructor assigned to be present in a nonparticipatory capacity, would seem to have the impermissible effect of advancing religion. Moreover, the monitoring procedure itself seems to violate the entanglement aspect of the Establishment Clause.

This does not mean that a majority of the Burger Court will be unable to find some rationale to uphold constitutionality. But if it does, it may bring with it consequences not expected and certainly not welcome to perhaps all but the Catholic endorsers of the measure. What the statute does is to sever secondary from elementary schools, thus creating a new class in determining constitutionality under the Establishment Clause. In all preceding situations, both the legislatures and the courts recognized a distinction between schools of higher education on the one hand and elementary and secondary on the other.

The term equal access came from the Court's decision in *Widmar v. Vincent*, to be discussed more fully later in this chapter. That case, however, dealt with prayer at the college level and in it the Court expressly said: "University students are, of course, young adults. They are less impressionable than younger students and should be able to appreciate that the University's policy is one of neutrality towards religion."

In 1963, Congress enacted the Higher Education Facilities Act of that year; two years later came the Elementary and Secondary Education Act. With one exception, to be noted shortly, the Supreme Court recognized a differentiation between the two classes. Thus, in *Tilton v. Richardson* it upheld aid to church-related colleges while, on the same day, in *Lemon v. Kurtzman* and *Earley v. DiCenso*, it held unconstitutional aid at the elementary and secondary school levels. That differentiation was adhered to in all later cases relating to aid to education but was never extended to encompass one between elementary and secondary schools.

The one exception was the case of *Wisconsin v. Yoder*, discussed at the beginning of this chapter. But that case involved the Free Exercise Clause, not the Establishment Clause. It is difficult to defend the Equal Access Act as a measure adopted pursuant to Article I, Section 8, of the Constitution, which authorizes Congress to make all laws necessary and proper for carrying into execution the Constitution, including the Free Exercise Clause; it can hardly be claimed that students are deprived of the free exercise of religion or of speech if required to pray at home, in churches, or anywhere else but public schools at both the elementary and secondary school levels.

Should the Court recognize and predicate a determination of constitutionality in prayer cases on such a differentiation, it will not be easy for the non-Catholic advocates of prayer to challenge a similar differentiation in aid to school cases. This, assuredly, is not what they expected nor what they would welcome. Yet this seems to be the logical consequence of judicial acceptance of the Equal Access Act. If equal access is good for prayer, why not for funding?

BIBLE READING IN PUBLIC SCHOOLS

What might have been most significant about *Abington School District v. Schempp* and its companion case *Murray v. Curlett* is not what they held but what they did not hold: They did not hold that the Court had made a mistake in *Engel v. Vitale*. Notwithstanding the strong and often vituperative assaults upon the Court from fundamentalists, Catholics, and members of Congress in the year following *Engel v. Vitale*, it manifested no sense of repentance or a felt need to retreat. On the contrary, it extended the *Engel* ruling beyond prayer recitation to encompass Bible reading. Nevertheless, there are some indications that Warren, Burger's predecessor as Chief Justice, and other members of the Court felt it prudent to respond as tactfully as possible to those who had assailed the *Engel* decision.

In the first place, Warren designated Tom Clark to write the opinion rather than Black, the author of both the *McCollum* and *Engel* opinions. Notwithstanding his pro-busing opinion in the *Everson* case, Black was generally considered to be the most doctrinaire among the separationists on the Court and Warren might well have found it politic to choose another, particularly if he was a southerner, as Clark was.

Second, Clark included in his opinion a long accolade recounting the close identification of religion with American history and government, quoting from Douglas's opinion in *Zorach v. Clauson* that we "are a religious people whose institutions presuppose a Supreme Being"; that "the Founding Fathers believed devotedly that there was a God and that the unalienable rights of men were rooted in Him"; that oaths of office, "from the Presidency to the Alderman," end with the supplication "So help me 'God'"; that each House of Congress opens with prayer by its chaplain; and that the sessions of the Court itself "are declared open by the crier in a short ceremony, the final phrase of which invokes the grace of God." As a dissenter in the *Zorach* case it would not have been quite appropriate to suggest that Black include these quotes in the Court's opinion were he assigned to write it.

Third, Clark's opinion stressed the neutrality rather than the no-aid aspect in the *Everson* opinion; and last, and related to that, he relied primarily not on the no-aid but rather on the "purpose-effect" concept first suggested in Warren's opinion in the *McGowan v. Maryland* Sunday closing law case.

The challenged Pennsylvania statute, in the *Schempp* case, provided that "At least ten verses from the Holy Bible shall be read, without comment, at the opening of each public school on each school day. Any child shall be excused from such Bible reading, or attending such Bible reading upon the written request of his parent or guardian."

The Schempp family brought suit contending that such reading (as well as the recitation of the Lord's Prayer) violated the Religion Clauses of the First Amendment. The Schempps were not atheists but rather members of a Unitarian church where they and their children regularly attended religious services. Not so with respect to Madalyn Murray and her son, William, avowed and militant atheists, who in the companion case of *Murray v. Curlett*, challenged the practice in the Baltimore schools. (By a second marriage Madalyn became Madalyn Murray O'Hair but remained a militant and highly publicized atheist and is now head of the American

Atheist Center in Austin, Texas. On the other hand, William later became a born-again Christian who not only took out newspaper ads apologizing for his part in the *Schempp-Murray* suit but also committed himself to helping generate grassroots support for creation science.)

The Murray complaint challenged a rule promulgated by the Maryland school commissioners that provided for the holding of opening exercises in the schools, which consisted primarily in the "reading, without comment, of a chapter in the Holy Bible and/or the use of the Lord's Prayer." The commissioners manifested their tolerance toward Catholic pupils by providing that the "Douay version may be used by those pupils who prefer it." (They could hardly do less inasmuch as Maryland had been established by Catholics seeking refuge from intolerance and persecution in Protestant England. Nevertheless it required a protest by the Murrays to induce them to amend the rule so as to accept the Douay version.) They did not, however, go so far as to include a Jewish version, nor did they restrict the reading to Psalms or other parts of the Old Testament, such as Proverbs or Isaiah, which would be acceptable to all three faiths.

Originally they did not allow absence from the exercise on the part of Jews or nonbelievers, apparently unaware or indifferent to the letter written some three centuries earlier by Roger Williams to the Town of Providence. As quoted in part by Clark in his opinion for the majority of the Court in the *Schempp-Murray* case, it reads:

> There goes many a ship to sea, with many hundred souls in one ship, whose weal and woe is common, and is a true picture of a commonwealth, or a human combination, or society. It hath fallen out sometimes, that both Papists and Protestants, Jews and Turks, may be embarked in one ship; upon which supposal, I affirm that all the liberty of conscience I ever pleaded for, turns upon these two hinges, that none of the Papists, Protestants, Jews, or Turks be forced to come to the ship's prayers or worship, nor compelled from their own particular prayers or worship, if they practice any.

(Clark did not include in his quotation the sentence that follows this passage. It reads:

> I further add, that I never denied, that notwithstanding this liberty, the commander of this ship ought to command the ship's course, yea, and also command that justice, peace and sobriety, be kept and practiced, both among the seamen and all the passengers.

As can be seen, the sentence exemplifies the principle of church-state separation upon which Clark's opinion was based.)

On the insistence of the Murrays the school commissioners amended their rule so as to allow excusal from participation in or attendance at the opening exercises upon written request of a parent or guardian. Nevertheless, the Murrays were not content and proceeded to sue.

That voluntariness is a fiction in public school prayer, Bible reading, and other religious activities can be appreciated from the following extract in the *Schempp* trial record:

> Edward Schempp, the children's father, testified that after careful consideration he had decided that he should not have Roger or Donna excused from attendance at these morning ceremonies. Among his reasons were the following. He said that he thought his children would be "labelled as 'odd balls'" before their teachers and classmates every school day; that children, like Roger's and Donna's classmates, were liable "to lump all particular religious difference[s] or religious objections [together] as 'atheism'" and that today the word "atheism" is often connected with "atheistic communism," and has "very bad" connotations, such as "un-American" or "pro-red," with overtones of possible immorality. Mr. Schempp pointed out that due to the events of the morning exercises following in rapid succession, the Bible reading, the Lord's Prayer, the Flag Salute, and the announcements, excusing his children from the Bible reading would mean that probably they would miss hearing the announcements so important to children. He testified also that if Roger and Donna were excused from Bible reading they would have to stand in the hall outside their "homeroom" and that this carried with it the imputation of punishment for bad conduct. [The last sentence describes the experience of the McCollum boy some fifteen years earlier.]

Clark's opinion declared both the Pennsylvania and Maryland laws unconstitutional under the Establishment Clause, and this notwithstanding the fact that individual students could absent themselves from the exercises. He rejected the claim that unless the exercises were permitted a "religion of secularism" would be established in the schools, noting the absence of evidence that discontinuing the practices would manifest hostility to religion by preferring nonbelievers over believers. He made it clear that the decision was not to be understood as barring the study of comparative religion or the history of religion and its relationship to the advancement of civilization or the study of the Bible as a work of literature if it was presented objectively as part of a secular program of education. (It bears noting that many religiously motivated parents would resent the teaching of the Bible as a work of literature. To them the Bible is God's word to man and it would be sacrilegious to treat it as Shakespeare's plays or Byron's poetry.) Notwithstanding the Court's effort to avoid it, there was a good deal of hostility expressed from the same sources that condemned the *Engel* ruling. It was, however, considerably milder than that which followed the *Engel* decision just a year earlier, and this though the decision encompassed Bible reading as well as prayer. Moreover, the United Presbyterian church joined the Baptist Joint Committee on Public Affairs in defending the *Schempp-Murray* ruling and, even before it was handed down, the National Council of Churches, anticipating the Court's action, issued a statement declaring that "neither true religion nor good education is dependent upon the devotional use of the Bible in the public school program."

SILENT PRAYER AND/OR MEDITATION

The cases that have been considered in this chapter have dealt with articulated prayer. The Supreme Court's consistent rejection of the efforts to bring them into the public schools has led a number of states to enact legislation allowing or requiring some form of silent prayer and/or "meditation" in elementary and high schools. This must not be confused with the moment of silence audiences at professional football games are asked to observe as a token of respect to some recently deceased person of importance. It is highly doubtful that any court would hold this unconstitutional were a suit to be instituted to forbid this practice in public elementary schools, especially if the deceased was a teacher or fellow pupil.

A federal court judge in *May v. Cooperman* (1983) was faced with a challenge to a New Jersey law, which without mentioning the word "prayer" required a one-minute period of silence "before the opening exercise of each school day for quiet and private contemplation or introspection." (One wonders how the kindergarten teachers in DeKalb County would tell the children to engage in "contemplation," "introspection," or the more often used "meditation" before partaking of their milk and cookies but that they need or indeed may not meditate on anything religious.) The judge came to the conclusion after a long trial that the

experiences of various schools during the weeks when the minute of silence was enforced suggests that some students will use the minute of silence to pray; some will use it to engage in thoughtful meditation; some will tolerate it though considering it boring and stupid; some who believe it violates their religious convictions will nevertheless submit to it, not wishing to risk public ridicule; some who believe it violates their religious convictions will either refuse to observe it or will absent themselves from the place where others are observing it.

On the basis of the trial testimony the judge reached the conclusion that "omission of the word 'prayer' was a cosmetic change only, having no substantial effect." He ruled that the statute violated the First Amendment since its purpose was to advance religion, its effect was to advance the religion of some and inhibit that of others, and its net result was excessive entanglement of religion and state.

All in all, some twenty-three states have enacted laws relating to silent prayer or meditation, some mandating the exercise and some leaving it to the discretion of the principal or school superintendent in each district. The legislature in at least one of the states, Alabama, found these alternatives insufficient. In 1981 it enacted a statute authorizing silent prayer but a year later it added articulated prayers to the freedom of choice grab bag. There was, however, one limitation on the freedom: if a school chose articulated prayer it could employ only the prayer formulated by the legislature.

The following is the first enacted Alabama statute:

At the commencement of the first class of each day in all grades in all public schools, the teacher in charge of the room in which each such class is held may announce that a period of silence not to exceed one minute in duration shall be observed for meditation or voluntary prayer, and during any such period no other activities shall be engaged in.

The added statute reads:

From henceforth, any teacher or professor in any public educational institution within the State of Alabama, recognizing that the Lord God is one, at the beginning of any homeroom or any class, may lead the willing students in the following prayer to God: "Almighty God, You alone are our God. We acknowledge You as the Creator and Supreme Judge of the world. May Your justice, Your truth, and Your peace abound this day in the hearts of our countrymen, in the counsels of our government, in the sanctity of our homes and in the classrooms of our schools. In the name of our Lord. Amen."

Inasmuch as the Supreme Court had ruled in the *Engel* case that recitation of a prayer formulated by school authorities violated the Establishment Clause, it was practically mandatory for Brevard Hand, the trial judge in the case of *Wallace v. Jaffree*, to issue a temporary injunction against implementation of the law until the trial was held. Though the silent prayer aspect had never been passed upon by the Supreme Court, it was within the discretion of the judge to issue a temporary injunction against that part of the statute as well, and Hand did so, thereby indicating that there was at least some merit in the plaintiffs' suit. He went even further: his opinion on granting the plaintiffs' motion left no doubt that he deemed both laws to be unconstitutional.

It must therefore come as a shock to read his decision after the trial. He ruled that, notwithstanding the precedents established in the *Everson* case and followed in all subsequent cases, the Supreme Court was wrong in ruling that the First Amendment was applicable to the states. The Court, he said, misread history in these decisions. Accordingly, he dissolved the temporary injunction and ruled in favor of the state.

The plaintiffs thereupon rushed to Supreme Court Justice Powell, who reinstated the injunction with a short opinion stating that until the Supreme Court overrules the *Engel* and *Schempp* decisions they were binding upon all lower court judges, including Hand. In the *Schempp* opinion, Clark had gone out of his way—since none of the parties raised the question—to reaffirm the Court's earlier rulings that the Religion Clauses were applicable to the states by reason of the Fourteenth Amendment prohibition of state laws depriving a person of the right to due process of law, and contentions to the contrary "seem entirely untenable and of value only as academic exercises." This obviously did not bother Hand any more than the other holdings in the *Schempp* decision.

When the *Wallace v. Jaffree* case reached the Court of Appeals, Hand's decision was reversed. The Court held that the Establishment Clause was applicable to the states; that both sections of the statute violated that clause, since their common purpose was to advance religion; that this too was its effect; and that its enforcement would involve the state in religious activities. Undaunted, the State of Alabama, through its governor George C. Wallace, applied to the Supreme Court for review and reversal of the Court of Appeals decision. In April 1984, the Court agreed to accept the case for argument but only with respect to the silent prayer aspect; as to the vocal prayer, it affirmed the ruling of unconstitutionality as it had done two years earlier in *Treen v. Karen B.*, the then most recent of the many efforts to persuade it to overrule the *Engel* and *Schempp* decisions.

While the Supreme Court was still considering whether to accept the state's appeal in the *Wallace* case, a proposal to settle the question of constitutionality was made in the United States Senate. Several members, seeking to effect a compromise between vocal prayers and none at all, offered a measure that would amend the Constitution so as to authorize silent prayers in public schools. To advocates of vocal prayer, and particularly President Reagan, their determined leader, this was not enough. To opponents it was too much. A vote on the proposal was taken on March

15, 1984. The motion was defeated by a vote of eighty-one to fifteen.

Had the proposal carried, it would still have required a two-thirds vote in the House and approval in three-fourths of the states. Defeat of the proposal by no means ends the matter. The Supreme Court might still decide that no amendment is needed and that the Constitution as it now stands does not forbid silent prayer in the public schools. Should the Court decide that it does, it may safely be predicted that the bones of this effort to compromise between vocal prayer and none at all will rise again.

RELIGION IN STATE COLLEGES

The religion-in-school cases that have been considered in this chapter have dealt with teaching or practices in elementary and secondary schools. In *Tilton v. Richardson* the Supreme Court ruled that, while the purpose-effect-entanglement test applied to government financing of colleges, it did not apply equally so—that is, while financing which with respect to elementary and secondary schools would be held violative of the Establishment Clause, a contrary result could be reached where colleges were involved. The principal reason for this lies in the fact that students at college are less likely to be influenced with respect to their religious commitment than those who are younger. Realistically, this distinction explains the Court's 1981 decision in the case of *Widmar v. Vincent.*

In the *Bob Jones University* case the Court had ruled that in instances of conflict the guarantees of the First Amendment's Religion Clauses must yield to the nation's interest in racial equality. That, however, was not the first case in which the Court sacrificed the Establishment Clause for the benefit of another constitutionally protected right. Although denied by the Court, realistically that is what happened in the *Widmar* case, except that there the protected right was freedom of speech rather than racial equality.

The suit was a challenge to the refusal by the University of Missouri at Kansas City, a state institution, to allow a religious student group named Cornerstone to hold its meetings in university facilities. Cornerstone was an organization of Evangelical Christian students whose meetings included prayer, hymns, Bible commentary, and discussion of religious views and experiences. They brought suit claiming that the university's discriminatory action (since nonreligious groups were allowed to use the facilities) violated their right to free exercise of religion, equal protection of the laws, and freedom of speech.

In holding this action unconstitutional, Powell, speaking for the majority, stated that the Establishment Clause did not require exclusion of use of college facilities by religious groups, since permitting use would not have the purpose or effect of advancing religion nor would it result in entanglement with religion. Moreover, he said, whenever a state undertakes to regulate speech on the basis of its content, the Free Speech Clause requires that it prove the existence of a "compelling" interest to justify its action. The compelling interest for excluding Cornerstone, the state asserted in the *Widmar* case, was its felt need to achieve a greater degree of church-state separation than required by the Establishment Clause as construed by the Supreme Court. This, said Powell, did not constitute an interest sufficiently compelling to infringe upon Cornerstone's right to freedom of speech.

Powell recognized that university students are young adults, less impressionable than younger students, and thus could have justified his reasoning on that grounds, as the Burger Court had done in *Tilton v. Richardson,* to which he referred. Had he done so, he would not be faced with an apparent need to reverse the decision by the Court of Appeals in the case of *Brandon v. Board of Education.* Instead, he said, the *Brandon* case was different because there the religious groups claimed, "that the denial of facilities *not* available to other groups deprives them under the Free Exercise Clause" (Powell's emphasis). In addition, the lower court's ruling in the *Brandon* case rested "solely on rights claimed under the Free Exercise Clause," whereas in the present case the Supreme Court was basing its decision on freedom of speech rather than of religion.

A reading of the decisions in the District Court and the Court of Appeals in the *Brandon* case indicates that Powell was wrong on both counts. The school facilities there *were* available to nonreligious student organizations; indeed, the students asserted a claim, rejected by both courts, that this discrimination constituted a violation of the Fourteenth Amendment's Equal Protection Clause. Moreover, Powell was also wrong in asserting that the students' claim was limited to rights under the Free Exercise Clause. Besides the equal protection claim, both lower courts also considered and rejected the plaintiffs' claim that the school board's action violated their rights to freedom of speech and freedom of association.

Except for one reality, the *Widmar* decision could reasonably be construed as overruling, without expressly saying so, the *Brandon* decision; the reality is that it was *after* the *Widmar* decision that the Court rejected the appeal in the *Brandon* case. It is not usual for the Court to overrule a decision *before* it is handed down; but then perhaps the Burger Court's majority would not allow technicalities like that to stand in the way of compelling state colleges to provide rooms for those standing in need of prayer.

CHAPTER 4

Religion in Public Places

RELIGIOUS SYMBOLS: CRÈCHES

Lynch v. Donnelly, decided in March 1984, involved a challenge to the funding, with relatively small amounts, of the original placing and subsequent maintenance of a crèche or nativity scene in a park which, though owned by a nonprofit private organization, was located close to the city hall in the heart of Pawtucket's shopping district. The city-funded display consisted of figures and decorations traditionally associated with Christmas, including a Santa Claus house, reindeer pulling Santa's sleigh, a Christmas tree, carolers, cutout figures of a clown, an elephant, and a teddy bear, hundreds of colored lights, a larger banner that read "Season's Greetings," and a crèche.

The *Lynch* case, a taxpayer's suit prosecuted by the American Civil Liberties Union, challenged only the crèche aspect of the display. It had been designed by the city maintenance supervisor, was erected and dismantled annually by city employees, and was wired for lighting by the city's electricity. The figures in the crèche included a baby lying, with arms outstretched, in a manger, two angels, some animals, and several figures kneeling in a posture of worship to the baby.

The United States District Court and the Court of Appeals both ruled that the city's participation in the project violated the Establishment Clause. When the case reached the Supreme Court, Rex E. Lee, Reagan's Solicitor General, made a motion, which the Court granted, to be allowed not only to submit an *amicus curiae* brief but also to participate in the oral argument in support of what turned out to be a successful appeal by the city. Before considering the Court's five to four decision, something should be said about the Solicitor General's intervention.

There can hardly be any doubt that the motion to intervene was made with Reagan's approval and it is highly probable too that it was he who initiated it. It is quite common for the Solicitor General to intervene as an *amicus curiae* in litigation having a direct and substantial effect upon the government's interest. If the controversy involves a matter of major concern to the government, the Solicitor General will in all likelihood also ask to participate in oral argument and his request will usually be granted.

How did Lee explain the government's great concern about the constitutionality of a crèche in Pawtucket? "The United States," he said, "had a deep and abiding interest in maintaining the nation's long-standing tradition that the Federal Government be free to acknowledge and recognize that religion is part of our heritage and should continue to be an element in our public life and public occasions." He noted, too, that a nativity scene had been placed in the East Room of the White House at least since the time of the Trumans and perhaps even longer.

It is not easy to discern the relevancy of this evidence of religiosity. For so long as anyone is president the White House and Camp David are his homes, and the Constitution guarantees the privacy of a person's home, even if he happens to be President of the United States. Nor were other aspects of city-financed Christmas celebrations particularly relevant to the lawsuit since the plaintiffs carefully made it clear, as did both the District Court and the Court of Appeals, that only the crèche component was challenged in the suit and only it was the subject decided upon by the courts. It would hardly have been a serious threat to the integrity of the presidency or the survival of religion in America were the Supreme Court to affirm these courts' limited rulings.

A more realistic explanation for Reagan's intervention is the same as that which applies to his efforts to restore prayer to the schools. It is highly probable that in both instances the majority of Americans favor the challenged practices, and it would not hurt him in his campaign for reelection if he championed them in the courts as well as in the halls of legislatures.

Perhaps with an eye to the election, Lee told Jewish voters that Reagan was really on their side. He reminded them in his Supreme Court brief that in 1981 Reagan had issued proclamations to commemorate Jewish Heritage Week and Jewish High Holy Days and had later proclaimed 1983 to be the "Year of the Bible." (Presumably the Jews could interpret this to refer to the Old Testament.) In a broad hint to the Jews, Lee noted that a decision against the crèche would presumably invalidate the government's recognition of Jewish holidays. Lee noted the trial testimony of Pawtucket's mayor, indicating his willingness to display a menorah (candelabra lit during the Hanukah holiday in December) as part of the city's annual Christmas holiday celebration but nobody had asked for it.

Another, and perhaps more charitable explanation for the government's intervention, might be found in Reagan's sincere conversion to (Christian) religiosity sparked by Jerry Falwell and his Moral Majority. The following report in the February 1, 1984, *Daily News Bulletin* of the Jewish Telegraphic Agency presents a fair picture of the Jewish response to this conversion.

REAGAN'S SPEECH TO BROADCAST EVANGELISTS REPLETE WITH REFERENCES TO GOD AND JESUS
by Kevin Freeman

President Reagan told a group of broadcast evangelists yesterday in Washington that Americans had no need to fear the future because "we have a promise from Jesus to soothe our sorrows, heal our hearts and drive away our fears."

In a speech to 4,000 people attending the National Religious Broadcasters convention, Reagan made 24 references to God and Jesus and strongly attacked the Supreme Court's ban on prayer in public schools. "God, source of all knowledge, should never have been expelled from our children's classrooms," he declared to the thunderous approval of the audience which included the Rev. Jerry Falwell, the Christian Evangelist who heads the Moral Majority.

Joseph Berger, the religion editor of *Newsday* a Long Island daily, said Reagan's speech contained the "markings of a church sermon." He quoted Jeffrey Hadden, a Virginia sociologist who had written a book on broadcast evangelists, as saying he could not recall a more "explicitly Christian" speech by Reagan.

Reagan's address to the evangelists, considered an important potential political constituency for Reagan, was the President's first speech since his announcement Sunday that he would seek re-election.

Reagan's speech yesterday was similar in tone to one he made last March in Orlando to the National Association of Evangelicals, an organization of conservative churches and agencies, which came under stinging denunciation from leaders of the three branches of Judaism.

The President told the Orlando gathering that "there is sin and evil in the world and we are enjoined by Scripture and the Lord Jesus to oppose it with all our might." He said Soviet Communism "is the focus of evil in the modern world" and that those favoring a mutual freeze on nuclear weapons were ignoring "the aggressive instincts of the evil empire."

Jewish religious leaders said the use by the President of moral absolutes "in the name of Jesus" was morally offensive and possibly a violation of his constitutional obligations; that castigation of the Soviet Union as the "focus of evil" might unwittingly bring about the "catastrophe" of a nuclear holocaust; that it implied an attempt to silence opposition to the President's policies, including support of prayer in public schools; and threatened the nation's religious pluralism.

Lee's Supreme Court brief explains Reagan's supernationalism, religious fervor, and insistence upon a large military budget. They are apparently based upon a letter by President John Adams to his wife explaining the reason for a fast day that he had proclaimed:

We have appointed [the letter read] a Continental fast. Millions will be upon their knees at once before their Great Creator, imploring His forgiveness and blessing; His smiles on American councils and arms.

(It is difficult to reconcile the last two words of this proclamation with the views of Benjamin Franklin, upon whom Burger placed such great reliance to support the decision in *Marsh v. Chambers*. It was Franklin who said "there never was a good war or a bad peace.")

The Court's opinion in *Lynch v. Donnelly* was written by the Chief Justice. Total separation of church and state, he said, was not possible; the Court's function was to reconcile the inescapable tension between the objective of preventing unnecessary intrusion of either the church or the state upon the other. It should not take a simplistic or absolutist approach in applying the Establishment Clause to invalidate mechanically all statutes "that confer benefits or give special recognition to religion in general or to one faith." He quoted Supreme Court Justice Joseph Story, who in his *Commentaries on the Constitution of the United States* written a century and a half ago, said:

"The real object of the [First] Amendment was . . . to prevent any national ecclesiastical establishment, which should give to an hierarchy the exclusive patronage of the national government.

This, it bears noting, is an abridged version of what Story wrote. Unabridged, and obviously more supportive of Burger's opinion, it reads:

The real object of the amendment was not to countenance much less to advance, Mohametanism, or Judaism, or infidelity, by prostrating Christianity; but to exclude all rivalry among Christian sects, and to prevent any national ecclesiastical establishment which should give to an hierarchy the exclusive patronage of the national government.

(It is somewhat surprising that Burger should quote Story as an authority on the meaning of the First Amendment's Religion Clauses; his interpretation of the amendment has consistently been rejected by the Court—and Burger himself, as indicated by the *Lemon* opinion—at least since the *Everson* decision in 1947. The idea probably came from Solicitor General Lee's brief, which also quoted Story, though not the same sentence. The sentence cited by Lee reads:

> An attempt to level all religions, and to make it a matter of state policy to hold all in utter indifference would have created universal disapprobation, if not universal indignation.)

It has often been found useful, Burger continued, to inquire whether a challenged law has a secular purpose, whether its principal or primary purpose is to advance or inhibit religion, and whether it creates an excessive entanglement with religion. The Court, however, has been unwilling to be confined to any single test or criterion. Nevertheless, Burger did examine the crèche situation in the light of this "often useful" test and by it he found no constitutional violation.

Based on the record in the case he was persuaded that the city had a valid secular purpose for including the crèche in the Christmas display, had not impermissibly advanced religion, and had not created an excessive entanglement between church and state. With respect to the first element, he said, it was not necessary that the crèche project should have an "exclusively secular" purpose; it was enough that it had such "a" purpose, else much of the conduct and legislation that the Court had approved in the past would have been invalidated. What Pawtucket's Mayor Lynch had done was simply to take note "of a significant historical religious event long celebrated in the Western World." All that the crèche did was simply to "depict the historical origin of this traditional event long recognized as a National Holiday." This display was "sponsored by the City to celebrate the Holiday and to depict the origins of that Holiday." Those, for Burger, were legitimate secular purposes sufficient to satisfy that prong of the purpose-effect-entanglement test.

Burger found it no more difficult to conclude that it was not the primary effect of the crèche presentation to advance religion. To do otherwise would require that it be viewed "as more beneficial to and more an endorsement of religion, for example, than expenditure of large sums of money for textbooks supplied throughout the country to students attending church-sponsored schools." And the same is true in regard to public funding of transportation to such schools, to federal grants for college buildings in church-sponsored colleges and universities, to exemptions for church properties, to enforcement of Sunday closing laws, to released time programs for religious training, and to legislative prayers.

Finally, said Burger, there was no proof of impermissible entanglement and certainly not the "comprehensive, discriminating, and continuing state surveillance" forbidden in previous Supreme Court decisions. As for a claim of political divisiveness, *Mueller v. Allen* had decided that only in cases of direct subsidies to religious institutions was potential political divisiveness a relevant fact in determining impermissible entanglement. Moreover, there was no evidence of political friction or divisiveness over the crèche in the forty-year history of Pawtucket's Christmas celebration. "A litigant cannot by the very act of commencing a lawsuit . . . create the appearance of divisiveness and then exploit it as evidence of entanglement." On the contrary, the display "engenders a friendly community spirit of good will in keeping with the season." "It would be ironic . . . if the inclusion of a simple symbol of a particular historic religious event, as part of a celebration acknowledged in the Western World for 20 centuries . . . would so 'taint' the City's exhibit as to render it violative of the establishment clause."

Before turning to O'Connor's concurring opinion and the dissents of Brennan and Blackmun, some comment on Jewish reaction to Burger's opinion is appropriate. His implication that only a troublemaking litigant commenced the lawsuit to "create the appearance of divisiveness" manifests either a lack of knowledge as to how American Jewry feels about government financing of a crèche or, what may be even more disturbing, a deliberate disregard of how the overwhelming majority of American Jews feel on the subject.

It was forty years ago when the crèche was financed and installed by the Pawtucket city authorities; by coincidence that was also the year in which the National Jewish Community Relations Advisory Council (NJCRAC) was formed. As indicated earlier in the book, today it represents one hundred and five local Jewish community councils or federations throughout the nation, as well as the major civic organizations, the American Jewish Congress, the American Jewish Committee, and the Anti-Defamation League of B'nai B'rith, among others. The Synagogue Council of America, representing the three branches of American Jewry, was established even earlier than that.

Initially, some of the more timorous constituent organizations were reluctant to express their views publicly and certainly to take legal action that might be construed to be anti-Christian or atheistic. (It should be noted that this trepidation was not an exclusively Jewish trait. As related in Chapter 3 of this book, it was for this reason that the Unitarian Schempps allowed their children to be present during the prayer-Bible reading ritual, as Jewish children earlier remained in the classroom during the Champaign religious instruction periods.) By 1948 the constituents in both the NJCRAC and the Synagogue Council felt sufficiently secure to vote unanimously for the submission of a joint *amicus curiae* brief in the *McCollum* case. Later, Jewish feelings of security had progressed to the point that the two organizations submitted briefs in the *Engel* and *Schempp* and other Supreme Court cases relating to the separation of church and state.

As to the unhappiness on the part of the overwhelming majority of American Jews over publicly financed crèches there can be no doubt. During practically the entire forty-year period, the Joint Policy Statement of the Synagogue Council and the NJCRAC included the following:

> We oppose the erection of religious statues or the placing of religious symbols on publicly-owned property, public parks, city halls, governmental office buildings, and similar premises that are purchased and maintained out of taxes imposed upon all persons, irrespective of their religious beliefs or affiliations. The presence on such premises of religious statues or symbols constitutes in effect a dedication of the premises to one sect or creed to the exclusion of others. The expenditure of governmental funds or the use of governmental property for religious purposes, moreover, is a serious impairment of the principle of separation of church and state. Experience has shown that the placing of religious statutes or symbols on public property divides the community along religious lines and brings about inter-religious disharmony and acrimony.

In his opinion Burger echoed the statement in Lee's brief that Reagan had issued two proclamations or messages relating to Jews: one to commemorate Jewish Heritage Week and the other a message relating to the Jewish High Holy Days. If Reagan's purpose was to assuage American Jews with respect to his efforts towards returning prayer to the public schools, or Burger's to appease them for the *Lynch* decision, they both failed. If the Court's majority relied upon the absence of vocalized Jewish protest as evidence that the plaintiffs brought the suit to create "the appearance of divisiveness" in order to "expose it as evidence of entanglement" where none existed, it was they rather than Donnelly's attorney who was responsible for misapplying the Establishment Clause. In a situation where tensions may be high and unhappy repercussions reasonably foreseeable, silence should not be taken to mean consent. It should be noted that it was not only Jews but nonfundamentalist Protestants affiliated with the National Council of Churches (which filed an *amicus curiae* brief urging affirmance of the lower court's determination of unconstitutionality) who expressed unhappiness with the crèche situation. Strong feelings of discontent were also expressed by Baptists, Unitarians, Ethical Culturists, and secularists, all of whom are protected by the First Amendment's Establishment Clause.

To Jews the disturbing error with respect to the Court's decision was its characterization of the birth of Jesus as an "historical" event meriting support out of tax-raised funds for its commemoration. At least implicit in this and the general tenor of the opinion is that America is a Christian country, with the consequence that, even if the presence of angels at the birth of Jesus might not be provable by generally accepted historical standards, for the purposes of constitutional law it must be accorded recognition as an historical fact. What is particularly troublesome about this is that Burger could have arrived at the same obviously desired conclusion of constitutionality with respect to the crèche endeavor by simply resorting to the justification employed by Chief Justice Warren in *McGowan v. Maryland* and *Braunfeld v. Brown* for compulsory Sunday closing laws even in regard to Jews who keep their stores closed on Saturdays.

In these cases the Court ruled that, although historically those laws were religiously based, they had since became secular efforts to assure to all one day's rest in seven. In the *Lynch* case the president of the Pawtucket Plaza Associates and the executive director of Downtown Pawtucket Revitalization, Inc., both testified that the principle impact of the city's Christmas display was to bring potential customers into the downtown Pawtucket area—surely an acceptable and constitutionally protected secular purpose, which Burger refused to adopt.

Instead he quoted Douglas's "we are a religious people" and added to it a recitation that has almost become a ritual in lawyers' briefs and judges' opinions in cases involving the Establishment Clause. In many cases (including *Lynch v. Donnelly*) the ritual set forth, in varying lengths, a recitation of the numerous instances of government acts favorable toward religion. The origin of both the "religious people" invocation and the governmental friendly-action litany is to be found in Justice David J. Brewer's opinion in *Church of Holy Trinity v. United States* (1892). The following is the penultimate paragraph of his opinion:

. . . If we pass beyond these matters to a view of American life as expressed by its laws, its business, its customs and its society, we find everywhere a clear recognition of the same truth. Among other matters note the following: The form of oath universally prevailing, concluding with an appeal to the Almighty; the custom of opening sessions of all deliberative bodies and most conventions with prayer; the prefatory words of all wills, "In the name of God, amen"; the laws respecting the observance of the Sabbath, with the general cessation of all secular business, and the closing of courts, legislatures, and other similar public assemblies on that day; the churches and church organizations which abound in every city, town and hamlet; the multitude of charitable organizations existing everywhere under Christian auspices; the gigantic missionary associations, with general support, and aiming to establish Christian missions in every quarter of the globe. These, and many other matters which might be noticed, add a volume of unofficial declarations to the mass of organic utterances that this is a Christian nation.

The last five words in the quotation merit additional comment, for they are the unarticulated yet basic premise of Burger's opinion in the *Lynch* case, notwithstanding his deletion of the words "Mohametanism" and "Judaism" in his quotation from Story. In his opinion in *Vidal v. Giraurd's Executor* (1844) Story stated that "the Christian religion is a part of the common law" (i.e., judicially made as distinguished from legislative law). Many years earlier Jefferson, who as a careful historian had made a study of the origin of the maxim, challenged such an assertion. He noted that "the common law existed while the Anglo-Saxons were yet pagans, at a time when they had never yet heard the name of Christ pronounced or that such a character existed . . . . What a conspiracy this, between Church and State." Common law is not part of constitutional law but, even if he did not intend to, what Burger was doing in his opinion was trying to make Christianity part of our constitutional system.

Returning to the opinions in the *Lynch* case, it should be noted that while O'Connor concurred with Burger's opinion, she felt sensitive enough to find that "Pawtucket did not intend to convey any message of endorsement of Christianity or of disapproval of non-Christian religions." "The evident purpose of including the crèche in the larger display," she continued, "was not promotion of the religious content of the crèche but celebration of the public holiday through its traditional symbols. Celebration of public holidays which have cultural significance even if they also have religious significant aspects, is a legitimate secular purpose."

O'Connor concluded her concurring opinion by reaffirming commitment to the Establishment Clause.

Every government practice [she said] must be judged in its unique circumstances to determine whether it constitutes an endorsement or disapproval of religion. In making that determination, courts must keep in mind both the fundamental place held by the Establishment Clause in our constitutional scheme and the myriad, subtle ways in which Establishment Clause values can be eroded. Government practices that purport to celebrate or acknowledge events with religious significance must be subjected to careful judicial scrutiny.

Brennan's dissenting opinion, for himself, Marshall, Blackmun, and Stevens, was, as often is the case with him in church-state litigation, a comparatively long one, about twice as long as Burger's for the majority. Moreover, it manifested considerably more scholastic research than Burger's. (The same is frequently true even when he votes with the majority. For Clark's majority opinion in the *Schempp* case, twenty-four pages were enough; Brennan's concurring opinion was three times as long.)

Initially he noted with satisfaction the fact that, although the purpose-effect-establishment test had earlier been ignored in the *Marsh v. Chambers* case, it had now been returned to the arena of constitutional law. He did express concern that the commitment might be only superficial and suggested that the Court seemed to be willing to "alter its analysis from Term to Term in order to suit its preferred results."

It must be recognized that the majority's willingness to alter analysis to suit a preferred result is hardly unique with the Burger Court. There are three ways the Supreme Court can meet the problem of uncomfortable prior decisions in a legal system predicated upon adherence to former decisions. (Lawyers call this *stare decisis.*) Most often the Court will find some distinguishing factor that justifies a contrary result. Occasionally it will admit that it had committed an error and will expressly overrule the earlier decision. In still other instances it will simply ignore it. (You can't take the court to court for this offense, although if you are a law school professor you can call your students' attention to it or write a book or law review article exposing the offense.) It was the first of these alternatives that, according to Brennan, Burger chose.

Applying the three-part test to Pawtucket's crèche, Brennan was unable to find a "clearly secular purpose." He rejected Pawtucket's claim that it sought only to participate in the celebration of a national holiday, to attract people to the downtown area in order to promote pre-Christmas sales, and to help engender a spirit of good will and neighborliness. In the first place, said Brennan, these purposes could have been served by a display of Santa Claus, reindeer, and wishing wells without the crèche. In addition, Pawtucket's celebration was constitutional only if it was non-denominational and not intended to promote religion. The purpose of keeping "Christ in Christmas" could hardly be called secular.

The "primary effect" [he said] of including a nativity scene in the City's display [was] . . . to place the government's imprimatur of approval on the particular religious beliefs exemplified by the crèche. Those who believe in the message of the nativity receive the unique and exclusive benefit of public recognition and approval of their views. For many, the City's decision to include the crèche as part of its extensive and costly efforts to celebrate Christmas can only mean that the prestige of the government has been conferred on the beliefs associated with the crèche, thereby providing a significant symbolic benefit to religion. The effect on minority religious groups, as well as on those who may reject all religion, is to convey the message that their views are not similarly worthy of public recognition nor entitled to public support. It was precisely this sort of religious chauvinism that the establishment clause was intended forever to prohibit. In this case, as in *Engle v. Vitale,* [w]hen the power, prestige and financial support of government is placed behind a particular religious belief, the indirect coercive pressure upon religious minorities to conform to the prevailing officially approved religion is plain.

Finally, he said, it was evident that Pawtucket's inclusion of a crèche as part of its annual Christmas display posed a significant threat of fostering "excessive entanglement." Jews and other non-Christian groups, prompted perhaps by the mayor's remark that he would include a menorah in future displays, could be expected to press the city for inclusion of their symbols in city-financed events. This would result in governmental accommodations to the various demands and thus divide the city along religious lines.

Brennan could not accept Burger's assertion that the crèche was a mere representation of "a particular historic religious event." To him it was instead a mystical recreation of an event that lies at the heart of Christian faith. To suggest, as Burger did, that it was merely a "traditional" symbol and therefore no different from Santa's house or reindeer was, in Brennan's view, "not only offensive to those for whom the crèche [had] profound significance, but insulting to those who insist for religious or personal reasons that the story of Christ is in no sense a part of 'history' nor an unavoidable element of our national 'heritage.'"

This thought was echoed in Blackmun's short addition (with Steven's concurrence) to Brennan's opinion.

. . . [I]ironically [he said] the majority does an injustice to the crèche and the message it manifests. While certain persons, including the Mayor of Pawtucket, undertook a crusade to "keep Christ in Christmas" the Court today has declared that presence virtually irrelevant. The majority urges that the display, "with or without a crèche," "recall[s] the religious nature of the Holiday," and "engenders a friendly community spirit of good will in keeping with the season." Before the District Court, an expert witness for the city made a similar, though perhaps more candid, point, stating that Pawtucket's display invites people "to participate in the Christmas spirit, brotherhood, peace, and let loose with their money." The crèche has been relegated to the role of a neutral harbinger of the holiday season, useful for commercial purposes, but devoid of any inherent meaning and incapable of enhancing the religious tenor of a display of which it is an integral part. The city has its victory—but it is a pyrrhic one indeed.

The evolution (or perhaps devolution) of the pre-*Lynch* status of Jews in American constitutional law was manifested by substituting for "Christian," terms such as "nonsectarian" or "Judeo-Christian" or "American civil religion." This, at least, is how the legislative chaplain in *Marsh v. Chambers* justified his status as a paid chaplain. What the *Lynch* decision did was to bring the status of Jews back to its earliest stage. Burger's opinion in the *Lynch* case would seem to have made it unnecessary for a chaplain to engage in even this act of self-censorship, as legislative prayers addressed only to Jesus are part of a tradition that is considerably older and more widespread in the United States than Christmas crèches.

In a listing, headed by *Dred Scott v. Sanford* (1857), of the Supreme Court's most unhappy decisions, *Lynch v. Donnelly* must be included. Both are predicated upon the same basic concept: the inherent inferiority of ethnic groups, either because of color of skin or religious commitment.

It is appropriate to conclude discussion of government-financed crèches with the following eloquent expression by Norman Redlich, Dean of the New York University School of Law, a recognized scholar in the field of constitutional law and chairman of the American Jewish Congress' Commission on Law and Social Action. The essay, published in the March 26, 1984, issue of the *New York Times,* is set forth in its entirety. Under the heading "Nativity Ruling Insults Jews," it reads:

> The United States Supreme Court's decision in the Pawtucket, R.I. crèche case insults American Jews and all others who do not share what the Court's majority perceives as the country's dominant belief, Christianity.
>
> After the 5-4 decision, in *Lynch v. Donnelly,* a Jewish student approached me in the hall of our law school and said, in anguish, "I feel as if we have been betrayed." Indeed, we have been.
>
> For the first time, the Supreme Court has upheld direct government approval and financial support of an avowedly religious symbol relating to the beliefs of only one faith. While the Court's flagrant departure from the constitutional principle of church-state separation is, in this instance, particularly threatening to Jews, it should be equally troubling to members of all

religious faiths. We all are partners in the American enterprise: what diminishes my freedom will ultimately diminish yours.

The Constitution requires that, in their professional capacity, judges must stand outside any parochial religious perspective. A majority of today's Supreme Court Justices may indeed view the Nativity scene as a rather harmless religious symbol that is part of a broader observance of a secularized holiday. But non-Christians do not. To us, the support of a city-owned display that depicts the birth of Jesus to the Virgin Mary represents official endorsement of a religious message that we do not accept—although we fully respect and defend the rights of those who do.

The Supreme Court argued that government, and other religions, should "accommodate" to this religious symbol as long as it is linked with songs, reindeer, a Christmas tree and other decorations. But this is not a country in which Jews, or anyone else, should be asked to accommodate to a dominant religion.

Constitutionally there are no minority religions here, just as there is no established religion. We are all equal—all religions, all believers, all non-believers. When I see a government-supported crèche, I suddenly feel as if I have become a stranger in my own home, to be tolerated only as long as I accept the dominant religious values. But that is not the American way. It is not the philosophy of the great religion clauses of the First Amendment, which say: "Congress shall make no law respecting an establishment of religion, or prohibiting the free exercise thereof."

In America, Jews are all equal participants in the national experience of religious freedom. We do not ask to be tolerated. We belong here. When government, at any level, lends support to a Christian religious observance, Jews and other non-Christians are automatically excluded. President Reagan may believe that this is a Christian nation—indeed, the Administration joined Pawtucket's appeal after it reached the Supreme Court from two lower Federal courts—but the Constitution clearly rejects such an un-American, sectarian notion, and the Court should know better.

Supporters of the Court's decision may argue that Jews simply do not understand, that the Court's opinion merely views the crèche as part of a celebration, along with other expressions of Christmas such as songs, decorations or even "masterpieces" depicting "explicit Christian themes and messages" in public supported art museums. But the Court's opinion clearly recognizes the crèche as a Christian symbol that depicts the origins of Christmas. This constitutes official recognition of a profoundly religious event. A Nativity scene in a municipal park is not the same as a religious painting; it represents government support for a central tenet of a religious belief that many Americans do not share.

The experience of Jews worldwide adds to the profound significance of the Constitution's guarantee of religious neutrality. We have too long a history of living in countries where at best we were tolerated, at worst persecuted. In those countries, government-supported religious symbols have been the norm. Will we next be told that, as part of the secular observance of Easter, with eggs and bunnies, we should also accept the Crucifix as a simple recognition of a historical event?

We cannot accept, or understand, the Supreme Court's insensitivity to our rightful place in American society. The Court's opinion, by seeking to "accommodate," does exactly what the Constitution was designed to prevent: It denigrates religion by trying to convert a religious symbol into a secular observance, and it shuts the door on those of us who cannot accept a religious symbol because it conflicts with our deepest religious beliefs.

Jews should not be asked to accommodate. The most accommodating Jews in the contemporary history of the western world were the German Jews.

There is now pending before the Supreme Court an application to review the decision of the United States Court of Appeals in the case of *Stone v. McCreary*.* The case is the converse of *Lynch v. Donnelly*. There suit was brought by an opponent of the crèche; in the *Stone* case it was brought by its proponents, residents of Scarsdale, New York, who were denied a request that they be allowed to place a crèche at their own expense in a public park during the Christmas season.

The request was made before the *Lynch* decision was handed down and was rejected by the village authorities on the ground that granting it would violate the Establishment Clause. In reversing a District Court's decision upholding the denial, the Court of Appeals ruled that under the *Lynch* decision, which came down after the District Court acted, to deny a license to the plaintiffs while licenses for a wide variety of other displays were freely granted, would violate the Establishment Clause.

The Court rejected the contention that the *Lynch* case was different because there the crèche was placed on privately owned property rather than on publicly owned land. Since in the *Lynch* case, the Court said, public funds were used to install the crèche, the electricity used to illuminate it came from city-owned electric lines, and the project was sponsored by the city, there was no critical difference between the two cases. It did, however, require that a sign of adequate size disclaiming any public ownership be placed near the crèche.

The Supreme Court can respond to the petition for certiorari in *Stone v. McCreary* in any one of three ways: It can simply deny it; it can accept jurisdiction and affirm the decision; or it can by the change of but one vote reverse the decision on the ground, perhaps, that while the crèche in the *Lynch* case had been placed on privately owned property, in the *Stone* case it was to be placed on public property.

---

* Since this was written the Supreme Court has agreed to review the decision.

RELIGIOUS SYMBOLS: FLAG LOWERING

Lynch v. Donnelly involved a symbol which, at least in its origin, was obviously Christological. *Brown v. Thomson* (1978) challenged the constitutionality of governmental recognition of Good Friday, the day of Christ's death on the Cross rather than his birth in a manger. The symbol utilized for the purpose was the American flag, a patriotic and hence obviously not intrinsically religious symbol.

The chief character in the drama was Governor Meldrim Thomson of New Hampshire, who according to a report in the *New York Times* of March 25, 1978, had earlier been involved in controversies that encompassed Martin Luther King, United States Representative at the United Nations Andrew Young, a number of state university instructors whom he ordered discharged, and President James Carter, whose pardon of Vietnam draft resisters impelled Thomson to order a lowering of the flag in protest.

In 1976 and 1977 Thomson had ordered flags on state buildings to be lowered to half-mast on Good Friday. On the Tuesday before Good Friday in 1978 he issued a similar order, accompanied by a declaration that "all of us are more conscious [then ever] of the everlasting debt we owe to our Creator," and that "we appreciate the moral grandeur and strength of Christianity as the bulwark against the foes of destructive ideologies."

The next morning four clergymen, with the assistance of the New Hampshire Civil Liberties Union, instituted a suit and obtained a temporary injunction from a federal court judge forbidding the ceremony on the ground that the governor's proclamation was "no less than an exhortation to Christians to participate in a religious observance of critical significance in Christian theology."

> There is [the judge continued] not even a pretense of neutrality in this document. It contains all the seeds of divisiveness that the establishment provision was designed to prevent. It not only seeks to advance religion, but a particular religion.

Accordingly, he ordered the governor to "publicly withdraw" his proclamation and not lower the flags on Good Friday unless he issued a substitute declaration "putting such action in a secular context without officially endorsing the tenets of any other religion."

On the same (Wednesday) evening an appeal was taken to a judge of the Court of Appeals, who issued an order the next afternoon setting aside the injunction, thereby allowing the flag to be flown at half-mast. Off the American Civil Liberties Union's attorneys flew to Washington, and at nine o'clock the next morning (Good Friday) they got from Brennan a temporary order directing that the flags, which had been lowered that morning, be raised to their secular level. As a result, office flags were raised that morning with one exception; the exception was the flag on the capitol building, which had been left up from the beginning so that Thomson could lower it to half-mast for the benefit of the newspaper and television photographers. For some reason Thomson was delayed and by the time he arrived the entire Supreme Court had acted upon Brennan's order.

Working hastily from handwritten papers, that Court, without a formal opinion, voted five (Brennan, White, Marshall, Blackmun, and Stevens) to four (Burger, Stewart, Powell, and Rehnquist) to reinstate the District Court's order. Up went the flags, presumably until the next year's Good Friday replay. But it did not happen that way. On the first Tuesday in November 1978, Thomson was voted out of office and his successor pledged not to lower the flag on Good Friday. The result was that no final decision and opinion on the merits was issued.

All this happened before *Lynch v. Donnelly* came to the Supreme Court. In the interim Stewart had been replaced by O'Connor (probably no change there) and White had returned to his more natural habitat with Burger and Rehnquist in aid-to-religion cases. The net result of all this is that the Court's determination of the next flag-lowering ceremony on Good Friday will likely depend on how White chooses between permissible crèches and impermissible lowered flags.

RELIGIOUS SYMBOLS: CROSSES

Lynch v. Donnelly upheld the use of taxpayers' funds to erect and maintain a crèche on property which, for Establishment Clause purposes, can realistically be considered public property. As of now, the Supreme Court has not definitely decided whether the same or a contrary ruling would be applied if the controversy involved a cross, rather than a crèche, erected on a public street or a public park. The Court has had opportunities to issue an opinion upon the question but until now has declined to do so.

The *Lynch* decision manifests the general attitude of the Court's majority towards the issue of religious symbols on public property and, were one to wager on how it would decide the question of crosses on public property, the odds would have to be in favor of a determination of constitutionality. Not that there is an absence of distinguishing factors that could justify a contrary result. The crèche, for example, is a seasonal rather than an all-year phenomenon, even though for shopping purposes the season starts the day after Thanksgiving and continues until a week or two after Christmas. The cross cases, on the other hand, concerned a permanent fixture, in earlier days of wood but now most often of stone or granite.

A second distinguishing factor, were the Court inclined to rule against constitutionality, could be the setting of the cross as against that of the crèche. The latter is surrounded by inherently secular symbols: Santa Claus and his reindeer, holly, a Christmas tree (a tree is a tree is a tree all twelve months of the year but is generally not tinselled eleven of the year's twelve months). The exclusive religiosity of a cross is hardly open to question; one kneels in prayer before a cross but not in front of a crèche, at least not when it is part of a mercantile endeavor as it was in Pawtucket.

One of the earliest cases challenging the erection of a permanent cross on public property was that of *Lowe v. City of Eugene, Oregon.* For some thirty years before the case reached the courts in 1966, various civic groups in that city erected, on what was known as "Skinner's Butte" (named after the city's founder), a series of simple wooden crosses, some of them lighted during various periods connected with Christmas or Easter. It was located on a hill within the city limits several hundred feet from the business center but it rose high above the center and presented a commanding view of the city.

As each cross fell into disrepair and disappeared, it was replaced within a few years by a similar cross also made of wood. The last wooden cross erected by the local chamber of commerce was either blown down or fell down, or perhaps was destroyed by vandals. Thereafter, Alpha Phi Omega, a service fraternity located at the University of Oregon, undertook in cooperation with the chamber of commerce to erect a permanent lighted cross made of concrete.

When the fraternity applied to the city council for the necessary permit, it found to its surprise that there were some residents who were not happy about the endeavor and claimed that it was unconstitutional. A vote at the council was overwhelmingly in favor of the project but the opponents' protest resulted in a decision not to go forward with the project pending receipt of an opinion by the city's attorney on the question of constitutionality. While the attorney was researching the law, the fraternity, surprised at the opposition and not desirous of getting involved in the controversy, withdrew from the project, thereby apparently bringing it to an end.

It did not work out that way. The Eugene Sand & Gravel Company, acting on its own and without any expense to the city, erected a concrete cross with necessary electric fittings for its illumination. This was done during the night, when everybody was asleep at home. While the mayor and some others were disturbed the next morning about how the affair was handled, most of the council members were quite satisfied, particularly since the cross was deemed to be a very attractive work of art. To make sure that it would remain where it was, the city council voted to put the matter to the residents in the form of a resolution accepting the cross as a gift, appointing the American Legion post to affix a suitable plaque, and directing the city park department to light it on Memorial Day, Independence Day, Thanksgiving Day, during the Christmas season, and on Veterans Day.

The malcontents were not ready to accept the event as a *fait accompli.* They engaged the voluntary services of a New York specialist in church-state relations to act as chief counsel in a suit challenging the erection of the cross and calling upon the state court to compel its removal. The defendants named in the suit were the City of Eugene and the Eugene Sand & Gravel Company.

The institution of the suit brought the matter to national attention, with the result that the ensuing trial was reported in many newspapers throughout the nation. Both the plaintiffs' complaint and the defendants' answer to it were limited to the question of constitutionality under the Establishment and Free Exercise clauses of the First Amendment. Nevertheless, the trial judge expressly decided not to rule on that question but instead invoked a long-standing principle that where a case can be adjudged independently of any constitutional determination the court should not pass upon the question of constitutionality. In the case before it, the court stated, no charter provision or ordinance had been called to its attention that either expressly or by implication granted the city council authority to allow the erection of a permanent religious symbol in a city park, nor was there any state statute to that effect.

Having decided that the cross had been erected without lawful authority, the court decided that it had to be removed and, since it was the Eugene Sand & Gravel Company that erected the cross in the first place, the court ordered the company to remove it. Had the plaintiffs' counsel possessed prophetic vision, they would not have added the company as a defendant in the first place, for as it transpired, that ultimately turned out to be what may have been their fatal error. The reason for this lay in the fact that the city council voted not to appeal the decision, but the company decided that it would, with the result that removal of the cross was postponed until the final appeal was decided.

When the case reached the Supreme Court of Oregon, a majority voted to reverse the lower court's decision and uphold the constitutionality of the action taken by the company. At the time the appeal was argued one of the regular justices had been absent for a number of months and a lower court judge had been appointed to serve in his place. The temporary judge's vote had made a majority favoring reversal, but when the regular judge returned the reversal decision was itself reversed and a new one was issued requiring removal on the ground that the enterprise violated both the United States and the Oregon constitutions.

The next step was now up to the company and it accordingly filed an appeal to the United States Supreme Court. The appeal, however, was dismissed on the basis of a long-standing principle that where a state court decides that a particular law violates both the state and United States constitutions, the Supreme Court will not accept an appeal by the losing party. The reason for this lies in the fact that all federal courts must accept a state court's decision with respect to validity under its own constitution. It follows from this that there is no need for a federal court to decide that it also violates the national constitution. Put in simple terms, this means that there is no need to shoot a corpse.

The company then did what the plaintiffs' had successfully done, that is, move for a rehearing. Unlike the Oregon Supreme Court, the United States Supeme Court did not change its mind, but rather denied the motion for a rehearing.

Was the cross removed and the controversy ended? By no means. Although the city had decided not to contest the first decision, the citizens of Eugene by a majority vote decided to amend its charter. The amendment had four sections: The first constituted an acceptance of the cross as a gift from the company; the second, a dedication of the cross as a memorial to the war veterans of all wars in which the United States participated and the naming of the gift as the "Veterans War Memorial Cross"; the third, authorizing the local American Legion post at its own expense to prepare and affix an appropriate plaque; and the fourth, turning over to the city's department of parks responsibility for maintaining the cross and lighting it up on Memorial Day, Independence Day, Thanksgiving Day, during the Christmas season, and on Veterans Day.

This time the pro-cross forces succeeded. A majority of the Oregon Supreme Court ruled the new provision in the city's charter called for a judgment of constitutionality. The cross, said the court, was a religious symbol but that undeniable fact did not require a determination of unconstitutionality. The requirement of a secular purpose in determining constitutionality was satisfied since the new charter provision related the cross to Christmas as a secular day, as of course were Memorial Day, Thanksgiving Day, and Veterans Day. Nor could it be held that the display of the religious symbol had a primary effect of advancing religion, particularly in view of the fact that the display was sponsored by a secular organization and was lit up during secular holidays, festivals, and pageants.

Finally, said the court, the display of the religious symbol did not involve excessive government entanglement with religion. It would have been a different matter if the city had actively participated in the planning and organization of activities involving such a display. But the mere fact that the city paid for the maintenance of the religious symbol did not constitute excessive entanglement.

This time it was the anti-cross plaintiffs who called on the United States Supreme Court to review and reverse the Oregon decision. Again the Court in *Lowe v. Eugene Sand & Gravel, Inc.* (1977) refused, over Brennan's dissent, to do so, but unlike the prior application by the company, it gave no reason for its refusal. It could not have been, as in the prior case, because the Oregon court had ruled the practice a violation of the state's constitution and there was therefore no need for consideration under the First Amendment. On the contrary, the Oregon Supreme Court's opinion expressly said that the purpose-effect-entanglement formula was applicable in cases challenging validity under the state's constitution and application of that test required a ruling in favor of the company. There was, therefore, a real controversy that only the United States Supreme Court could resolve.

Three years after the second *Lowe* decision, the Supreme Court, in *Stone v. Graham*, ruled invalid under the Establishment Clause a Kentucky law mandating posting of the Ten Commandments in public school classrooms, and this even though under the statute all costs had to be paid out of private contributions without any expense on the part of the state. It may be that the difference between the *Stone v. Graham* and the *Lowe* cases lay in the fact that in the former the display was within public schools, while in the latter it was on a public street. It should be noted, however, that the Oregon Supreme Court's opinion in the *Lowe* case deemed valid "the passive display of a religious symbol in a public school," so that the result would have been the same in both situations.

In *Gilfillan v. City of Philadelphia* (1980) the erection of a cross on public property and at the city's expense was only part of a lawsuit challenging the city's expenditure of its funds to welcome a visit by Pope

John Paul II. As set forth in the opinion of the United States Court of Appeals, the factual situation of the controversy was as follows.

In September of 1979 the pope announced that he would undertake a "pastoral mission" to the United States and that his trip would include a stop in Philadelphia. City officials then began a series of meetings with the leaders of the Archdiocese of Philadelphia in preparation for the pope's visit. Out of these meetings grew plans for a Mass at Logan Circle. In accordance with those plans and with the approval of the Archdiocese, the city designed and built a large platform to be used as the dais from which the pope would celebrate Mass, distribute Holy Eucharist (a sacrament of the Roman Catholic church), and bring his message to Philadelphia.

Shortly thereafter, two taxpayers residing in Philadelphia brought suit for an injunction against use of city funds to finance the building of a red-carpeted platform on one corner of which a white thirty-six-foot-high cross was erected. They contested only the city's payment for the construction of a platform that was to be used exclusively for a religious service and for a few other items, such as the costs of installing a sound system, leasing chairs, planting shrubbery and flowers, and building another smaller platform for the choir.

The City of Philadelphia defended the action under an agreement with the Archdiocese of Philadelphia to reimburse the city should the plaintiffs prevail. Prevail they did, but over the strong dissent of one of the three judges of the Circuit Court of Appeals.

Applying the three-pronged purpose-effect-entanglement test, the majority rejected the claim that the expenditures were justified by two secular purposes: first, the protection of the pope and the crowd, and second, the possibility of a "public relations bonanza" for the city. The Court of Appeals upheld the lower court's determination that the platform was not designed, constructed, or used for a "civil" (i.e., secular) purpose but for the celebration of the Holy Mass by the pope assisted by the bishops of the Catholic church. Nor could the Court of Appeals see how the erection of a thirty-six-foot-high cross, the purchase of approximately fifty thousand dollars in flowers, and the installation of a fifty-six thousand dollar sound system contributed to the protection of the pope.

The Court of Appeals also rejected the public relations purpose of helping put Philadelphia in a good light.

By so arguing [the Court said] the City places itself in a difficult position. Viewers of the ceremony that do not know of the city-sponsorship are likely to believe only that the Archdiocese, not the City, will receive the public relations "bonanza." But if the city-sponsorship is known, that aid connotes the state approval of a particular religion, one of the specific evils the Establishment Clause was designed to prevent. An auspicious aspect of our pluralistic society is its rich religious diversity. The essential purpose of the Establishment Clause reflects this pluralism. Finally, if some peripheral public relations benefit can constitute a sufficient secular purpose, then the purpose test is destroyed, for it is hard to imagine a city expenditure that will not look good in someone's eyes.

Nor could the majority accept the claim that a one-time expenditure would not "have the effect of placing the City's imprimatur of approval on the Catholic religion." City officials, it said, went out of their way to align themselves and collaborate with the Archdiocese. The effect of the city's imprimatur of approval on the Catholic religion could not but benefit the Catholic religion. Besides this, the city's expenditure of funds effectively enabled the pope to reach a large number of persons to attend the performance of a religious ceremony.

Finally, the Court of Appeals held, there was sufficient entanglement of church and state to require a determination of unconstitutionality. This was manifested by the fact that, although the city designed the platform, it had to be approved by the Archdiocese and that for each aspect of the preparations the Philadelphia official in charge had a counterpart in the Archdiocese. Moreover, the city's expenditures tended to prompt divisiveness among and between religious groups, causing impermissible entanglement.

The dissent was predicated on the fact that the pope was the head of the secular state of the Vatican City, geographically within the city of Rome but nevertheless an independent national entity, even though the United States did not then have direct diplomatic relations with it. That the Holy See was a theocratic state was not material, nor was it unique. Israel was its Jewish counterpart and its religious nature had not prevented the United States from entering into diplomatic relations with it, as with all other political entities, and nobody disputed its permissibility.

The City of Philadelphia sought to appeal the decision but the Supreme Court rejected its application. That, however, took place in 1981. Within three years, the United States entered into formal diplomatic relations, not with the Vatican City (the pope would not accept that) but with the Holy See. Were some foolhardy taxpayer to institute a suit challenging validity under a Constitution that forbids entanglement of church and state, the chances of success would be small. This would have been so even with a pre-Burger Court; our government's relations with other foreign governments is generally not considered to be a matter for judicial determination. Our political structure reserves for presidential determination how much of taxpayers' funds should be used to welcome a visiting head of state, whether the state be the Holy See or the Union of Socialist Soviet Republics.

In *American Civil Liberties Union v. Rabun County* (1983), the United States Court of Appeals in Georgia reached a determination directly opposite to that of the Oregon Supreme Court in the *Lowe* case. Moreover, it did so in what might be considered disregard of the Supreme Court's decision in the *Valley Forge Christian College* case, discussed in Chapter 2 of this book.

Challenged in the *Rabun County* case was the erection by a local chamber of commerce of a lighted cross in Georgia's Black Rock Mountain State Park. Besides the American Civil Liberties Union, the plaintiffs in the suit were two Georgia residents who were unwilling to use the park for camping purposes because of the cross and its physical and "metaphysical" influence. One of the plaintiffs was the director of a religious camp; the cross was clearly visible from the porch of his cabin in the camp and from the roadway that had to be used to reach the camp. The injury to him, the Court noted in its opinion upholding his standing to sue, was particularly disturbing and intrusive because the cross was visible from his special place of religious contemplation and retreat.

The Federal District Court decided in favor of the plaintiffs. It held that the state's action in initially approving the request by the local chamber of commerce to erect the cross on the state's property and later failing to remove it constituted state action sufficient to bring the case within the prohibitive scope of the First and Fourteenth amendments. It also held that the project violated all three aspects of the purpose-effect-entanglement test, in that the state's action lacked a secular purpose, had as its principal or primary effect the advancement of religion, and fostered an excessive government entanglement with religion.

The Court of Appeals agreed with the District Court's determination that the state action required by the Fourteenth Amendment was present and also with its decision holding the action to be a violation of the Establishment Clause.

The District Court's finding of religious purpose, the higher court said, was supported by ample evidence. Numerous qualified witnesses had testified at the trial that the Latin cross was universally regarded as a symbol of Christianity. In addition, the selection of an Easter deadline for completion of the cross, the decision to dedicate the cross at Easter Sunday services, and the several inspirational statements contained in the chamber's press releases all pointed to the existence of a religious purpose.

Moreover, the Court of Appeals continued, even if the purpose of constructing the cross was to promote tourism, this alleged secular purpose would not have provided a sufficient basis for avoiding conflict with the Establishment Clause.

Nor, the Court concluded, did the fact that for many years a cross had shone over the mountains of itself provide a rational basis for ignoring the mandate of neutrality imposed by the Establishment Clause. The Court noted the apparently contradictory decisions in the *Lowe* case and in other cases but their correctness was questionable and, in any event, the cases were distinguishable.

In view of its determination of unconstitutionality under the purpose aspect of the Establishment Clause, the Court did not find it necessary to consider the effect and entanglement aspects of the clause. Instead, it concluded its decision with the words, "the cross must be removed."

RELIGIOUS SYMBOLS: THE DECALOGUE

Stone v. Graham, discussed in the preceding chapter, related to the posting of the Ten Commandments on the walls in public schools. While referred to in Rehnquist's dissenting opinion in that case, the Court of Appeals' 1973 decision in *Anderson v. Salt Lake City Corp.*, which the Supreme Court refused to review, is not mentioned in the majority opinion. Nor is any mention of it to be found in any of the four opinions in *Lynch v. Donnelly*, although it was clearly relevant to both these cases.

The *Anderson* suit challenged the action of the Salt Lake City Board of Commissioners in permitting the Fraternal Order of Eagles to erect on the courthouse grounds a permanent three-by-five-foot granite monolith inscribed with a version of the Ten Commandments and certain other symbols representing the All Seeing Eye of God, the Star of David, the Order of Eagles, letters of the Hebraic alphabet, and Christ. After erection of the monolith, the commissioners authorized the installation and maintenance, at the city's expense, of lighting equipment to illuminate and enhance the display.

Similar monoliths had been erected in public places across the United States as part of the Eagles' established and continuing "youth guidance program" and were intended ". . . to inspire all who pause to view them, with a renewed respect for the law of God, which is our greatest strength against the forces that threaten our way of life."

Reversing the District Court's contrary decision, the Court of Appeals upheld the constitutionality of the city's action. It ruled that the monolith was primarily secular and not religious in character and that neither its purpose nor effect was to advance religion. (For some unexplained reason, the opinion makes no reference to entanglement, although that was the principal ground for the Supreme Court's decisions in the *Walz* and *Lemon* cases, both of which are cited in it.)

The fact, the Court said, that the decalogue has an ecclesiastical background does not necessarily mean that it is primarily religious in character—it also has substantial secular attributes. "Although one of the declared purposes," the Court continued, "was to inspire respect of God, yet at the same time secular aspects were also emphasized. It [was] not a religious organization—it [was] a fraternal order which [advocated] ecclesiastical law as the temporal foundation on which all law is based, but the creed [did] not include any element of coercion concerning these beliefs, unless one considers it coercive to look upon the Ten Commandments. (Although they are in plain view, no one is required to read or recite them.)"

It may be that *Stone v. Graham* does not overrule *Anderson v. Salt Lake City Corp.* If (or when) a situation such as that of the latter case reaches the Supreme Court, it can make a distinction between the two cases. The former relates to children, who by virtue of compulsory school attendance laws must attend public schools, while no one is compelled by law to walk in a street from which the monolith is visible. And the fact that the city may pay the cost of illuminating the cross does not of itself render the project unconstitutional; the *Lynch v. Donnelly* decision attests to that. Moreover, the monolith in Salt Lake City did not stand alone; it was accompanied by what might be deemed secular objects—the Order of Eagles and letters of the Hebraic alphabet, just as the crèche in Pawtucket had for its companions a Christmas tree, a Santa Claus house, and reindeer pulling Santa's sleigh, not to mention such patently nonreligious articles as cutout figures of a clown, an elephant, and a bear.

On the other hand, it is conceivable, if not likely, that a majority of today's Supreme Court would find no legal distinction between streets in a city and the classrooms in Kentucky. Logic could support such a decision. If for business reasons or to see his doctor or dentist a Salt Lake City resident has to pass the monolith, he should not be required to blindfold himself and engage the use of a seeing-eye dog.

Finally, the Court could, if it wished, avail itself of the escape route resorted to in the *Salt Lake City* case—that is, simply deny a petition for a writ of certiorari without giving any reasons for its denial, whichever way the lower court decided the case.

RELIGIOUS TESTS FOR STATE OFFICES

In *McDaniel v. Paty* (1978) the Burger Court was called upon to decide whether Tennessee could constitutionally exclude McDaniel, an ordained minister, from serving as a member of a legislative body. Appreciation of the question raised in this case requires a brief examination of its historical background.

At the time the Constitution was written clergymen were barred from holding public office in seven of the original thirteen states: Maryland, Virginia, North Carolina, South Carolina, Georgia, New York, and Delaware. Later, six new states, including Tennessee, wrote the same disqualification into their own constitutions. The practice in the states came from England, where clergymen, though eligible to serve in the House of Lords, were barred from being elected to the House of Commons. The purpose of the states in America for excluding clergymen was primarily to assure the success of a new political experiment, the separation of church and state.

Originally, Thomas Jefferson advocated such a position in his 1783 draft of a constitution for Virginia, but James Madison persuaded him to change his mind.

> Does not [Madison wrote] the exclusion of Ministers of the Gospel as such violate a fundamental principle of liberty by punishing a religious profession with the [de]privation of a civil right? does it [not] violate another article of the plan itself which exempts religion from the cognizance of civil power? does it not violate justice by at once taking away a right and prohibiting a compensation for it? does it not in fine violate impartiality by shutting the door [against] the Ministers of one religion and leaving it open for those of every other?

When, therefore, the Constitution was drafted in 1787 there was a general though not universal acceptance of the prohibition of religious tests for public office in Article VI. A reasonable interpretation of that article would encompass not only parishioners but also clergy; Robert F. Drinan, S. J., served in the House of Representatives for three terms (until he was ordered by the Vatican to choose between Congress and the church and chose the latter), and there was no contention that he could have been constitutionally disqualified.

In the course of time, all but two of the states, Maryland and Tennessee, amended their constitutions or otherwise nullified their barriers against clergymen seeking to serve in public office. In *Torcaso v. Watkins* (1961) the United States Supreme Court, without dissent, held unconstitutional under the First Amendment a Maryland law that barred an atheist from qualifying as a notary public because he would not take the oath required of all public officials that he believed in the existence of God. (Maryland later amended its constitution to repeal the disqualification clause.)

Logic would seem to require a similar decision of unconstitutionality with respect to a provision in the Tennessee constitution that barred clergymen from serving in the state's legislature. McDaniel, a clergyman so barred, brought suit in the state's courts challenging his disqualification. Unsuccessful there, he appealed to the Burger Court and won an unanimous judgment of reversal. But that was as far as unanimity would go. Indeed, even a bare majority could not be mustered to agree upon an opinion to justify the decision.

Burger, speaking for himself, Powell, Rehnquist, and Stevens, held that *Torcaso v. Watkins* was not in point, since there the oath requirement was "focused on *belief*" (emphasis in original) whereas the Tennessee requirement was "directed primarily on status, acts, and conduct" of the clergy. What this means is that those who drafted the Tennessee law did not care whether or not you were an atheist in belief so long as you did not assume the status and act or conduct yourself as a clergyman. Nevertheless, the statute did violate the Free Exercise Clause because it required surrender of a free exercise right as a prerequisite for seeking public office. However, the Burger opinion refused to declare that Tennessee's action violated the Establishment Clause and, at the same time, rejected the state's argument that the disqualification was based on its interest in preventing a state religion.

Brennan, speaking for himself and Marshall, was of the view that the Tennessee law violated both the Establishment and Free Exercise clauses. (As was to be expected, his opinion was almost twice as long as Burger's.) Stewart, in a short opinion, agreed with Brennan that *Torcaso v. Watkins* was in point and mandated a determination of unconstitutionality. White was unable to agree with the other justices that the First Amendment, establishment and/or free exercise, was in any way relevant. To him, the controlling principle was the Fourteenth Amendment's Equal Protection Clause. Together Burger, Powell, Rehnquist, Stevens, Stewart, Brennan, Marshall, and White make eight; the ninth, Blackmun, took no part in the consideration or decision of the case.

How's that for fragmentation?

Religion in Military, Penal, and Legislative Service

Basically, the scope of this chapter encompasses two constitutional aspects of religion in times of war: exemption from military service and utilization of chaplains to achieve military success. Although not directly concerned with military service, the related subjects of access to chaplains by persons in civil prisons and the employment of chaplains to open legislative sessions with prayer are also considered in this chapter.

PREPARATION FOR POSSIBLE WAR: CONSCIENTIOUS OBJECTION TO MANUFACTURE OF ARMAMENTS

The cases considered in this section deal with conscientious objection to preparation for possible ultimate participation in actual combat. One of these is *Thomas v. Review Board* (1981), in which the Burger Court was faced with the question whether in times of peace a person could constitutionally be denied unemployment insurance benefits for refusal by reason of religious conscience to work in a plant that manufactured armaments for possible use in combat. In *Sherbert v. Verner* (1963) the Warren Court had ruled that denial of benefits to Sabbatarians who refused to accept jobs that required them to work on Saturdays violated the Free Exercise Clause. Over the sole but almost inevitable dissent by Rehnquist, the Burger Court ruled that the same conclusion was applicable in the *Thomas* case.

At the hearing before the Unemployment Review Board, Thomas had stated that he would not object to working in a plant that produced steel that could be used to manufacture tanks but his conscience would not allow him to actually hammer the steel into a tank. However, a fellow Jehovah's Witness testified that working on tanks was scriptually "acceptable."

The majority, in an opinion by the Chief Justice, held that these facts did not justify the board's decision. As to the first aspect, he said, so long as Thomas was acting in good faith, which was not challenged, it was not for the Court to say that the line he drew was an unreasonable one. Nor could it pass judgment between differing interpretations of intrafaith doctrine. The guarantee of free exercise was not limited to beliefs that are shared by all members of a religious sect. Courts were not arbiters of scriptural interpretations, including those relating to the commandment not to kill. It was therefore not the Court's function to pass judgment on whether Thomas or his fellow worker correctly perceived the commands of their common faith.

While granting unemployment benefits to Thomas might manifest tension between the mandates of the Free Exercise and Establishment clauses, it did not involve the state in fostering a religious faith in violation of the latter. It reflected no more than the governmental obligation of neutrality and did not constitute the involvement of religion with secular institutions that the Establishment Clause sought to forestall.

Until the Court overruled *Sherbert v. Verner,* it was binding in the *Thomas* case. Since the Court was not prepared to do that, Burger concluded, Thomas was entitled to judgment that he could not be denied unemployment compensation benefits.

In his dissent, Rehnquist expressed his view that in most cases the majority of the Court had been applying incorrect interpretations of both the Free Exercise and Establishment clauses. As to the former, the Court should have remained faithful to the interpretation applied by Warren in *Braunfeld v. Brown* in holding that a state did not violate the free exercise rights of a Sabbatarian in its enactment of Sunday closing laws. A statute that did not make unlawful any particular religious practice but simply made it more expensive to exercise did not violate the clause. As for the Establishment Clause purpose-effect-entanglement test, Rehnquist said, it should be "wholly abandoned" (blithely forgetting that he expressed no dissatisfaction with it when it was applied in the *Walz* and *Lemon* cases). Instead, he would adopt the test urged by Stewart in his dissent in *Abington School District v. Schempp.* Stewart's view was that the clause was limited to "government support of proselytizing activities of religious sects by throwing the weight of secular authorities behind the dissemination of religious tenets."

In sum, Rehnquist concluded, the Court, in both the *Sherbert* and *Thomas* cases, should have ruled that a state could constitutionally allow but was not compelled to accord unemployment compensation benefits to applicants who refused to accept employment they consider forbidden by their religious conscience.

PREPARATION FOR POSSIBLE WAR:
CHAPEL ATTENDANCE IN MILITARY ACADEMIES

Another aspect of preparation for war deals with the military academies at West Point, Annapolis, and Colorado Springs. Regulations applicable to them required that cadets and midshipmen attend chapel services every Sunday under penalty of dismissal for repeated absences. Some rather courageous (or perhaps foolhardy) students brought suit asserting the unconstitutionality of the regulations under the First Amendment Religion Clauses. At the trial of the case, *Laird v. Anderson* (1972), Assistant Secretary of Defense Roger Kelley and Admiral Thomas Moorer (later Chairman of the Joint Chiefs of Staff) testified that the regulations did not require the cadets and midshipmen to *worship* but only to *attend,* and that the purpose and primary effect were to make better and more effective combat officers of them. How? Because if a cadet observed young men at prayer and worship he would learn how they responded to religion, and when the cadet became a combat officer he would be able to put this knowledge to use on the battlefield. As Secretary Kelley testified:

> The opportunity to observe others at worship is clear manifestation of the manner and extent to which they draw upon God or a supernatural being in the conduct of their lives.

Attendance at religious services, said Admiral Moorer, "is a vital part of the leadership package, and it would be as inconsistent with the responsibility the Academies have to train complete combat officers to ignore this necessity as it would be to ignore the most obvious physical and tactical education."

The purpose and effect of the regulations, the Department of Defense argued, were therefore secular; the regulations were not to inculcate faith but to make better military officers, and that in fact is what they did. It follows therefore that they were entirely constitutional.

The justices in the Burger Court were not persuaded. Without any recorded dissent, they rejected an appeal by the Department of Defense from the lower court's decision of unconstitutionality. Yet a reasonable argument even under the Free Exercise Clause could be made for requiring cadets and midshipmen to attend religious services.

In his expression of opposition to military chaplains as an "establishment" prohibited by the Constitution, Madison recognized, although he rejected, a possible exception in the "case of navies with insulated crews," since church attendance was obviously impracticable. Today, American soldiers who are or have been serving in Lebanon or Grenada or South Korea or El Salvador may be practically as "insulated" as navy men at sea. A soldier drafted into the armed forces and sent to battle far from home is deprived of the opportunity to fulfill his sacred obligation to pray in the church of his choice, and military chaplains serve as a substitute. There are times, however, when a chaplain may not be available in an area of actual combat. In such instances, commissioned army officers may have to serve as substitute chaplains and, if so, it would seem reasonable that they should undergo some training in military academies so as to minimize as much as practicable war's intrusion upon the enlisted man's freedom to exercise his religion.

PREPARATION FOR POSSIBLE WAR: CONSCIENTIOUS OBJECTION TO COMPULSORY REGISTRATION

From earliest times war has been generally viewed as a man's business. The Amazons of ancient Greece do not count, since they came from a mythology that antedates history. Deborah, according to Judges 4, could be a prophetess and judge but joined Barak in combat only with extreme reluctance, warning him unsuccessfully that he would lose his honor since it would be said that the Lord delivered Sisera, commander in chief of the enemy forces, into the hands of a woman. The same chapter also relates that another woman, Jael, disposed of Sisera by driving a nail into his head, really a man's work. Centuries later, Joan of Arc, with the reluctant approval of Poitiers' theologians, was allowed to raise an army and lead it in war until her unsuccessful efforts at Paris and Compiègne culminated in her capture and ultimate death at the stake, this with the approval of the same Christian church that had earlier approved her entry into battle.

These were exceptions and, while Florence Nightingale was able to break the sex barrier with respect to nursing services on the battlefield, the aversion to women's participation in the killing of human beings rather than the healing of them continued until the middle years of the twentieth century, and even then was tolerated only in relation to voluntary rather than conscripted service.

More recently, however, as in many other areas the rising tide of gender equality has impinged even upon the arena of the mass killing that is known as war. The decision makers in Congress and in the armed forces found that within reasonable limits (i.e., excluding actual combat) women could contribute to our efforts in a total war, which by definition means total effort including that of women.

When, therefore, in 1980 the Soviet armed invasion of Afghanistan impelled President Jimmy Carter to recommend enactment of a law requiring all eighteen-year-old persons to register for possible war service should that become necessary, he deemed it quite natural to include women. There was sound constitutional basis for this assumption. In *United States v. Bland* (1931) a majority of the Supreme Court upheld the denial of naturalization to a Canadian woman who refused to take the congressionally prescribed oath to defend the Constitution and laws of the United States against all enemies, except with the written interpolation of the words, "as far as my conscience as a Christian will allow."

The majority considered it immaterial that throughout its history the government had never drafted women and that Bland was a nurse, who during World War I spent nine months as a volunteer nurse serving with the American armed forces in France, so that registration of women could be of help in military service, even without engaging in actual combat. Notwithstanding this precedent, Congress refused to go along with Carter and limited the registration requirement to males, a deletion the president found necessary to accept in order to get the measure enacted.

In *Rostker v. Goldberg* (1981) the Court, in an opinion by Rehnquist and over the dissents of White, Brennan, and Marshall, held that the exclusion of women did not violate the constitutional mandate relating to the equal protection of the laws. (Although the Equal Protection Clause appears in the Fourteenth Amendment which relates to state action, beginning with *Barrows v. Jackson* in 1954 the Supreme Court has consistently held that it is applicable to Congress by virtue of the Due Process Clause in the Fifth Amendment.)

While the registration law as enacted excluded women, it made no exception with respect to men whose religious conscience forbade not only participation in armed conflict but also in its preparation. In 1918 the Supreme Court, in the *Selective Draft Law Cases (Arver v. United States)*, had ruled that there was no constitutional right to exemption from military service by reason of religious conscience and that Congress could, if it saw fit, abolish all religious exemptions. Logically, then, Congress could take the lesser step of requiring registration by conscientious objectors as well as everybody else, so that in case of an emergency it could call upon all persons to take up arms or otherwise assist in the defense of the country.

On the other hand, our nation is not a military dictatorship; Article II designating the president, a civilian, as commander in chief of all armed forces guarantees this. Moreover, our constitutional rights are never suspended, even in times of war. Thus, Article I, Section 9, forbids denial of the writ of habeas corpus except in cases of actual rebellion (which happened only once) or invasion (which has never happened); and the Third Amendment permits quartering of soldiers in any person's home in time of war only "in a manner prescribed by law."

> The Constitution of the United States, [the Supreme Court said in *Ex parte Milligan* (1866)] is a law for rulers and people, equally in war and peace, and covers with the shield of its protection all classes of men, at all times and under all circumstances. No doctrine, involving more pernicious consequences, was ever invented by the wit of man than that any of its provisions can be suspended during any of the great exigencies of government.

In later cases, the Court held that freedom of speech could be abridged to a limited extent when our nation was at war but certainly not when it was at peace and the purpose of the challenged speech was to express opposition to our entering into war.

In *West Virginia State Board of Education v. Barnette* (1943) the Court ruled that the First Amendment's guarantee of free speech encompassed symbolic speech, as by saluting the flag, and freedom of silence, as by refusing to do so. The same is obviously true where (as, indeed, was the situation in the *Barnette* case) the refusal is based on religious conscience. It could reasonably be argued that only a serious national crisis could justify a law requiring citizens to violate their religious beliefs by registering for a draft that might never by invoked.

There is no religious conscience exemption in the 1980 draft registration but the Department of Justice did not prosecute those who did not register so long as they kept silent about it. Rather it adopted a policy of limiting prosecution to the few registrants who articulated their nonconformance, even if it was only in a letter to the government stating why their religious conscience forbade them to conform. Among those, the sentences imposed by the trial judges varied. In one case, the defendant was placed upon probation and required to perform at least two hundred and fifty hours of community service. In another, the defendant was sentenced to thirty months in prison.

Two of the cases have been appealed to the Supreme Court. One, *United States v. Wayte,* has already been accepted by it for consideration during the term beginning in October 1984. The other, *United States v. Schmucker* (decided too late for the filing of a petition for review before the Court's recess), in all probability will also be accepted for consideration during the same term.

In the first case, Wayte had been indicted for failure to register but the trial court dismissed the indictment on the ground of impermissible selective prosecution based on the fact that the government prosecuted only those who articulated their refusal to register. Wayte had written to the Selective Service declaring that he had not registered and did not plan to do so. Six months later he wrote another letter stating that he still had not registered and that he would be traveling around the nation "encouraging resistance and spreading the word about peace and disarmament."

The trial court dismissed the indictment on the ground that Wayte had been selected for prosecution because of his exercise of First Amendment rights. Initiation of the prosecution, the Court said, was part of the government's deliberate policy of prosecuting only those who wrote to the government to report their noncompliance or communicated it to others. This policy of prosecuting only "vocal" but not "quiet" nonregistrants, it held, violated the Constitution.

The Court of Appeals, by a vote of two to one, reversed the decision. Selectivity in prosecution was not of itself impermissible; it was unconstitutional only on proof that the selection was deliberately based upon an unjustifiable standard. The government had explained that its selective system was necessary because the identities of other violators were not known, whereas violators who publicly expressed their refusal to register made clear their violation of the law and at the same time identified themselves, thereby making prosecution feasible. The Court upheld the validity of this explanation. Since, it said, Wayte had failed to prove that the government focused its investigation on him not because of this plausible explanation but only to punish him for his protest activities, the indictment should have been upheld.

What brought about the prosecution in the second case, *United States v. Schmucker*, was the defendant's letter to the Selective Service advising it of his intention not to register for the draft and stating that the act of registration would itself violate his religious conscience, even if he were never to be called for actual service.

The record in the case disclosed that of the approximately half million young men who failed to register by November 1982, only thirteen had been indicted, and in each case the defendant had expresed his opposition to the law either by letter to the government or by public speech. On the basis of this fact, the Court of Appeals reversed the District Court's decision against Schmucker and ruled that a prosecutorial policy violates the First Amendment if it is directed solely at the vocal nonregistrant who openly objects to the law on religious, moral, or political grounds.

The reason for this, the Court said, was that by adopting a policy that excludes from prosecution the thousands of potential draftees who engage in noncompliance and evasion of the law but keep silent about it, the government discourages dissenters from expressing their criticisms of that policy. Coerced silence in these circumstances could not be reconciled with freedom of speech.

The *Schmucker* case also involves the Free Exercise Clause. The Court's opinion noted that he was a sincere Mennonite and that the prosecution against him was based on a letter he wrote to the government in which he said that registering would violate his religious conscience. Neither the District Court nor the Court of Appeals addressed itself to that question.

As will be noted in the next section of this chapter, there is no constitutional right to exemption from war service because of religious conscience. Perhaps this principle could be extended to include a time in which we are in actual combat though not legally at war in the sense that there was no formal declaration of war required by Article I, Section 8, of the Constitution. In situations such as the Korean and Vietnam encounters, approval by Congress of expenditures to finance them might be deemed the equivalent of a declaration of war, with the consequence of constitutional power not to exempt conscientious objectors if Congress so saw fit.

But compulsory registration based on the possibility that at some time in the future Congress may declare war, either expressly or implicitly, is a different matter. The Supreme Court could conceivably hold that under the Free Exercise Clause the possibility of a future war is not sufficient cause to override conscientious objection to register for a war that hopefully may never come. It is unlikely that this will happen; it is more probable that the Court will address itself only to the questions of freedom of speech, freedom of petition, and the equal protection of the laws. If so, what will remain unanswered is the serious question whether religious conscience must be recognized at a time when we are not at war but only engaged in protecting friendly nations such as El Salvador or friendly insurgents against unfriendly nations as in Grenada and Nicaragua.

Elton Eller was another of the thirteen conscientious objectors found guilty for refusal to register. By reason of conscience he elected not to appeal. (He was sentenced to perform two years of unpaid public service.) However, an extract from a letter he had earlier sent to his congressman merits quoting here in part:

The obvious consequences are $10,000 fine and up to 5 years in prison. Not so apparent are things like an interruption of my education, loss of my right to vote, a prison record which could and most probably will interfer [sic] with any job for which I might apply, loss of friends and acquaintances and respect . . . .

I am not trying to oppose the United States government, nor am I attempting to cause problems for the Selective Service. Simply, I cannot conscientiously register for the draft. I feel that God has called me to not register. Therefore, I will not register. True, as a Christian I am called to obey my government at all times that to do so would not conflict with my following God and Jesus Christ (I Peter 2:13-17; Romans 13:1, 5-8). However, registration for the draft for me has fallen into the area of conflict, and my belief is that when God and the government conflict, God must be obeyed.

As has been noted, Congress refused to include women in the registration measure and in the *Rostker* case the Supreme Court upheld their exclusion. But it had no intention of exempting males who attended college; on the contrary, it was concerned that too many of them were not complying with the law. Accordingly, in 1983 it enacted a measure excluding from eligibility for federal loans male students who had not registered.

The constitutionality of this measure was upheld by the Supreme Court in the case of *Selective Service System v. Minnesota Interest Reserve Group* (1983). The appeal was by the government from a District Court decision striking down the law on two grounds: first, that it constituted a bill of attainder (a legislative determination of guilt and infliction of punishment without a court trial) forbidden by Article I, Section 9, of the Constitution; and, second, that it violated the Fifth Amendment's ban on self-incrimination in that the student's silence by failure to register during the required period (within thirty days after his eighteenth birthday) of itself constituted a punishable offense.

The Supreme Court, in an opinion by Burger and over the dissents of Brennan and Marshall, rejected both contentions and upheld the constitutionality of the statute. The law, Burger said, did not punish for past conduct, since a provision in it gave nonregistrants thirty days after receiving notice before they became ineligible for college aid. Indeed, it did not inflict or intend to inflict any punishment at all; it merely sought to promote a fair allocation of scarce federal resources by limiting aid to those who were willing to meet their responsibilities to the United States.

Nor, the Court said, did the 1983 law violate the Fifth Amendment's ban on compulsory self-incrimination since it did not compel the nonregistrant to disclose anything or make any statement to anyone as to whether or not he had registered during the required registration period.

It should be noted that, as in the *Rostker* case, neither of the claims of unconstitutionality was based upon the Free Exercise Clause, but Reagan's Department of Education may have supplied the missing link. Unsatisfied with the adequacy of the 1982 law, it bypassed Congress and issued a regulation going considerably further than Carter's efforts to include women. Its regulation barred from eligibility for government loans all college students regardless of age or sex who failed to sign forms stating that they had either registered or, by reason of age or sex, were not subject to the draft.

In 1984, a suit, *Alexander v. Department of Education,* challenging the regulation under the Free Exercise Clause was brought by three Boston University theology students, a man and two women, none of whom was Mennonite but were rather members of the United Methodist church. A temporary injunction against enforcement of the law was issued by a federal judge in Boston.

> The Secretary of Education [the judge said in his decision] established a new ground for denial of aid. In other words, the sanction that Congress reserved for a small group of lawbreakers was imposed by the Secretary on a potentially much larger group of persons who have not broken any law and who have met all the statutory requirements for aid. The imposition of this sanction is beyond the powers delegated to Congress.

Unless a temporary injunction were ordered, the judge continued, the students would have been

> . . . forced to make a choice between complying with Federal regulations or abiding by their religious principles.
> Denying aid to those whose only offense is refusal out of religious convictions to fill out a form stating that they are not required to register raises constitutional issues.

It is quite possible, therefore, that with this case the constitutional issue arising under the Religion Clauses of the First Amendment will finally reach the Burger Court.

CONSCIENTIOUS OBJECTION TO MILITARY SERVICE

In *United States v. Macintosh* (1931) the Supreme Court rejected as "astonishing" the assertion that it was a "fixed principle of our Constitution, zealously guarded by our laws, that a citizen cannot be forced and need not bear arms in a war if he has conscientious scruples against doing so." The Court said:

> . . . Of course, there is no such principle of the Constitution, fixed or otherwise. The conscientious objector is relieved from the obligation to bear arms in obedience to no constitutional provision, express or implied; but because, and only because, it has accorded with the policy of Congress thus to relieve him . . . . The privilege of the . . . conscientious objector to avoid bearing arms comes not from the Constitution but from the acts of Congress. That body may grant or withold the exemption as in its wisdom it sees fit.

This does not mean that Congress has unrestricted discretion in determining who shall and who shall not be granted the privilege of exemption. The First Amendment's ban on preferring some religions over others precludes limiting exemption (as Congress had directed in World War I) to the traditional pacifist faiths, such as the Friends and the Mennonites.

Congress recognized this unwelcome reality—unwelcome because it required it either to eliminate all religious exemptions, something it was not ready to do, or extend them to encompass such disfavored faiths as that of Jehovah's Witnesses. It chose the latter alternative and provided in the 1940 Selective Service Law that exemption should be granted to anyone who "by reason of religious training and belief" possessed conscientious scruples against "participation in war in any form." On third thought it decided that it might have been more liberal than it intended. (Not that there was lack of precedent for a considerable broader exemption. The Mosaic Code exempted, among others, the "fainthearted" [Deuteronomy 20:8]. So open-ended an exemption could result in a purely voluntary army—which American history had shown to be ineffective—since too many draftees would claim that they had become infected with acute faintheartedness.)

In 1948, the law was again amended to limit exemption to persons who by reason of religious training possessed a "belief in a relation to a Supreme Being [capitals in original] involving duties superior to those arising from any human relation" but the exemption was not to include persons possessing "essentially political, sociological, or philosophical views or a merely personal code."

Unfortunately, this effort presented its own difficulties, primarily in the constitutional arena. Ever since the *Everson* decision in 1947 it had been the law of the land that under the Establishment Clause government could not prefer some religions, e.g., theistic ones such as Christianity, Judaism, and Islam, over others, such as Buddhism and Taoism, which do not encompass belief in a personal God. Moreover, even if the term "Supreme Being" could be interpreted to encompass religious faiths other than the "Big Three," under the Establishment Clause as construed in the *Everson* decision and applied in *Torcaso v. Watkins* (1961), the government could not prefer all religions over nonreligion any more than some religions over others.

Thus it befell to the Supreme Court to find a constitutional way of separating the good (believers) from the bad (those guilty of possessing "essentially political, sociological, or philosophical views or a merely personal code"). It achieved this task by invoking the well-established principle of statutory interpretation that, where a law enacted by Congress can conceivably by interpreted in such a way as to avoid having to pass upon its constitutionality, that interpretation must be accepted. By using the term "Supreme Being" rather than "God," Congress, said the Court, did not intend merely the traditional personal deity of the faithful but rather a "religious belief" that "is sincere and meaningful and occupies a place in the life of its possessor parallel to that filled by the orthodox belief in God of one who clearly qualifies for the exemption."

That is how, during the Vietnam War period, the Court, in an opinion by Clark, was able to find in three cases decided under the name of *United States v. Seeger* (1965) that a registrant who admitted his "skepticism or disbelief in the existence of God" but avowed a "belief in and devotion to goodness and virtue for their own sakes and a religious faith in a purely ethical creed," another who stated a belief in "Godness horizontally through Mankind and the world," and a third who avowed a commitment to religion defined by him as "the supreme expression of human nature, man thinking his highest, feeling his deepest, living his best" were all entitled to exemption under the statute as it had been amended in 1948.

In *Welsh v. United States* (1970) the Court, over the dissent of three members, including Burger, who had been appointed Chief Justice a year earlier, went even further; it ruled that a registrant who struck out the words "religious training" from his application was nevertheless entitled to exemption and this notwithstanding the fact that in his original application in April 1964 he stated that he did not believe in a "Supreme Being," apparently no matter how that term was defined. (In a letter to his local board in June 1965, three months after the *Seeger* decision was handed down, he requested that his original negative answer be stricken and the question as to his belief in a Supreme Being be left open.)

Welsh v. United States was as far as the Burger Court would go in protecting the rights of religious objectors to war. A year after that decision it held, in *Gillette v. United States,* that in limiting exemptions to persons whose conscience forbade participation in all rather than only some wars, Congress did not thereby violate the Establishment Clause (by preferring some religions over others) nor abridge the free exercise rights of selective objectors. It accordingly upheld the conviction of a devout Catholic who, in adherence to church doctrine, was willing to participate in "just" wars but not in those that were "unjust" and who put the Vietnam War in the latter category. Only Douglas, the sole dissenter from the judgment in the *Walz* tax exemption case, dissented from the Court's judgment in the *Welsh* case. To the other members of the Court, including the liberal block of Black, Brennan, and Marshall (who wrote the majority opinion), the question of whether the Vietnam War was a just or unjust war was political rather than religious and was therefore to be answered by voters on election day rather than by five of nine Supreme Court justices who were neither elected nor could be removed by a majority of the people.

Douglas was also the lone dissenter in *Johnson v. Robison* (1974). In that case the Supreme Court passed upon a challenge by conscientious objectors to a provision in the Veterans Readjustment Benefit Act that excluded conscientious objectors from veterans' educational benefits even if they had satisfactorily completed alternative civilian service, such as service in hospitals within the United States. Two grounds were asserted in support of the objectors' claim. First, their exclusion from benefits denied them the Fifth Amendment's due process guarantee of equal protection of the laws. Second, the law violated the Free Exercise Clause of the First Amendment.

In an opinion by Brennan, the Court ruled against the objectors with respect to both claims. While privileges were unequal between veterans engaged in military service and those performing alternative civilian service, so too were their obligations. Under the challenged law an objector served for two years and then was free of any obligations to the government; on the other hand, after two years of active duty the veteran remained subject to active reserve and standby reserve obligations for an additional four-year period. Moreover, only active soldiers became part of the military establishment, subject to its discipline and potentially hazardous duty; conscientious objectors performing noncombative service did not.

Military service with educational benefits, said Brennan, was obviously more attractive to a registrant than service without them and Congress could without violating the equal protection guarantee seek to induce him to volunteer for military service or not to seek a lower Selective Service classification.

Finally, as to the free exercise claim, under the *Gillette* decision, Brennan said, a conscientious objector to service in what he considered to be an unjust war could be imprisoned for his refusal to serve. It could hardly be ruled a denial of free exercise if the consequence of refusal to serve in any war was no more than the withholding of educational benefits.

Douglas's dissent was applicable to both the equal protection and free exercise aspects of the majority decision. It was predicated upon the fact that under that decision educational benefits could be withheld from a conscientious objector to active military service who could nevertheless be required to perform alternative civilian service twenty-four hours daily far from home, while it was not withheld from a draftee who did not serve overseas but lived with his family in a civilian community and worked from nine to five as a file clerk on a military base and attended college in his off-duty hours.

One month after the Court had decided the *Gillette* case, it handed down a *per curiam* decision in the case of *Clay* (also known as *Muhammad Ali*) *v. United States*. It there set aside Ali's conviction for willfully refusing to serve in the armed forces during the Vietnam War period. In order to qualify for classification as a conscientious objector, the Court said, the applicant must satisfy three basic tests: That he was conscientiously opposed to war in any form, including "just" wars; that his opposition was based on religious training and belief; and that it was sincere. The government and the Court agreed that the Department of Justice was in error in ruling that Ali's beliefs were not based upon religious training and belief.

> It seems clear, [the Department had said] that the teachings of the Nation of Islam preclude fighting for the United States not because of objection to participation in any form but rather because of political and racial objections as interpreted by Elijah Muhammad . . . . It is therefore our conclusion that registrant's claimed objections to participation in war insofar as they are based upon the teachings of the Nation of Islam, rest on grounds which are primarily political and racial.

The government conceded, and again the Court agreed, that the department had erred in finding that Ali had not been sincere inasmuch as he had not asserted his conscientious objector claim until military service became imminent. The Court did not find it necessary to decide whether the department was correct in ruling that Ali was not opposed to war in any form but only selectively opposed to certain wars. Since it was wrong with respect to two of the tests, the conviction had to be set aside without regard to the question of justness or unjustness. Implicitly, this left the government the option of retrying Ali on the third ground alone; but to the satisfaction of millions of boxing fans, it decided to abandon the whole endeavor.

The Court's decision did not make any reference to the constitutional aspects of the case and the Appeals Board gave no reasons for its over-ruling the hearing officers' recommendation that Ali's claim should be sustained. Yet it is difficult to escape the conclusion that were Ali merely a nonprominent Black Muslim and not its most famous believer the result of the proceeding might have been different.

Evidence to support this assumption may perhaps be found in the case of *Rosenfeld v. Rumble* (1975). In the *Gillette* case, the Court recognized an area of permissible resort to force that did not entail sacrifice of conscientious objection status—force used in defense of home, family, or other persons in the community against immediate acts of aggressive violence. Notwithstanding this, in the *Rosenfeld* case, the Supreme Court left standing a decision by the Court of Appeals denying conscientious objector status to a person of Jewish upbringing and faith who, in answer to a hypothetical question by a hearing officer, stated that he would personally bear arms, though not in a military unit, if a foreign nation crossed the territorial boundaries of the United States with the avowed purpose of exterminating all Jews. The fact, the Court of Appeals held, that he was profoundly influenced by his understanding of the holocaust of atrocities perpetrated against Jews by the Nazi regime did not entitle him to exemption.

The reason for this, the Court said, was that the *Gillette* exemption applied only where the draftee's limitation in both time and geographic area were objective and not subjective criteria. This was not the situation with Rosenfeld, and therefore as to him, what was applicable was the *Gillette* ruling that excluded from exemption persons who were willing to participate in "just" wars.

MILITARY CHAPLAINS

Like conscientious objectors, clergymen do not have a constitutional right to exemption from military service. National self-preservation is the first law even in a nontotalitarian state; in Lincoln's day we fought a bloody civil war predicated on that premise. A democratic nation can survive without a constitution (England and Israel are examples) but a constitution without a nation is meaningless. Conscientious objectors are exempt from military service by reason not of any constitutional right but of legislative grace, and what Congress gives it can take away. The same is true even with respect to ordained clergymen, who may praise the Lord (indeed they are urged to do so) but must, if commanded, pass the ammunition.

Both exemption of clergymen from compulsory military service and the reason for it can be traced to the days of Moses. Before the Israelite soldiers went into combat the priests, exempt from participation in battle, were commanded to exhort them: "Hear, O Israel, ye approach this day into battle against your enemies; let not your hearts be faint, fear not and do not tremble, neither be ye terrified because of them; for the Lord your God is he that goeth with you, to fight for you against your enemies, to save you" (Deuteronomy 20:1-4)

It can hardly be doubted that this morale-building function is today a service expected of clergymen at home no less than of chaplains on the battlefield. Since defensive wars (are there any other?) justify utilization of all the nation's resources, it would seem reasonable that religion should be available when it can help in recruiting young men and making better soldiers of them in military service after they are recruited. This is illustrated by the following report in the March 1, 1969, issue of the Jewish Telegraphic Agency *News Bulletin*:

> A U.S. Army private who embarked on a "death fast" because he claimed his religious conviction as an Orthodox Jew prevented him from serving "an army practicing violence" in Viet Nam has been taken into custody and confined in a mental [*sic*] ward at Madigan General Hospital, Tacoma, Wash., military authorities revealed today.
>
> The soldier, Pvt. Robert Levy, 22, of Kansas City, Mo., started a hunger strike two weeks ago at Fort Lewis, Wash. For 14 days he ate only milk and honey. Yesterday, he stopped eating altogether stating that "as an expression of my religious conviction as an Orthodox Jew, I break the law of the United States and refuse to remain a soldier."
>
> Defense Department officials disclosed that the Army is trying to get rabbis to convince Levy that the war is righteous and his fast unjustified.

A more recent instance of what might be called a chaplain's gung ho contribution toward more effective fighting rather than to providing religious services to the soldiers is reported in the *New York Times* issue of March 4, 1984.

When [the *Times* reported] Capt. Jay Romans, an Army chaplain, is faced with young soldiers too frightened to jump out of a military plane flying high at this [Fort Benning] base, he stops for a moment and whispers a little prayer. Then he walks to the door of the airplane and leaps out.

As the trainees watch the 36-year old chaplain's white parachute open 1,200 feet above the ground, they say they invariably feel better about what they are about to do.

"I've got my rosary in my pocket," Lieut. Sharon Smith of Buffalo, N.Y. said Thursday just before her second jump for an airborne training course. "And when I see the chaplain, I've got double reassurance."

The government is not reluctant to present the justification. The chaplaincy, it said in its brief in the case of *Katcoff v. Marsh* (1984), is necessary for the maintenance of good morale. *Katcoff v. Marsh* merits further consideration.

Although handed down by a Federal District Court judge, the decision will in all likelihood reach the Supreme Court. The suit was instituted in 1980 by two Harvard Law School students, probably after studying *Flast v. Cohen* in their constitutional law course. Relying on that decision they sued as taxpayers and charged in their complaint that the government's employment of paid chaplains to serve in the armed forces violated the Establishment Clause of the First Amendment.

Unexpectedly, before the judge could decide the case, the Supreme Court handed down its decision in *Valley Forge Christian College v. Americans United for Separation of Church and State*, holding that taxpayers did not have standing to challenge in court a law allowing the government to dispose of surplus property even by handing it over free of charge to a church. Although the Supreme Court expressly stated in its opinion that it was not overruling *Flast v. Cohen*, the *Valley Forge* decision was widely assumed to foreclose all taxpayers' suits except those limited to challenges against federal aid to parochial schools.

By what to nonlawyers might be deemed a technicality of the highest order, the District Court judge in the *Katcoff* case ruled that the Harvard law students did have standing to sue, notwithstanding the *Valley Forge* ruling. The difference between the *Flast* and *Valley Forge* cases was that the former was a challenge under Article I, Section 8, of the Constitution, which deals with the power of Congress to tax and spend, while in the latter case, the issue was whether the plaintiff's challenge was aimed at the government's authority under a different part of the Constitution, Article IV, Section 3, which empowers Congress to dispose of property belonging to the federal government. A taxpayer has standing to sue if he attacks action by Congress but not (as in the *Valley Forge* case) a bureaucratic implementation of a congressional directive to an executive department such as the Department of Health, Education and Welfare. The Army's budget enacted into law by Congress specifically included funds to employ chaplains as the 1965 Elementary and Secondary Education Act challenged in the *Flast* case did in relation to financing religious schools. It followed from this that the plaintiffs in the *Katcoff* case had standing to sue.

Should the case be appealed it will not be by the government. The reason for this lies in the fact that, after having found that the plaintiffs had standing to sue, the District Court ruled that the Army's Chaplaincy Program was not unconstitutional and the Army could go on employing chaplains.

In *Marsh v. Chambers*, discussed more fully later in this chapter, the Supreme Court said that in some areas it need not measure constitutionality on the basis of the purpose-effect-entanglement test but could rely instead upon American history as it related to a particular practice, in that case the employment of legislative chaplains. The judge in the *Katcoff* case followed suit. The most appropriate test of constitutionality with respect to the military chaplaincy program, he said, was whether it constituted "a real threat to the Establishment Clause." That the Army Chaplaincy Program did not pose such a threat was evidenced by the fact that when the Congress drafted the First Amendment it authorized, at the same time, employment of a paid chaplain for service in the army.

The government also contended that not only was the Army Chaplaincy Program immune from attack under the Establishment Clause, but it was actually required under the Free Exercise Clause. Since the trial judge found that the program did not violate the Establishment Clause, he did not find it necessary to determine validity under the free exercise claim. Yet a good case can be made to support the free exercise contention.

A soldier drafted into the armed forces and sent to battle thousands of miles from home is deprived of the opportunity to exercise his religion by attending the church of his choice. The deprivation is acceptable but only to the extent that it is necessary to the overriding consideration of national defense; if the government can practicably furnish a substitute in the form of a traveling church in the person of a chaplain, the soldier might have a constitutional right thereto.

Even opponents of military chaplaincies recognize the need many soldiers have for this spiritual help, particularly in periods of stress and crisis. They argue, however, that the churches could provide this even more effectively and certainly more honestly if the chaplains were not part of the military establishment, if they were paid by the churches rather than the government, and if they did not wear military uniforms and did not hold military rank. Godly men are human too, and in the military if you want good efficiency reports, promotions in rank, and decorations, you don't go around making waves. A commanding officer who thinks all conscientious objectors are cowardly frauds, and in any event should be made to do their duty as everybody else, is not likely to recommend for promotion a chaplain who seems to be much too trusting in attesting to the sincerity of soldiers who newly discover a conscientious objection to war they did not previously know they possessed.

Yet there is another side to the matter. Military chaplains, besides building morale, fill a need which civilian chaplains without official rank, status, and pay could not fill or could not fill so effectively. When a young man of eighteen or nineteen, away from home and family perhaps for the first time in his life, finds himself in some kind of trouble with the overwhelmingly large, disciplined, and impersonal institution known as the army, he may need a trusted ombudsman and need him desperately. In such a situation, a chaplain who has the same military rank and wears the same uniform as the commanders, who eats with them, and calls them by first name can be more valuable to the troubled soldier than one who eats, sleeps, and associates himself entirely with the foot soldier. Thus considerations of humaneness justify military chaplaincies.

RELIGION IN PRISONS

To some extent, free exercise law applicable to a person confined in prison is comparable to that relating to one who is conscripted into the armed forces. In both instances it cannot be said that he voluntarily agreed to restrictions upon his First Amendment rights. Nor, in either case, can it be urged that it is unconstitutional to impose any restrictions upon those rights; in neither case, for example, does the individual have the right to attend the church of his choice.

There is, obviously, one difference between the two situations: in one the individual involved is a person confined because he has committed a crime, whereas this is not true with regard to the other. But, as will be seen later, a majority of the Supreme Court does not consider that necessarily a critical factor in determining constitutionality. In any event, it should not justify different privileges between persons adhering to conventional faiths and those belonging to unpopular religions or "cults," such as Black Muslims, the faith which Muhammad Ali joined.

In *Cruz v. Beto* (1972) the Burger Court ruled, somewhat briefly, on the religious rights, not of prisoners belonging to the Black Muslim faith as did many of the cases that reached the courts, but rather of a Buddhist convict. Cruz, an inmate of a Texas prison, alleged that while prisoners who were members of other religious sects were allowed to use the prison chapel, he was not. Because he shared his Buddhist religious material with other prisoners he was placed in solitary confinement on a diet of bread and water for two weeks and spent twenty-two hours a day in total idleness without access to newspapers, magazines, or other sources of news. He also alleged that he was prohibited from corresponding with his Buddhist religious advisor.

He further alleged that the state encouraged inmates to participate in other religious programs, provided at state expense, and made available access to chaplains of the Protestant, Catholic, and Jewish faiths, copies of the Christian and Jewish Bibles, weekly Sunday school classes, and religious services, all at the state's expense. In addition, he claimed that points of good merit were given prisoners as a reward for attending orthodox religious services, those points enhancing a prisoner's eligibility for desirable job assignments and early parole consideration. None of these privileges, he asserted, were accorded to him.

In a *per curiam* opinion (i.e., one not attributed to any of the justices) the Supreme Court refused to accept the lower court's ruling and reasoning in rejecting Cruz's complaints. While obviously, it said, a prisoner could not enjoy the exercise of his religion to the same extent as non-prisoners, he was nevertheless protected by the Free Exercise Clause subject only to the necessities of prison security and discipline and could not be discriminated against simply because his religious beliefs were unorthodox. This did not mean that every religious sect or group within a prison, no matter how few in number, had to have identical facilities. While it was not necessary that chaplains, priests, or ministers be provided without regard to the extent of the demand, reasonable opportunities had to be afforded to all prisoners to exercise their religious freedom without fear of penalty.

Cruz v. Beto was not the first instance in which the Supreme Court ruled that a prison inmate was constitutionally entitled to religious privileges available to other prisoners. In *Cooper v. Pate* (1964) it had held it unconstitutional to deny a prisoner, solely because of his religious beliefs, permission to purchase certain religious publications and to avail himself of other privileges accorded to prisoners. (With respect to another aspect of discrimination in prisons, the Court held in *Lee v. Washington* [1968] that a law requiring racial segregation in prisons violated the Equal Protection Clause of the Fourteenth Amendment.)

Rehnquist could not agree with the determination of his colleagues in the *Cruz* case. To him, the most rational explanation for the plaintiff's obviously meritless suit was the opportunity "to obtain a short sabbatical in the nearest Federal courthouse." Temporary relief from prison confinement, he continued, "is always an alluring prospect, and to the criminal the possibility of escape lurks in every excursion beyond prison walls."

Rehnquist's skepticism regarding sincerity of motivation in suits by prisoners seeking relief under the Free Exercise Clause undoubtedly has some basis in reality. The availability of a law library in many penitentiaries and free time for inmates, coupled with judicial willingness to accept handwritten petitions for relief and the fact that the prisoner has nothing to lose if his suit fails, make lawsuits under the Free Exercise Clause quite attractive.

Yet there can be little doubt about the sincerity of Orthodox Jews whose life-long religious conscience forbids them to eat non-kosher foods, or of American Indians whose religious tenets forbid the cutting of their hair, or even of new faiths, such as that of the Black Muslims, which practically originated in prisons. Of course, even where sincerity is established the prisoner's free exercise rights must yield to the authority of officials to impose reasonable restraints so as to assure safety and security in prisons. It should nevertheless be noted that in the 1973 case of *Elam v. Henderson* the Burger Court rejected an appeal by Black Muslims, who complained that the prison authorities refused to provide meals strictly in compliance with their religion's dietary laws, to specially prepare foods in accordance with their religious practice, and to provide various requested foods and other items at the commissary for sale to the inmates. It was uncontroverted, however, that these prisoners were allowed substantial time each week to practice their religion and there were no allegations that the absence of a special dietary menu had resulted in malnutrition.

To the Court of Appeals the plaintiffs had not alleged anything more than "very minor inconveniences" which might, in a very limited way, impinge on the full exercise of their religious "preferences." But it is difficult to reconcile this decision with the appropriate test for determining free exercise rights as it was formulated in *United States v. Ballard* (1944). There the Court held that it is the sincerity of the individual's belief (and not its acceptability to government officials as a conventional, established faith) that calls for judicial determination. Under the Establishment Clause it would seem to be outside the competence of secular courts to determine what are major and what minor infractions of a religious code. If there is such a differentiation it must be made within the church, not outside of it.

The *Ballard* sincerity criterion relating free exercise claims of prisoners was the issue in *Theriault and Dorrough v. Carlson*, a case which, in 1975, the Supreme Court refused to review. While in a federal penitentiary in Atlanta, Theriault together with a fellow prisoner, Dorrough, jointly founded the Eclatarian faith, or Church of the New Song. It originally started as a game, with Theriault adopting the title of "Bishop" and Dorrough that of "Pope." However, according to Theriault's trial testimony, by the time he brought suit "he realized that he was affecting other people's feelings and so he started to get more sincere." Dorrough came forward with the suggestion which they adopted: "You put yourself down, you be the head of the church, that's the Bishop, you put yours, and put me down as the First Minister."

A church, however, needs more than a bishop and a first minister; it also needs a name, prophecies, and a mission. The name they chose was the "Eclatarian" faith, or "Church of the New Song." The prophecies came in the form of messages Theriault received from "Eclat" informing him that he was the "Eclatarian Nazarite" and directing him to establish the Church of the New Song. The mission and the antichrist were identified by Dorrough in the trial as follows:

> In our Free Exercise Seminars, our revelation ministry is basically to destroy the Nicolaitans which we believe are the repressive rulers and the powercrats of the system. That means the prison system, the people in the prison system, the people in the parole system, the people in government in general, the judiciary, et cetera. And we believe in destroying them or changing their minds with the power of our mouth.

Theriault acquired a Doctor of Divinity certificate through a mail order application. Then, as self-appointed "Bishop of Tellus," he ordained Dorrough as First Revelation Minister of the Church of the New Song, conferring upon him in the courtroom on the day of the trial the degree of Doctor of Divinity, Doctor of Philosophy, and Bachelor of Philosophy.

The defendants in their suit were the Catholic and Protestant chaplains at the penitentiary and the prison officials. Seeking an injunction the plaintiffs alleged various deprivations of their establishment and free exercise rights, including the use of taxpayers' money to compensate the chaplains for their services, the denial to themselves of the right to freely exercise their own religion, and various other infringements upon their First Amendment rights.

The District Court accepted their suit and issued a decree according them some of the relief they requested. The Court of Appeals reversed.

> While it is difficult [it said] for the courts to establish precise standards by
> which the bona fides of religion may be judged, such difficulties have
> proved to be no hindrance to denials of First Amendment protection to
> so-called religions which tend to mock established institutions and are
> obviously shams and absurdities and whose members are patently devoid
> of religious sincerity.

CHAPLAINS IN THE HALLS OF LEGISLATURES

Chapter 3 considered the constitutionality of prayers in public schools.
The most recent opinion issued by the Supreme Court in a case relating
to prayer in government institutions, *Marsh v. Chambers* (1983), dealt
not with schools but with a state capitol and concerned not recitation by
children but by an official chaplain. A rather courageous member of the
Nebraska legislature brought suit challenging the constitutionality of a
long-standing practice of starting each day it met with a prayer recited by
a salaried chaplain who had occupied the office for sixteen years before
the suit was brought. During most of this period his prayers were Christological, as indicated by part of an invocation delivered in March 1978 and
quoted in Stevens's dissenting opinion:

> Father in heaven, the suffering and death of your son brought life to the
> whole world moving our hearts to praise your glory. The power of the
> cross reveals your concern for the world and the wonder of Christ crucified.
>   The days of his life-giving death and glorious resurrection are ap-
> proaching. This is the hour when he triumphed over Satan's pride; the time
> when we celebrate the great event of our redemption.

In 1980, after a complaint by a Jewish legislator, the chaplain removed
all references to Christ and at the trial he characterized his later prayers
as "nonsectarian," "Judeo Christian," and "with elements of the American
civil religion." (In fairness to the chaplain it should be noted too that he
had added to one self-composed prayer the first eight verses of Psalm 22
in the Old Testament.) Until the *Marsh* suit was started the prayers were
collected from time to time and were published at public expense, but the
District Court ruled this to be unconstitutional and counsel informed the
Supreme Court that the legislature decided not to challenge this facet of
the ruling.

The District Court held, and it was this holding that was appealed, that the state's appropriation of funds used to pay the chaplain's salary was unconstitutional but that the practice itself was not. The Court of Appeals went further and ruled that the practice was unconstitutional in its entirety and that it did not matter whether or not the chaplain received any salary for his services. The Supreme Court decided that they were both wrong and held that the practice was valid and so too was the chaplain's receipt of monetary compensation for his services. Of itself, the Court held, the fact that the same chaplain served for fourteen years was immaterial; it noted that for the twenty years between 1949 and 1969 the same chaplain had served in the United States Senate.

In reaching their decisions, both lower courts had relied upon the purpose-effect-entanglement test but, beyond mentioning this fact, the Supreme Court paid no further attention to it. This is rather surprising inasmuch as it was Burger, the author of the majority opinion in the *Marsh* case who, in the *Walz* case, had contributed a third of the test, that which related to entanglement. There he had relied primarily upon that test to uphold tax exemption for churches, and referred to the historic background of the practice in just a few paragraphs towards the end of the opinion. In the *Marsh* opinion, on the other hand, his reliance was exclusively on history, perhaps because, as Brennan suggested in his dissenting opinion, the Nebraska law could not escape invalidation under any of the facets in the three-pronged test of constitutionality, especially the one relating to his own contribution.

After noting in his opinion the invocatory prayer "God save the United States and this Honorable Court" that initiated every Supreme Court session, Burger cited as precedent the action of the Continental Congress, which beginning in 1774 adopted the traditional procedure of opening its sessions with a prayer offered by a paid chaplain. He also pointed out that the First Congress, as one of its early items of business, adopted a policy of selecting a chaplain to open each session with prayer. Moreover, he said, they continued the practice after the First Amendment was adopted, thus indicating quite clearly that they did not consider it to be a violation of the amendment. These precedents were followed consistently in "most of the states" and this too testified to its constitutionality.

It may be that Burger's use of the word "most" rather than "all" manifests a significant flaw in the history-based recognition of constitutionality. He pointed out in his opinion in the *Walz* case that *all* of the original thirteen and today's thirty-eight additional states have always provided for tax exemption of places of public worship. Unanimity might evidence constitutionality, although as suggested in the first chapter of this book it might also indicate fear of not returning to the capital after the next election day. But even if unanimity were evidence of legislative belief in constitutionality, it is still the function and obligation of courts rather than legislatures to make the final decision; otherwise there would be no point to judicial review.

Burger acknowledged that prayers were not offered in the convention that drafted the Constitution but he had an explanation for the omission. History, he said, indicates that this might simply have been an oversight. At one point, Benjamin Franklin suggested "that henceforth prayers imploring the assistance of Heaven, and its blessings on our deliberations, be held in this Assembly every morning before we proceed to business." His proposal was rejected, said Burger, "not because the Convention was opposed to prayer, but because it was thought that a mid-stream adoption of the policy would highlight prior omissions and because the Convention had no funds."

This is not exactly what occurred, or at least not the complete story. According to Madison, who was there and took copious notes, the following is what happened after the convention had been in session for more than a month:

> Mr. Hamilton and several others expressed their apprehensions that however such a resolution might have been at the beginning of the convention, it might, at this late day, 1. bring on it some disagreeable animadversions, and 2. lead the public to believe that the embarrassments and dissentions within the convention, had suggested this measure. It was answered by Doctor Franklin, Mr. Sherman and others, that the past omission of a duty could not justify a further omission—that the rejection of such a proposition would expose the Convention to more unpleasant animadversions than the adoption of it: and that the alarm out of doors that might be excited for the state of things within, would at least be as likely to do good as ill.
>
> Mr. Williamson observed that the true cause of the omission could not be mistaken. The Convention had no funds.
>
> Mr. Randolph proposed in order to give a favorable aspect to the measure, that a sermon be preached at the request of the convention on 4th of July, the anniversary of Independence,—and thenceforward prayers be used in the Convention every morning. Dr. Franklin seconded this motion. After several unsuccessful attempts for silently postponing the matter by adjourning, the adjournment was at length carried, without any vote on the motion.

In later years, Madison, in a letter he wrote to a correspondent, said:

The proposition was received and treated with the respect due it; but the lapse of time which had preceded, with considerations growing out of it, had the effect of limiting what was done, to a reference of the proposition to a highly respectable Committee [a polite way which even today is used to kill a bill]. This issue of it may be traced in the printed Journal. The Quaker usage, never discontinued in the State, and the place [Philadelphia] where the Convention held its sittings, might not have been without an influence as might also, the discord of opinions within the Convention, as well as among the Clergy of the Spot.

As far as they are relevant to the issue of legislative chaplaincies, the following facts relating to *Marsh v. Chambers* appear from this incident:

1. The Constitutional Convention had proceeded for more than a month without prayers.

2. Some of the members feared that resort to prayer at so late a date might give rise to unwelcome criticism from some of the public.

3. It might also lead to the inference of dissention within the Convention with respect to the constitution under consideration.

4. Franklin's motion provided that "one or more Clergy of the City" be requested to officiate in the prayer service but one member objected on the ground that "the Convention had no funds."

5. It could therefore be inferred that clergymen could not be induced to officiate unless they were paid for their services and that officiating by a lay member of the Convention was unthinkable.

6. The Convention's meetings were held in Philadelphia, a Quaker city which did not permit legislative prayers.

Burger pointed out that James Madison, the drafter of the Establishment Clause, voted in favor of a bill authorizing payment of congressional chaplains, thereby obviously even if only implicitly attesting to its constitutionality. He did note in his opinion that many years later in "Detached Memoranda" Madison "expressed doubts concerning the chaplaincy practice." (This occurred long after he retired from the political arena and thus was free from the demands of politics.)

In view of Madison's paramount role in framing not only the Constitution but the First Amendment as well, a somewhat more extended presentation of his views is merited. The following is the full quotation from the "Detached Memoranda" relevant to the question of prayers in the halls of legislatures. (It is obvious from the opening sentence in the second paragraph that what Madison expressed was more than "doubts.")

Is the appointment of Chaplains to the two Houses of Congress consistent with the Constitution, and with the pure principles of religious freedom?

In strictness the answer on both points must be in the negative. The Constitution of the U.S. forbids everything like an establishment of a national religion. The law appointing Chaplains establishes a religious worship for the national representatives, to be performed by Ministers of religion, elected by a majority of them: and these are to be paid out of the national taxes. Does not this involve the principle of a national establishment, applicable to a provision for a religious worship for the Constituent as well as of the representative Body, approved by the majority, and conducted by Ministers of religion paid by the entire nation?

The establishment of the chaplainship to Congress is a palpable violation of equal rights, as well as of Constitutional principles. The tenets of the chaplains elected [by the majority] shut the door of worship against the members whose creeds and consciences forbid a participation in that of the majority. To say nothing of other sects, this is the case with that of Roman Catholics and Quakers who have always had members in one or both of the Legislative branches. Could a Catholic clergyman ever hope to be appointed a Chaplain? To say that his religious principles are obnoxious or that this sect is small, is to lift the evil [*sic*, probably "veil" intended] at once and exhibit in its naked deformity the doctrine that religious truth is to be tested by numbers, or that the major sects have a right to govern the minor. If Religion consist in voluntary acts of individuals, singly, or voluntarily associated, and it be proper that public functionaries, as well as their Constituents shall discharge their religious duties, let them like their Constituents, do so at their own expense. How small a contribution from each member of the Congress would suffice for the purpose? How just would it be in its principle? How noble in its exemplary sacrifice to the genius of the Constitution, and the divine right of conscience? Why should the expense of a religious worship be allowed for the Legislature, be paid by the public, more than that for the executive or Judiciary branch of the Government?

In one respect Madison was wrong. Catholics have achieved the status of legislative chaplaincies, as they have the presidency and chief justiceship of the Supreme Court. Quakers don't want it and Jews, unmentioned by Madison, have yet to be asked.

Burger recognized that John Jay and John Rutledge (both later to become, like him, Chief Justice of the Supreme Court) opposed adoption of a motion to begin the first session of the Continental Congress with prayer.

We do not agree [Burger said] that evidence of opposition to a measure weakens the force of the historical argument; indeed it infuses it with power by demonstrating that the subject was considered carefully and the action taken thoughtlessly, by force of long tradition and without regard to the problems posed by a pluralistic society. Jay and Rutledge specifically grounded their objection on the fact that the delegates to the Congress "were so divided in religious sentiments . . . that [they] could not join in the same act of worship." Their objection was met by Samuel Adams, who stated that "he was no bigot, and could hear a prayer from a gentleman of piety and virtue, who was at the same time a friend to his country."

The difficulty with this rationalization lies in the fact that the incident occurred in a period when invocations to God were the usual and universal practice in governmental sessions and in the documents they produced. The Declaration of Independence issued by the Continental Congress was considerably shorter than the Constitution written eleven years later, yet it had no less than four references to the deity. By contrast, the Constitution the Court was called upon to interpret in the *Marsh* case contains no prayer or even mention of God. It would seem that in construing the document the absence of prayer would be considerably more significant than its presence eleven years earlier in the Declaration of Independence or in the sessions of the first Continental Congress two years before that. Another Chief Justice, John Marshall, generally considered the greatest of them all, once said: "We must never forget that it is a constitution we are expounding"; to which might be added "not the records of a Continental Congress."

Brennan opened his dissenting opinion with what lawyers call a confession of error. In his concurring opinion in the *Schempp* case he had said:

> The saying of invocational prayers in legislative chambers, state or federal, and the appointment of legislative chaplains, might well represent no involvements of the kind prohibited by the Establishment Clause. Legislators, federal and state, are mature adults who may presumably absent themselves from such public and ceremonial exercises without incurring any penalty, direct or indirect.

He admitted he had been wrong, as, he said, Burger was now wrong in the *Marsh* case.

Having expressed his repentance, Brennan turned to the Chief Justice's opinion. He found it a "good thing" that Burger did not subject the Nebraska practice to inquiry under the Establishment Clause; had he done so he might have reshaped the Establishment Clause rather than only carve out an exception to it. (The implication of this is that Burger was determined to uphold the challenged practice even if it required altering the purpose-effect-entanglement test.) That, however, was the only "good thing" he could find in the opinion. In a rather uncharitable expression (probably reflecting his deep unhappiness with the Court's other post-*Marsh* decisions) he said:

> I have no doubt that, if any group of law students were asked to apply the principles of *Lemon* to the question of legislative prayer, they would nearly unanimously find the practice to be unconstitutional.

To Brennan, the Nebraska prayer situation violated all three prongs of the Establishment Clause. The purpose of the prayer was preeminently religious; so was its primary effect; and there could be no doubt that the practice led to excessive entanglement between the state and religion, the last not only in terms of divisiveness in the selection of a suitable chaplain but also in terms of its political consequences. Moreover, he said, it violated the constitutional prohibition of aid to religion, its mandate of neutrality between religion and religion and between religion and nonreligion, and its ban on religious discrimination in the absence of a compelling governmental interest that would justify it. In addition to all this, it also violated the Free Exercise Clause of the First Amendment in that it imposed an unjustifiable burden on religious belief or practice.

The *Engel* and *Schempp* cases, Brennan said, "hang over this one like a reproachful set of parents." In addition to all else, the majority's opinion could not be reconciled with the decision in *Torcaso v. Watkins* (1961), which struck down a state statute requiring a religious oath as a qualification to hold office because it violated both the Free Exercise and Establishment clauses.

As has been noted, Stevens, in his dissenting opinion, set forth the text of an invocation given March 1878 by Chaplain Palmer, a Presbyterian. He would not expect, he said, to find a disciple of Mary Baker Eddy (founder of Christian Science) or the Reverend Moon (founder of the Unification Church) serving as the official chaplain in any state legislature. It was plain to him that "the designation of a member of one religious faith to serve as the sole chaplain of a state legislature for a period of 16 years constitute[d] the preference of one faith over another in violation of the Establishment Clause of the First Amendment."

It may be added that were it a congressional chaplaincy that was involved, the exclusionary practice would have also violated Article VI of the Constitution, which states that "no religious test shall ever be required as a qualification to any office or public trust under the United States." Suppose the nation's foremost atheist, Madalyn Murray O'Hair, after intensive study of everything in Protestant, Catholic, and Jewish theological seminaries, ranked top in a civil service test for congressional (not military) chaplain. The rest can be left to the reader's imagination.

By way of postscript, the following is an extract from an article appearing in the January 29, 1983, issue of *America*. Entitled "Paying for Prayers Before the Legislatures," by Robert F. Drinan, S. J., it reads:

> If prayers before legislative bodies go the way of prayer and Bible reading in the schools, crèches on public property and subsidies to church-related primary and secondary schools, many will be disappointed.
>
> The U.S. Supreme Court will decide the issue no later than June 1983. If the High Court decrees that legislatures must somehow get along without voluntary or compensated prayers, it is hard to think the republic will fall.

Drinan was wrong in anticipating invalidation of legislative prayers and was later shown to be wrong with respect to crèches.

6

Religion in Labor Law

HISTORIC BACKGROUND

Laws relating to labor can be broadly classified into two categories—ameliorative law and labor relations. The former deals with government-imposed restrictions upon employers to insure humane treatment of their employees; the latter requires employers to negotiate with representatives of the employees, commonly called labor unions, in matters relating to employer-employee relations such as wages, hours, tenure, vacation periods, etc.

Ameliorative law can be traced back to the Code of Hammurabi in ancient Mesopotamia issued about 1750 B.C., a time more or less contemporary with the Biblical Abraham. The earliest complete legal code known to history, it was civil, not religious, and its primary purpose was to protect the weak and poor laborers from inhumane treatment by the rich and powerful masters.

Mosaic law had a far greater direct influence on current labor law than Hammurabi's Code (although it may itself have originated in that code). There are a number of reasons for this—among others, its development over a period of some fifteen hundred years, measured from Abraham to Ezra, and its acceptance as the basis of much of Christian law (e.g., in the outlawing of usury). Among instances relevant to the subject of American labor law, notice can be taken of Deuteronomy 25:25, 26, which reads:

> Thou shalt not oppress an hired person that is poor and needy, whether he be of thy brethren, or of thy strangers that are in thy land within thy gate.
>
> At his day shalt thou give him his hire, neither shall the sun go down upon it; for he is poor, and setteth his heart upon it; lest he cry against thee unto the Lord, and it be sin unto thee.

Reference may also be made to Deuteronomy 23:15, 16, and Jeremiah 8-17, which forbid the return or oppression of escaped slaves. (It took a bloody civil war to nullify the Supreme Court's decision in *Dred Scott v. Sanford* upholding the constitutionality of the Fugitive Slave Law.) Also relevant is the commandment's mandate of a six-day workweek so that one's "manservant and maidservant may rest as well as thou" (Deuteronomy 5:14).

Over the centuries, remedial labor laws developed within the English common law system and from time to time were enacted within the United States into laws often challenged on constitutional grounds. Here, however, our concern is limited to the arena of constitutional law that deals with ameliorative and labor relations laws that affect religions and churches.

AMELIORATIVE LEGISLATION

In four 1961 cases the Warren Court resorted to the states' inherent power to legislate for the protection of the health and welfare of their citizens (technically known as the police power) to uphold the constitutionality of compulsory Sunday closing laws. Two of these cases, *McGowan v. Maryland* and *Two Guys from Harrison-Allentown, Inc. v. McGinley,* concerned owners of highway discount stores that were open for business seven days a week. The other two, *Gallagher v. Crown Kosher Super Market* and *Braunfeld v. Brown,* involved stores owned by Orthodox Jews, who by reason of religious conviction, abstained from all business activity on Saturdays.

In the first two cases the challenge was based upon the Establishment Clause. In the other two, the Free Exercise Clause was also invoked on the ground that competition with stores open for business six days a week other than Sunday economically impelled either violation of the Old Testament Sabbath or of the state Sunday laws. All the challenged statutes were upheld as permissible exercises of the states' police power.

With respect to the establishment claim, the Court ruled that, while the historic origin of Sunday laws was religious, their present purpose had become the secular one of assuring a weekly day of rest and family togetherness. The difficulty of enforcement justified designating the same day of rest for all merchants and quite naturally the states would choose the day that was historically used for that purpose by the majority of storekeepers. For this reason too the Free Exercise Clause was not violated even when the laws were enforced against Sabbatarians. The constitutionally permissible solution for the Sabbatarian's problem, said the Court, was the enactment of laws allowing them to remain open for business on Sundays but the states were not constitutionally obliged to enact such laws.

Two years later, in the case of *Sherbert v. Verner,* the Warren Court reached what on its face appeared to be a contrary result. There it held as a violation of the Free Exercise Clause denial of unemployment compensation to a Seventh Day Adventist, who by reason of religious conscience, would not accept a tendered position requiring work on Saturdays. The consequence of this decision was that Sabbatarians could not be denied judicial relief by reason of the state's refusal to amend its laws to accommodate them. The decision, however, accorded Sabbatarians only partial relief, since to most persons out of work employment is preferable to unemployment compensation. On that assumption, Congress amended Title VII of the Civil Rights Act of 1964 to forbid discrimination against an employee whose religious beliefs forbade him to work on his Sabbath.

Although the act itself came about as result of the struggle for equality on the part of blacks, it was not aimed solely against racial discrimination. Section 703 (c) (1) provides:

> (a) It shall be an unlawful employment practice for an employer to fail, to refuse to hire or to discharge any individual, or otherwise to discriminate against any individual with respect to his compensation, terms, conditions, or privileges of employment because of such individual's race, color, *religion,* sex, or national origin. (Emphasis added.)

The act provided for the establishment of the Equal Employment Opportunity Commission (EEOC) with authority to issue "guidelines" for enforcement of the law. Accordingly, in 1967, the EEOC adopted a guideline that read:

> [S]ection 703(a) (1) of the Civil Rights Act of 1964 . . . includes an obligation on the part of the employer to make reasonable accommodations to the religious needs of employees and prospective employees where such accommodations can be made without undue hardship on the conduct of the employer's business.

The life of the statute and guideline has been one of triple, triple, toil and trouble for the Supreme Court. First, was a challenge to constitutionality. Second, was the need to determine what was meant by the terms "reasonable accommodations" and "undue hardship." Third, was the question of who had to prove that the terms were or were not present in any particular case—the company, the union, or the employee?

Three times, moreover, in the score of years since the Civil Rights Act was adopted, the Court has sought to answer these questions, and still has been unable to answer them satisfactorily to Congress or the EEOC or the parties to the controversies—the companies and the employees.

The first of the three cases, all of which involved dismissal for refusing to work on one's religious day of rest, was *Dewey v. Reynolds Metal Company*. There the company was willing to permit and in the past had permitted Dewey to exchange shifts with fellow workers whose conscience did not forbid them to work on Sundays. However, he refused to continue this practice because his conscience would not allow him to induce others to violate the Christian Sabbath, and therefore he insisted that the company make the arrangements. The Court of Appeals upheld the company's rejection of his demands, noting that no such arrangements were required by the Civil Rights Act of 1964. Dewey then appealed to the Supreme Court.

The toil and trouble became apparent almost as soon as the Supreme Court agreed to hear the case. The Solicitor General asked the Court for permission to participate in the argument as an *amicus curiae* in support of Dewey's claim. This seemed to be entirely appropriate: what was challenged in the case was a federal law and a regulation adopted for its enforcement. However the Court would decide, its ruling would affect innumerable other observers of the Sabbath throughout the nation, and Dewey was a member of a class that could hardly afford to engage attorneys matching those representing the company. (As has been noted earlier in this book, the Court allowed the Solicitor General to intervene and argue in a case involving a crèche on private property in a small city in Rhode Island, even though no federal law or regulation was involved in the controversy.) Despite all this, three of the justices, Black, Douglas, and White, objected to the Solicitor General's intervention in the *Dewey* case but gave no reason for their objections.

It was all for naught. For some unexplained reason, Harlan did not participate in the Court's consideration and decision in the action and the result was a tie vote of four to four. Under Supreme Court rules, this meant that the lower court's decision (in this case in favor of the company) was affirmed, no opinion was issued by any of the justices, it was not indicated how any of the justices voted, and the affirmance was not to constitute an endorsement of the lower court's opinion or a precedent in future similar cases.

All this occurred in 1971. The following year, Congress amended Title

VII of the 1964 Civil Rights Act to do what the Supreme Court was unable to do in the *Dewey* case: First, make the 1967 guideline a mandatory law of the land and, second, shift from the employee to the company the burden of proof respecting the reasonableness or unreasonableness of the required accommodations.

The pertinent parts of the amendment read as follows:

> The term "religion" includes all aspects of religious observance and practice, as well as belief, unless an employer demonstrates that he is unable to reasonably accommodate to an employee's or prospective employee's religious observance or practice without undue hardship on the conduct of the employer's business.
>
> The employer has the burdern of proving that an undue hardship renders the required accommodations to the religious needs of the employee unreasonable.

There can be little doubt about the fairness of the second sentence. It recognizes the reality that the company's management is far better suited than a single employee to prove the existence or nonexistence of reasonable accommodation to the employee's religious needs, as, for example, finding a willing and competent substitute.

If Congress or the EEOC were under any illusion that the Court would provide a definitive answer on the questions of interpretation and constitutionality, the 1976 case of *Parker Seal Company v. Cummins* brought quick disillusionment. This time the Court of Appeals ruled in favor of the employee and it was the company that urged the Supreme Court to reverse the decision and to rule the statute and guideline unconstitutional under the First Amendment's Establishment Clause.

Its claim was that they violated each of the three parts of the purpose-effect-entanglement test. That the purpose provision was violated, the company argued, was indicated by the statement made on the floor of the Senate by the statute's principal sponsor, Senator Jennings Randolph (himself a Seventh-Day Baptist):

> I say to the distinguished chairman of the Labor and Public Welfare Committee, who manages this bill that there has been a partial refusal at times on the part of employers to hire or continue in employment employees whose religious practices rigidly require them to abstain from work in the nature of hire on particular days. So there has been, because of understandable pressures, such as commitments of a family nature or otherwise, a dwindling of the membership of some of the religious organizations because of the situation to which I have just directed attention.

. . . . .

My own pastor in this area, Rev. Delmar Van Horne, has expressed his concern and distress that there are certain faiths that are having a very difficult time, especially with the young people and understandably so, with reference to a possible inability of employers on some occasions to adjust to work schedules to fit the requirements of the faith of some of their workers.

There also can be no doubt, the company argued, that the principal or primary effect of the law and guideline was to advance the religion of Sabbath observers, whatever their particular Sabbath might be, as against all nonbelievers. Finally, the statute and guideline fostered divisive entanglement of governmental and religious activity. They spoke not simply of "religion" but of "all aspects of religious observance and practices, as well as belief." The government's task in determining whether an employee met these qualifications resulted in impermissible entanglement.

Cummins's brief and the *amicus curiae* briefs of such organizations as the American Civil Liberties Union and the American Jewish Congress sought to respond to each of these arguments and to urge that the purpose and effect of the statute and guideline were to insure Cummins's free exercise of the religion to which he was committed.

It was all for naught. What the Court did in the *Dewey* case, it did again in the *Cummins* decision. The only difference was a slight change in the cast: the nonparticipant this time was Stevens (Harlan was no longer on the Court.) The result was affirmance without opinion of the Court of Appeals' decision, which this time was in favor of the Sabbatarian rather than the company.

What can be said for *TransWorld Air Lines, Inc.* (TWA) and *International Association of Machinists* (IAM) v. *Hardison* (1977) is that in it the Court was finally able to muster a majority decision but it did so by announcing that it had found no constitutional question that needed to be answered. To achieve this happy consummation, it extracted and discarded pretty much all that was meaningful in the guideline and statutory amendment.

This is how it was done: Hardison had been hired to work as a clerk in TWA's supply shop, which operated twenty-four hours a day, three hundred and sixty-five days each year. In accordance with the company's contract with the aerospace workers union (IAM), he, as well as all other employees, was subject to a seniority system in determining shift assignments.

A year after he started working, Hardison, like Cummins, converted to the faith of the Worldwide Church of God. (There was no challenge to the sincerity of his conversion.) One of the tenets of that religion was the observance of the Sabbath by not working from sunset on Friday to sunset on Saturday, and he accordingly requested the company to change his shift so that he could refrain from working on that day. The problem appeared to have been solved when Hardison transferred to the 11 p.m. to 7 a.m. shift, thereby enabling him to observe his Sabbath.

Unfortunately, the problem reappeared when Hardison bid for and received a transfer from Building 1 to Building 2, where he would work the day shift. The two buildings had entirely separate seniority lists; and while in Building 1 Hardison had sufficient seniority to enable him to make the transfer, he was second from the bottom on the Building 2 seniority list and the union would not agree to accord him priority over those ahead of him in choosing the non-Saturday shift. A proposal by Hardison that he work only four days a week was rejected by the company on the ground that to employ someone not regularly assigned to Saturday work would have required TWA to pay premium wages. The net result was that after a hearing Hardison was discharged for insubordination in refusing his designated shift.

Claiming that the company was required to make reasonable accommodation to his religious needs and that such accommodation would not represent an "undue hardship," Hardison instituted a suit in the Federal District Court against both TWA and the union. The Court ruled that TWA had satisfied the "reasonable accommodations" requirement and that any further accommodation would have been an "undue hardship." Its decision, however, was reversed by the Court of Appeals, whereupon the company appealed to the Supreme Court.

There the company and the union prevailed. In an opinion from which only Brennan and Marshall dissented, White asserted that in using the term "reasonable accommodations" Congress could not have intended to require that, in meeting the demands of Sabbatarians, employers must disregard the contractual seniority rights of some employees in order to accommodate the religious needs of others. Nor, he said, could the term "undue hardship" be construed as anything more than a *de minimis* cost. (The complete relevant common law maxim reads: "*de minimis non curat lex*, which translated means 'the law does not concern itself with trifles.'")

White concluded his opinion with the following sentence:

As we have seen, the paramount concern of Congress in enacting Title VII was the elimination of discrimination in employment. In the absence of clear statutory language or legislative history to the contrary, we will not readily construe the statute to require an employer to discriminate against some employees in order to enable others to observe their Sabbath.

Marshall, in his dissenting opinion, remarked that if the Court was correct in interpreting the 1972 amendment as applying only where the effect was *de minimis*, the statute, while brimming with sound and fury, ultimately signified nothing. The reason for this was that, even if there were no accommodation requirement, the courts would simply ignore objections to accommodation that were *de minimis* in significance. The amendment made sense only if interpreted to effectively meet an existing need, which meant something more than *de minimus*.

Yet Marshall's dissent presented problems of its own, as indicated by the above quoted concluding paragraph of White's opinion. Offhand, it would seem difficult to justify discrimination against some employees in order to enable others to observe their Sabbath. Marshall himself agreed that accommodation would require "unequal treatment" in favor of the religious observer but, he said, this was hardly unprecedented in constitutional law. In *Wisconsin v. Yoder* (1972) the Court had found no constitutional barrier to exemption of Amish from laws requiring attendance by others beyond elementary school years. As has been noted, in *Sherbert v. Verner* (1963) it forbade denial of employment insurance benefits to persons who, like Hardison, would not accept employment compelling them to work on Saturdays even though the same privilege was not accorded to persons who for nonreligious grounds would prefer not to work on Saturdays. Finally, Marshall cited *Zorach v. Clauson* (1952), in which the Court upheld the practice of releasing pupils to receive religious instruction while the same privilege was not available to those desiring to use the time for secular off-school activities. In none of these cases, he said, was the privilege adjudged violative of the First Amendment's Establishment Clause in according preferential treatment to some religions over others or over nonreligion.

Between its decision in *TWA v. Hardison* and its acceptance of jurisdiction in *Thornton v. Caldor, Inc.*, to be considered shortly, the Burger Court was faced with two cases relating to forfeiture of benefits for refusing to accept a position that would violate religious conscience. *Thomas v. Review Board*, which involved conscientious objection to employment in a factory manufacturing armaments, has been considered in the preceding chapter. Challenged in the other, *Kentucky Commission on Human Rights v. Kerns Bakery, Inc.*, was the application of a state law, fashioned practically word for word after Title VII of the Civil

Rights Act of 1964, to a situation which, with one exception to be noted later, was similar to that in the *Hardison* case.

In the production department of the Kerns Bakery Company the employees worked five days a week, including Sundays, the "off-days" being Tuesday and Saturday. For two and a half years, Frank Goins, an employee, had no problem complying with the work schedule but then he began attending services at the Free Pentecostal Holiness Church and was later "saved, baptized and accepted into membership of the Church." One of its tenets was that, as in most other Christian denominations, Sunday was the Sabbath and members were required to refrain from working on that day.

Goins advised his supervisor of his new religious belief and sought accommodation by way of a transfer to an available non-Sunday job or by being excused from Sunday work. The company made no effort to accommodate him and when he failed to report for work he was fired. Following this, he filed a complaint with the Kentucky Human Rights Commission, which after a hearing determined that Kerns Bakery had engaged in acts of religious discrimination in violation of the statute. The commission found that the company could have easily accommodated Goins without "undue hardship" to its business by either transferring him to an available non-Sunday job or simply excusing him from Sunday work.

The commission's decision was set aside by a lower court on the ground that the statute violated the Establishment Clause of the First Amendment (as well as a similar provision in the state's constitution). On appeal, the state's highest court reversed the decision and reinstated the commission's determination. The purpose of the law, the lower court said, was to remedy the situation in which an employee is forced to abandon a precept of his religion in order to retain his job. By adopting the challenged statute the state's legislature was merely seeking to promote equal employment opportunities for members of all religious faiths.

Nor, the lower court said, did the law have a primary effect of advancing religion, since in no way was the legislature authorizing sponsorship or financial support to any religion. Finally, its action did not involve excessive entanglement of government in religion; outlawing religious discrimination in employment could not be held to constitute forbidden entanglement. The statute, the lower court concluded, did not provide that the employer must in all cases make accommodations to an employee's religious beliefs; accommodation was required only if it could "reasonably" be effected "without undue hardship on the conduct of the employer's business."

It is this last sentence which may distinguish the *Kerns Bakery* case from that of *TWA v. Hardison*. The record in the *Hardison* case showed that the employer there did make a bona fide effort to achieve accommodation but failed because of the union's objection. There was no such evidence in the *Kerns Bakery* case and this may explain the Supreme Court's refusal (in 1983) to review the decision. The Court gave no reason for its refusal but implicit in its action might well be the conclusion that accommodation may be required where the employer does not show "undue hardship."

Notwithstanding the suggestion of possible unconstitutionality implicit in the last paragraph of his opinion in *TWA v. Hardison*, White did not specifically say that preferential treatment would actually be unconstitutional; he said only that the regulation and statute in issue did not clearly mandate it, thus leaving the question of constitutionality unanswered. Nor can it be deemed clearly answered in the denial of review in the *Kerns Bakery* case. The Court will, however, not find it easy to avoid deciding the constitutional issue in *Thorton v. Caldor, Inc.* There the only question in the petition for certiorari, granted by the Court in March 1984, was:

[w]hether a Connecticut statute that protects religious observers against being compelled to work on the day of the week they observe as their Sabbath violates the Establishment Clause of the First Amendment.

The statute forbade employers to compel employees to work more than six days a week. It also provided that:

[n]o person who states that a particular day of the week is observed as his Sabbath may be required by his employer to work on such day. An employee's refusal to work on his Sabbath shall not constitute grounds for his dismissal.

No employer may, as a prerequisite to employment, inquire whether the applicant observes any Sabbath.

In 1975, a year before the law was enacted and at a time when the state's Sunday closing law was still in effect, Thornton accepted employment as department manager in one of Caldor's Connecticut stores. After the Sunday law was repealed, Caldor required its workers to be available for work in its stores on Sundays and Thorton acceded to the company's request until November 1979. At that time he asked to be excused from work on Sundays because he observed that day as his Sabbath.

The company offered him the option of transfer to a store in Massachusetts that was closed on Sundays or of demotion to a non-supervisory capacity at a substantially lower salary but without the requirement that he work on Sundays. Thorton rejected both alternatives, ceased coming to work, and brought suit under the state's law.

Connecticut's highest court ruled the statute unconstitutional under all three parts of the purpose-effect-entanglement test. It rejected Caldor's contention, based upon the Sunday closing law cases, that the purpose of Connecticut's law was the purely secular one of assuring all persons one day of rest in seven and that accordingly the term "Sabbath" in the law was utilized simply as a synonym for "time of rest" without any religious overtones. Connecticut's statutes, the Connecticut court said, already prohibited employment for more than six days in any calendar week, thereby assuring one day of rest, so that there was no need for any additional legislation. Moreover, use of the term "Sabbath," especially when capitalized, indicates quite clearly a religious purpose.

The effect of the law, the Connecticut court continued, was to advance religion. Only those employees who designated a "Sabbath" were entitled to refrain from working on that day; the privilege did not extend to persons who chose a day of the week that had no relationship to religion.

Finally, it ruled that the law failed under the ban of excessive governmental entanglement with religion. Inevitably, as employers challenged the employees' Sabbath observance, the state's inquiry would have to encompass an analysis of particular religious practices and would require a decision concerning the scope of religious activities that might fairly be labelled "observance of the Sabbath." Especially in an age of unparalleled religious freedom and diversity, that kind of state intervention was fraught with the sort of entanglement forbidden by the First Amendment. The enforcement mechanism prescribed by the statute was exactly the type of comprehensive, discriminating, and continuing state surveillance that creates forbidden excessive entanglement between church and state.

It should be noted that the Connecticut statute forbids employers from questioning applicants for a position as to whether they observe any Sabbath. The justification for this is quite reasonable in that, on receiving an affirmative answer, the company's hiring official might suddenly decide that the applicant did not really have the qualifications or experience or personality to fill the vacancy in the plant.

The sincerity of a recent conversion to Sunday observance can be challenged after the employee gets the job but cannot easily be disproved. Nonattendance at church will not suffice; as with President Reagan, prayer at home will be equally acceptable, whether the arbiter be the voting public or the EEOC. (This is true even with respect to the recently enacted Equal Access Act, discussed in Chapter 3.) In none of the cases discussed in this chapter did the employer question sincerity, notwithstanding the fact that in most if not all of the cases the applicant was a recent convert. It is a fair guess that if the employee prevails in the *Thornton* appeal, many employers, on advice of counsel, will not be so liberal as in the past in accepting the sincerity of recent conversions to Sunday observance. As in the *Hardison* case, the unions are likely to insist upon equal treatment in observance of contracted priorities.

These problems are not insoluble. The attractiveness of time and a half or double overtime pay for Sunday work may assure a sufficient number of employees who will not raise the religion issue. Ultimately the added cost of production will be paid by the consumers but this is hardly unprecedented in American economic history. Measured in the scale of competing values, those relating to religious freedom should rank high, as is attested to for example in the history of military exemptions for religious conscience.

The significance of the *Thornton* case and its national importance is indicated by the fact that it is prosecuted by counsel for the Committee on Law and Public Action, a lawyers' organization representing Orthodox Judaism, together with counsel for the American Jewish Congress; the State of Connecticut has been granted leave by the Supreme Court to participate in the appeal; and *amicus curiae* briefs have been submitted by the Solicitor General of the United States, the Council of State Governments, the American Civil Liberties Union, the American Jewish Committee, the Anti-Defamation League of B'nai B'rith, Americans United for Separation of Church and State, and the Conference of Seventh Day Adventists.

Whether the Burger Court hands down a definitive answer to the constitutional question or again finds a way to avoid it will have to await determination some time before adjournment about the end of June 1985.

Another aspect of ameliorative legislation was presented in the case of *Kings Garden, Inc. v. Federal Communication Commission*, decided by the Court of Appeals in 1974. This was a suit by a religious organization whose basic goal was to "share Christ world wide," in part through the operation of radio stations. The lawsuit came about as a result of a complaint by a job applicant who was asked "Are you a Christian?" and "Is your spouse a Christian?"

The suit was based on Section 3 of the Equal Opportunities Act of 1972, which amended Section 702 of the 1964 Civil Rights Act, banning religious discrimination in employment. The earlier act exempted from its coverage "a religious corporation, association, or society with respect to the employment of individuals of a particular religion to perform work connected with the carrying on by such corporation, association or society of its religious activities." The 1972 statute stated in part that it should not apply "to a religious corporation, association, educational institution, or society with respect to the employment of individuals of a particular religion to perform work connected with the carrying on by such corporation, association, educational institution or society of its activities," with the word "religious" deleted with respect to activities so as to appear to allow religious discrimination whether the position to be filled was that of broadcaster or janitor.

The suit before the Court of Appeals challenged the FCC's refusal to alter its anti-bias policy of exempting only employment "connected with the espousal of the licensee's religious views." In rejecting the challenge, the Court of Appeals noted that acceptance of the licensee's interpretation of the statute would mean that if a religious sect should own and operate a trucking firm, a chain of motels, a race track, a telephone company, a fried chicken franchise, or a professional football team, the enterprise could lawfully limit employment to members of the sect, whereas no such exemption would be allowed if the enterprise were privately owned.

As interpreted, the Court of Appeals said in a decision the Supreme Court refused to review, serious constitutional questions would be raised under the Establishment Clause invalidating laws that do not have a secular purpose or primary effect that advances religion. Moreover, it said, the statute would be vulnerable to challenge under the Fifth Amendment's guarantee of the equal protection of the law.

A religious sect, the Court of Appeals continued, has no constitutional right to convert a licensed communication franchise into a church. A religious group, like any other, may buy and operate a licensed radio or television station. But, like any other group, its franchise is subject to enforceable public obligations.

The commission, the Court of Appeals concluded, has set itself the difficult task of drawing lines between the secular and religious aspects of broadcasting. This was a delicate operation, but one that the First Amendment thrust upon every public body that had dealings with religious organizations.

To complete this discussion on religion in ameliorative legislation, notice should be taken of *Tony and Susan Alamo Foundation v. Donovan*, now before the Supreme Court on a petition to review. The case raises the question whether provisions of the Fair Labor Standards Act relating to minimum wages, overtime compensation, and record keeping can be constitutionally applied to the nonprofit business activities of a religious organization.

The controversy in the case relates to the status of some three hundred persons designated as "associates" of the Alamo Foundation. The foundation's evangelical efforts are carried on among derelicts, drug addicts, and criminals. In their rehabilitation these "associates" perform work in some thirty diversified commercial businesses operated by the foundation. As volunteers they receive no monetary compensation but are given lodging, food, transportation, and medical care, without which they could not survive except through resort to public assistance or to crime.

It was clear, the Court of Appeals said in its decision upholding the applicability of the Fair Labor Standards Act, that an individual such as a prosperous lawyer, taking a few hours from his legal practice to ring the bell for the Salvation Army, was not an "employee" but a bona fide volunteer donating his time to the advancement of a worthy cause, and the same was true of persons caring for children on Sunday during church services or preparing and serving meals at a church dinner. On the other hand, it was no less clear that there comes a time when voluntary endeavors must be recognized as passing beyond the line that exempts them from minimum wage laws.

Upon careful reflection, the Court felt impelled to conclude that the foundation overstepped the dividing line and was subject to the statute. Having reached that conclusion, it was therefore necessary for the Court to determine whether its application to "associates" violated the First Amendment and free exercise guarantees.

Measured by the purpose-effect-entanglement test, the Court said, the Establishment Clause was not violated. The statute was clearly social legislation enacted for the secular purpose of eliminating conditions detrimental to the health and economic welfare of workers. For the same reason, there was no violation of the effect aspect of the test. The law had nothing to do with religion; it neither advanced nor inhibited religious concerns.

The entanglement aspect presented a somewhat more formidable barrier but the Court was able to overcome it. The doctrine of excessive entanglement, it said, arose in connection with church schools rather than with church-operated charities or commercial enterprises. (A rather surprising statement in view of the fact that it was first announced and applied in the *Walz* case, which dealt with all church-owned properties.) The role of public officials in enforcing wage and hour requirements is more analogous to the task of accountants and auditors examining the books and other written records of a business enterprise than that of state officials evaluating the "live" activities of teachers within the framework of administrative policy. The officers of the foundation are not being compelled by government to frequent or support any religious activity or institution. All that they are required to do is to pay the standard living wage for work done in their commercial enterprises.

Rejected, too, was the foundation's contention that the Free Exercise Clause would be violated if the statute applied to activities of its officers. It could not possibly have any direct impact on their freedom to worship and evangelize as they pleased. The only effect would be a somewhat smaller net revenue from their business enterprise by being required to pay the standard living wage to workers. And the Supreme Court had squarely held that Sunday closing legislation does not violate the Free Exercise Clause merely because financial detriment results.

In sum, the Court concluded, there is surely no constitutional right under the Religion Clauses of the First Amendment to pay substandard wages.*

UNIONIZATION OF PAROCHIAL SCHOOL TEACHERS

As was indicated at the beginning of this chapter, ameliorative legislation can be traced back to Biblical times. Surprisingly, so too, although not quite as directly, are laws that mandate collective bargaining through negotiating committees and that sanction walkouts (strikes) after negotiation proves fruitless. Exodus 5 and some other verses relate how a committee consisting of Moses and Aaron (Moses was chairman but Aaron was more articulate and therefore acted as spokesman) dealt with Pharaoh.

The committee's initial demand was moderate. All they asked for was a three-day vacation, but not only did the boss (Pharaoh) reject it, he sought to break up the union and put an end to all further demands. Moses and Aaron were the troublemakers, he said, and did not really reflect the feelings of the labor force, a contention often made today in collective bargaining controversies. He decided to terminate such nonsense and accordingly instructed the taskmasters (foremen) to double the workload. Quite naturally the workers laid the blame on the shoulders of Moses, but he was able to appease them, and the ultimate consequence was a walkout that proved disastrous to the company.

Leaping now several thousand years to the Burger Court, we consider the case of *National Labor Relations Board v. Catholic Bishop of Chicago* (1979). In this case the Court was presented with the contention that it would violate the First Amendment's ban on laws respecting an establishment of religion or prohibiting its free exercise to compel parochial

---

*Since this was written the Supreme Court has agreed to review the decision.

schools to bargain collectively with unions representing their lay (non-clerical) teachers. In deciding the case, the Court, as we shall shortly see, neatly avoided answering the question by invoking the device of statutory interpretation, just as it had done in *TWA v. Hardison* and earlier in *United States v. Seeger*, discussed in Chapter 5 of this book. Understanding this decision and its implications requires a brief examination into its more recent historic and sociological background.

Unionization of parochial school teachers is a comparatively recent phenomenon, a consequence of the effect of American cultural values upon religion in general and most particularly but by no means exclusively (as can be attested by the case of *National Labor Relations Board v. Yeshiva University*, shortly to be considered) upon those of the Catholic church. The root of the development is to be found in the Americanization of Roman Catholicism. When Catholics did not practice birth control and, thus had large families, it was quite acceptable and indeed expected that they would give a son or daughter to the church and thus provide a supply of priests and sisters, the latter constituting an ample source for parochial school teacher staffs. But during the last half of the twentieth century Catholic couples have been practicing birth control and limiting their families almost to the same extent as non-Catholics, with the result that the church now finds it necessary to employ lay Catholics as parochial school teachers. Like their non-Catholic counterparts in the public schools, these teachers have families to support and are faced with the problem of an ever-rising cost of living. The salaries they receive are generally if not universally lower than those received by public school teachers and they believe that salary increases, beyond those offered by the school managements, and other benefits available to public school teachers are called for. Hence, unionization and the demand for collective bargaining.

In 1937, the Supreme Court upheld the constitutionality of the National Labor Relations Act as a valid exercise by Congress of its power to regulate interstate commerce. The act imposes upon an employer an affirmative duty to bargain collectively with a union representing a majority of its employees. Refusal to do so constitutes an unfair labor practice on the part of the employer and, in such case, the board can issue an order, enforceable in court, requiring the employer to bargain in good faith with the employees' union.

While most nonlawyers would probably find somewhat suprising the determination by the National Labor Relations Board (NLRB) that a parochial school is engaged in "interstate commerce," previous Supreme Court decisions have tolerated a wide interpretation of that term; wide enough to encompass the operations of private schools and colleges—including, as in the *Catholic Bishop* case, those that are church-operated.

More difficult to resolve, however, is the claim by the church that government compulsion of collective bargaining would violate both the Establishment and Free Exercise clauses of the First Amendment. In justifying its assumption of jurisdiction in this and other cases involving parochial schools, the NLRB relied upon the Supreme Court's 1937 decision in *Associated Press v. National Labor Relations Board* that application of the National Labor Relations Act to the Associated Press did not violate the amendment's guarantee of freedom of the press.

The NLRB viewed that decision as justifying its intervention in all labor disputes involving religious organizations that affected interstate commerce, presumably by strikes that prevented teachers or students residing in another state to attend school or lessened the purchase of books and school supplies coming from another state. Notwithstanding this position, it voluntarily established a policy of declining jurisdiction with respect to organizations that were "completely religious" (e.g., churches or theological seminaries) but of acting where the employing organization was "just religiously associated." It regarded those parochial schools over which it asserted jurisdiction as being in that category. It had declared, however, that in its intervention with respect to schools that were "just religiously associated" it had gone even further than it was constitutionally required to go and had voluntarily excluded the priests and sisters teaching in them from the collective bargaining units.

In its *National Labor Relations Board v. Catholic Bishop* decision, the majority of the Court rejected the board's distinction between "completely" and "just" and held that in neither case did it have authority to act on the complaint of the teachers' union against the school's management. It did not pass on the question whether such an assumption of authority would be constitutional. Instead, Burger, speaking for himself and four of his colleagues, invoked the principle, first announced by Chief Justice Marshall in 1804 and utilized in the *TWA* and *Seeger* cases, to the effect that a court should avoid deciding on the constitutionality of an act of Congress if it can dispose of the case before it without doing so. Applied to the *Catholic Bishop* controversy, the Chief Justice said, this meant that the Court should not decide the constitutional question unless Congress had clearly expressed its intention that the National Labor Relations Act should cover controversies between parochial school teachers and management with respect to union contract negotiations.

Under previous decisions of the Court, notably *Lemon v. Kurtzman* and *Meek v. Pittenger*, discussed earlier in this book, a statute was deemed to violate the Establishment Clause if, among other factors, it presented a risk of excessive governmental entanglement in the affairs of church-operated schools. State financing of the operations of those schools, even with respect to secular subjects, the Court had held, presented such a risk and was therefore unconstitutional. In the *Catholic Bishop* case, Burger said, it was clear that the board's exercise of its jurisdiction, though limited to determining the factual issue of whether an anti-union animus motivated the school's refusal to negotiate, would result in some entanglement in the school's affairs. The Court did not need to decide at that time, he continued, whether the entanglement would in fact be excessive and hence a violation of the First Amendment; it was sufficient ground for not allowing the board to exercise jurisdiction if exercise presented a significant risk that the amendment *might* be infringed.

Acceptance of jurisdiction would necessarily involve inquiry into such matters as to how many masses or other liturgies were required at Catholic parochial schools. As an example, he included as an appendix to his opinion the following colloquy between the NLRB examining officer and Monsignor O'Donnell, the rector of one of the parochial schools involved in the controversy:

Q. [by Hearing Officer] Now, we have had quite a bit of testimony already as to liturgies, and I don't want to beat a dead horse; but let me ask you one question: if you know, how many liturgies are required at Catholic parochial high schools; do you know?

A. I think our first problem with that would be defining liturgies. That word would have many definitions. Do you want to go into that?

Q. I believe you defined it before, is that correct, when you first testified?

A. I am not sure. Let me try briefly to do it again, okay?

Q. Yes.

A. A liturgy can range anywhere from the strictest sense of the word, which is the sacrifice of the Mass in the Roman Catholic terminology. It can go from that all the way down to a very informal group in what we call shared prayer.

Two or three individuals praying together and reflecting their own reactions to a scriptural reading. All of these—and there is a big spectrum in between those two extremes—all of these are popularly referred to as liturgies.

Q. I see.

A. Now, possibly in repeating your question, you could give me an idea of that spectrum, I could respond more accurately.

Q. Well, let me stick with the formal Masses. If you know, how many Masses are required at Catholic parochial high schools?

A. Some have none, none required. Some would have two or three during the year where what we call Holy Days of Obligation coincide with school days. Some schools on those days prefer to have a Mass within the school day so the students attend there, rather than their parish churches. Some schools feel that it is not a good idea; they should always be in their parish church; so that varies a great deal from school to school.

Determination of the constitutionality of such entanglement, Burger said, should not be made if the act could reasonably be interpreted not to encompass parochial schools.

Burger explored the legislative history of the act to determine whether Congress actually intended to include parochial school teachers in its coverage. He found no clear expression to that effect and stated that this absence fortified the conclusion that Congress did not contemplate that the board would require church-operated schools to grant recognition to unions as bargaining agents for their teachers. Nor did he accept the board's conclusion that the 1937 *Associated Press* decision required a determination of constitutional validity.

There [he said] the Court held that the First Amendment was no bar to the application of the Act to the Associated Press, an organization engaged in collecting information and news throughout the world and distributing it to its members. Perceiving nothing to suggest that application of the Act would infringe First Amendment guarantees of press freedoms, the Court sustained board jurisdiction. Here, on the contrary, the record affords abundant evidence that the Board's exercise of jurisdiction over teachers in church-operated schools would implicate the guarantees of the Religion Clauses.

In the absence of a clear expression of Congress's intent to bring church-operated schools within the jurisdiction of the board, the Burger Court declined to construe the act in a manner that would call upon it to resolve the difficult and sensitive questions arising under the Religion Clauses.

Brennan, speaking for himself and White, Marshall, and Blackmun, said that he could find no difficulty in concluding that Congress did intend to extend National Labor Relations Act coverage to lay teachers in church-operated schools. He noted that Congress, in adopting the Taft-Hartley Act in 1947, had refused to enact a provision stating that the term "employer" was not to include organizations operated exclusively for "religious, charitable, scientific, literary, or educational purposes." The only inference that could fairly be drawn from this is that Congress did not intend to exclude parochial schools any more than other organizations operated exclusively for "educational purposes." Other aspects of the act's legislative history and the language of the act itself offered no evidence of an intent to exclude parochial school teachers. Hence, the Court should have reached and decided the constitutional question, one way or another.

The following comments with respect to this case seem appropriate.

1. The Catholic church must have found itself in an uncomfortable dilemma with respect to the First Amendment ban on entanglement. On the one hand, it deemed it necessary to cite *Lemon v. Kurtzman* nine times and *Meek v. Pittenger* six times in its comparatively short brief to the Supreme Court in order to support its claim that the NLRB's action violated that ban. On the other hand, in those cases the church vigorously challenged the relevancy of the ban to state financing of parochial school operations.

One cannot rightfully fault the church for its reliance on those decisions. So long as they were not overruled they were still the supreme law of the land and therefore binding upon the government in labor relations cases no less than in those involving aid to parochial schools. In any event, the church did not rely exclusively on the constitutional issue but invoked also the rationale of statutory interpretation.

> Congress [the brief read] did not intend for the Act to apply to private religious schools. When the Act was passed over 40 years ago, priests, nuns and brothers were charged with the Church's teaching mission, and disputes between religious faculty and the Church were then and now beyond the pale of civil authority. There is no affirmative intent clearly expressed by Congress to apply the Act to the Church's teachers and absent a clear expression of Congressional resolve, this Court should not construe the Act to approve the Board's newly asserted right to intervene in Church schools.

The Baptist Joint Committee on Public Affairs was not faced with any such difficulty in its brief *amicus* supporting the church. It had strongly opposed aid to parochial schools as violative of the Establishment Clause and therefore could consistently argue that the clause equally forbade entanglement with those schools in a labor relations case.

> The same constitutional principles [its brief said] under the Establishment Clause which this Court has held in many cases to bar governmental financing of the operations of religious schools beyond narrowly prescribed limits, bar equally governmental exercise of jurisdiction under the National Labor Relations Act. The reason for this is that the primary effect of the statutory provisions relevant to the present case would be the inhibition of religion and their enforcement would result in unavoidable government entanglement with religion.

2. Brennan, in his dissenting opinion, did not pass judgment on the constitutional issue but urged only that it should not be avoided "by a cavalier exercise in statutory interpretation." The following year, in the case of *National Labor Relations Board v. Yeshiva University,* the same five to four vote that decided the *Catholic Bishop* case ruled, in an opinion by Powell, that all full-time faculty members in an Orthodox Jewish university were "managerial employees" and therefore not within the purview of the act. It must be acknowledged that the members of a college faculty do stand in a higher professional and managerial status than do newspaper copy editors and secondary school teachers. Unlike them, college teachers participate in decisions relating to granting of tenure, selection of department chairmen, promotions, course content, and other managerial functions. Yet it must have been more than mere coincidence that the four dissenters in the *Yeshiva University* case were those who dissented in the *Catholic Bishop* case. *Yeshiva University* did not raise the Free Exercise and Establishment clauses, although there can be little doubt that Yeshiva University is a religious institution. Why it did not can only be a matter for speculation.

3. The *Catholic Bishop* suit involved collective bargaining on behalf of teachers. Burger's opinion shed no clear light on whether the majority would reach the same conclusion with respect to collective bargaining by nonteaching personnel (e.g., maintenance employees). Logic might seem to indicate that, if Congress did not intend to include church-operated institutions in the act, its intention to exclude encompassed all employees. On the other hand, the Court could very well hold that compulsory bargaining with maintenance personnel would not impinge upon First Amendment restrictions, since it is not likely that mandatory bargaining with unions representing them would result in an entanglement of church and state.

There is, however, a difficulty with this approach. In *Committee for Public Education and Religious Liberty v. Nyquist,* the Court ruled unconstitutional the use of tax-raised funds to finance maintenance and repair costs in parochial schools and this would obviously include the salaries of maintenance employees. The Establishment Clause forbids laws advancing or inhibiting religion. If financing salaries advances religion, does not compulsory bargaining respecting salaries inhibit it?

Should a *Catholic Bishop* case involving only maintenance employees reach the Supreme Court, it could dispose of it in one of three ways: It might interpret congressional exclusionary intent to encompass all employees, maintenance as well as instructional; it might accept congressional intent to include them but rule that the *Nyquist* decision impelled a ruling of unconstitutionality; or, reflecting Rehnquist's philosophy (as expressed in *Mueller v. Allen*) that, while the *Nyquist* decision was binding and should not be overruled (Powell, whose vote was necessary for a majority in the *Catholic Bishop* case would probably not stand for overruling *Nyquist*), the Court might hold that the establishment claim should be strictly limited to cases involving government financing. Accordingly, it could rule that the NLRB's jurisdiction could extend to controversies involving unionization. While that would have been a bitter pill for arch-conservative Rehnquist to swallow, he managed to do it in the *Yeshiva University* case.

4. The schools involved in the *Catholic Bishop* suit were Catholic but obviously the Court's determination applies equally to collective bargaining by teachers in Jewish, Lutheran, and fundamentalist all-day schools on the elementary and secondary school levels.

5. Of course, the decision excluded only mandatory collective bargaining. There has been considerable voluntary collective bargaining with respect to both Christian and Jewish schools and the probabilities are that much of it will continue notwithstanding the Court's decision. Factors other than NLRB-mandated union recognition may impel continuation or even expansion of collective bargaining. Among these are teachers' strikes, in no way restricted by the *Catholic Bishop* decision, departure of teachers to obtain higher wages and other benefits in public schools, and parental pressure upon the school's administrative officials to reach an agreement with the union so that the children might return to classes.

6. The Court's decision was based upon the language of the act as it now reads. It may be assumed that the unions will seek to persuade Congress to amend it to include church-related schools and that the church and its allies will make every effort to dissuade it from doing so. How this conflict between two politically powerful forces in the United States will ultimately be resolved is anybody's guess. Should the unions succeed, which in light of their anti-Reagan efforts in the 1984 presidential election campaign is unlikely but not impossible, it would seem that the Court would then have to decide the constitutional issue.

So much for the *Catholic Bishop* decision and its ruling that the NLRB could not assert jurisdiction in a labor dispute involving "church operated" schools. Two years after it was handed down, the Court, in the case of *National Labor Relations Board v. Bishop Ford Central Catholic High School,* was faced with the question whether the board could assert jurisdiction in a labor dispute relating to a religiously affiliated high school operated by an independent corporation with a board of trustees who were not priests but laymen.

The case came to the Court when the board sought to reverse a decision by the United States Court of Appeals that it had no such jurisdiction because the school was in reality "church operated." The school had been established by the local diocese which, though it transferred formal title to the corporation and its lay trustees, had not thereby altered the religious mission of the school to provide spiritual, educational, and social opportunities to help the students to become mature and fulfilled Christians.

The Court of Appeals observed that the agreement between the diocese and the school contained a provision stating that if the school ever ceased to operate as a Roman Catholic high school, title would revert automatically to the diocese, so that the diocese retained a significant degree of control over the school. The Court stated that any possible conflict with the Religion Clauses arose, not out of the legal title to the school property, but from the suffusion of religion into the curriculum and the mandate to the faculty to infuse the students with the values of the Catholic creed. It therefore concluded that the board's position that the school was "separate and distinct from the church" was irrelevant as well as inaccurate and that the board could not properly exercise jurisdiction over it in light of the Supreme Court's holding in the *Catholic Bishop* case.

Without writing any opinion, the Supreme Court refused to hear the NLRB's appeal and thus left standing the decision of the Court of Appeals.

At first glance, this would seem to be inconsistent with the ruling in *Bradfield v. Roberts* that tax-raised funds could be used to finance the operation of a hospital owned by a corporation that had been formed and was controlled by an order of Catholic nuns. The consequence of these rulings would seem to be that when it benefits the church to be a corporation, the Court will recognize it as such, but when it is not to the advantage of the church to be so recognized, the charter will remain undiscovered. This is like you win if a tossed coin comes up heads and you win if it comes up tails.

The fallacy of the analogy lies in the fact that (perhaps with the exception of abortion procedures) the services available in church-controlled hospitals do not differ from those available in hospitals not so controlled, but that it is not true with respect to religious schools below the college level. Were it not so, the constitutional difficulties relating to aid to religious schools could be avoided by the simple device of incorporating the schools.

The Court's decision in the *Catholic Bishop* case was based exclusively on its interpretation of the National Labor Relations Act, and its ruling therefore did not affect state labor relations laws. Where a state legislature clearly indicates its intention that religious schools shall be subject to its own labor relations law, the federal courts, presumably including the Supreme Court, might seem to have no choice but to rule on the question of constitutionality.

That was the situation which, in 1983, faced the United States District Court in the case of *Catholic High School Association of the Archdiocese of New York v. Culvert.* Although the Catholic High School Association (hereafter referred to as School Association) was organized as a corporation under the state's Education Law, both the state and the archdiocese agreed that high schools were "church-operated" within the meaning of that term as used in the *Catholic Bishop* case and that the School Association was an arm of the archdiocese. The faculties consisted of lay and religious teachers, teaching both secular and religious subjects, and both were intimately involved in fulfilling the purposes of the Catholic schools.

The Lay Faculty Association (hereafter called Faculty Association) was a labor organization consisting only of lay teachers certified by a majority as their exclusive bargaining representative. After a number of members were suspended for protesting the School Association's new teacher policy, the Faculty Association instituted a proceeding under the State Labor Relations Act charging unfair labor practices. (In his message approving a 1968 amendment to the State Labor Relations Law, Governor Nelson Rockefeller stated expressly: "This bill amends the Labor Law to guarantee the employees of charitable, *religious* and educational institutions the right of self-organization.") The School Association then brought suit in a federal court claiming that the State Labor Relations Board (SLRB) could not oversee labor relations involving parochial schools and lay teachers without thereby violating the First Amendment's Establishment Clause.

In ruling that SLRB's intervention violated the entanglement aspect of the establishment test, the District Court judge rejected the contention that the state's statute merely required the School Association "to bargain in good faith" but not necessarily reach agreement over salaries, hours, and other conditions of employment. Even if the SLRB's intervention was limited to scrutinizing and ascertaining whether the school authorities were negotiating in good faith, the Court said that might well lead to excessive administrative entanglement between church and state.

Suppose a controversy arose as to whether the cause of a teacher's dismissal was his advocating abortion and birth control, as asserted by the School Association, or for union activities, as claimed by the Faculty Association. The SLRB's investigation to determine the true cause of the dismissal might well require it to scrutinize Catholic doctrine to enable it to ascertain the School Association's asserted motive, and this could in itself constitute impermissible entanglement.

At the present writing the trial judge's decision against the SLRB and the Faculty Association has been appealed to but not yet decided by the Court of Appeals. It may safely be assumed that the losing party will appeal to the Supreme Court. What may not be assumed with the same degree of safety is whether the Supreme Court will be able to find a way of deciding the appeal without reaching the issue of constitutionality. All that can be predicted is that, if the personnel of the Court is still the same, the decision will not be reached unanimously but rather by a five to four vote, most likely in favor of the church.

Granfield v. Catholic University and *Broderick v. Catholic University* present the rather unusual situation of suits, based upon the First Amendment's Religion Clauses, brought by two members of religious orders (one Benedictine and the other Dominican) against the church in the person of the local Ordinary (in this case the Archbishop of Washington, D.C.). The plaintiffs were members of the University's Law School faculty and their grievance revolved around the disparity in salaries between lay and clerical members, the latter receiving only sixty-five percent of the comparable "lay scale." This ratio, termed "clerical discount," was prevalent throughout the nation and was justified by a tradition that church-related colleges had the right to expect some measure of sacrifice from clerical members of their faculties.

The plaintiffs' complaints in the lawsuits were based on both the Establishment and Free Exercise clauses. The Court of Appeals' decision against them (which the Supreme Court refused to review) noted that, unlike the usual First Amendment suits challenging government financing of church-related schools in which the defendant is the governmental body charged with effectuating the legislative grant, the United States Commissioner of Education was not named as a defendant in the action. The omission was even more startling in view of the fact that approximately twenty-five percent of the university's annual income came in the form of grants from the government, and this without counting the university's exemption from federal income tax liability as an educational institution and its eligibility to receive tax deductible contributions.

The obvious explanation for the omission lay in the reality that the last thing the plaintiffs wanted to do was to put in risk these government subsidizations. Accordingly, their suit was predicated upon the theory that the funding did violate the Establishment and Free Exercise clauses but only for so long as the university subjected its cleric-professors to a discriminatory wage scale.

It was clear from this, the Court held, that as to the absent commissioner there was really no "case or controversy" within the meaning of the provision in Article III of the Constitution that limits federal court jursidiction to such situations. Accordingly, the Court held, sound principles of judicial restraint forbade consideration of the establishment issue.

Nor did the claim that the university's action violated the Free Exercise Clause present a case for federal court jurisdiction. The plaintiffs' reduced salaries were set by an arm of their own religious organization, allegedly for the advancement of ecclesiastical objectives shared by the plaintiffs and the university. The wisdom—or lack thereof—on the part of the university, the Court concluded, must be resolved within the confines of the Catholic church.

CONSCIENTIOUS OBJECTION TO UNIONIZATION

In a number of cases that reached the Supreme Court the contested issue was whether the Free Exercise Clause protected from dismissal employees who for reasons of religious conscience refused to join unions or even to pay union dues without joining. Involved in these cases were Seventh Day Adventists who asserted varying Biblical texts to justify the refusal. In *Linscott v. Miller Falls Company* (1971), it was 2 Corinthians 17, which states "be ye separate, saith the Lord." In *Gray v. Gulf, Mobile and Ohio Railroad* (1971), the proof-text was the statement in 2 Timothy 2:24 that "the servant of the Lord must not strive." In *Cooper v. General Dynamics* (1976) it was the call upon the faithful to "stand fast in one spirit with one mind striving together for the faith of the gospel" (Philippians 1:27) as well as the commandment to love one's neighbor, a term that included one's employer even if it was a multimillion-dollar corporation.

In all of these cases, the Supreme Court refused to overturn lower court decisions against the Adventists, although in the *Linscott* and *Gray* cases two justices, Burger and Douglas, noted their dissents. The essence of all these cases lay in the Supreme Court's reluctance to adjudge the employers' policies to be contrary to the First Amendment.

The sincerity of the Adventists in that they were not "free loaders" seeking the benefits of union contracts without contributing to their cost was manifested by their offer, in all three cases, to contribute to mutually acceptable charities the amounts they would have to pay as union dues.

In many instances the controversies did not reach the courts, since the unions acquiesced in this compromise, but in the three cases considered here they did not. One probable reason for this may lie in the fact that the expenses of labor negotiations and contract enforcement would not be diminished by the charitable contribution but would have to be borne by the Adventists' co-workers, thus requiring an increase in union dues. Another might be that employees opposing a particular union or all union contracts might resort to a First Amendment right as an instrument against the union or all unionization.

Whatever the reasons, the conclusion reached in all three cases was that the amendment did not compel acceptance of the Adventists' offer, a conclusion which the Supreme Court refused to disturb.

CONSCIENTIOUS OBJECTION TO POLITICAL POSITIONS

The 1984 presidential election campaign and the concurrent campaigns for other federal and state offices were marked with heated and almost virulent controversy, especially within the Democratic party's primary campaigns with respect to the AFL-CIO's expenditure of funds in support of Walter Mondale against Gary Hart and Jesse Jackson. Supporters of the latter two (and of Reagan in the election campaign) were vocal in their protestations, on constitutional and ethical grounds, against such asserted misuse of union funds. Our concern here relates only to the establishment and free exercise aspects of the controversy.

The constitutionality of unions using members' dues in political campaigns was passed upon by the Burger Court in the case of *Abood v. Detroit Board of Education* (1977). Although the major First Amendment issue in the case concerned freedom of public association and speech, the Court's opinion made it quite clear that it was equally applicable to rights under the Religion Clauses. Specifically, the case involved a Michigan statute that authorized unionization of government employees such as teachers and other civil service employees but also permitted agency-shop arrangements under which employees might join the union chosen by a majority of the employees or pay to it a "service charge" equal in amount to union dues so that they would share in financing the benefits all the employees receive through collective bargaining.

An understanding of the Court's decision in the *Abood* case and its political significance requires a brief review of its earlier decisions in this arena. The first of these was *Railway Employees' Department, A.F.L. v. Hanson* (1956). There the Court upheld the constitutionality under the First Amendment of a union-shop clause, authorized by the Railway Labor Act, requiring all employees to support financially the union representing the employees. It held that this requirement did not violate the First Amendment's guarantee of freedoms of conscience, association, and thought.

Five years later, in *International Association of Machinists v. Street,* the Court was faced with a challenge to the constitutionality of a union's use of treasury funds to which all employees were required to contribute in order to finance the campaigns of labor-oriented candidates for public office and to promote "the propagation of political and economic doctrines, concepts and ideologies" with which the plaintiffs disagreed.

The Court avoided passing upon the constitutionality of the Railway Labor Act clause (which was applicable to this as it was to the *Hanson* case) by interpreting it as authorizing only expenditures relating to the union's functions in negotiating and administering collective bargaining agreements and in adjusting grievances. This solution of a difficult constitutional problem was not available to the Court in the *Abood* case. The reason for this was that, unlike the *Hanson* and *Street* cases, Abood's challenge involved a state rather than a federal law and the Supreme Court was therefore bound to accept the Michigan court's interpretation of its own laws. The Supreme Court's jurisdiction was limited to determining First Amendment constitutionality of the statute as so interpreted.

In the *Abood* case, Stewart's opinion for the Court stated initially that the principles upon which the *Hanson* and *Street* cases were decided were equally applicable to cases involving unionization of government employees. Accordingly, service charges could be imposed upon nonunion members for their fair share of the monies needed to finance collective bargaining on such questions as contract administration and grievance adjustments. Moreover, union funds could also constitutionally be used in support of or opposition to some political or ideological issue relating to the rights of labor.

However, Stewart said, First Amendment guarantees of freedom of speech, association, and religion preclude imposing upon nonconsenting employees any part of the expenditures used for these purposes. In regard to the religion issue, the Court referred to *Torcaso v. Watkins,* which invalidated a statute requiring applicants for a state license (e.g., a notary public) to affirm their belief in God. It also cited the rhetorical question by Madison, the First Amendment's author, that "who does not see . . .

that the same authority which can force a citizen to contribute three pence only of his property for the support of any one establishment, may force him to conform to any other establishment in all cases whatsoever?" Quoted, too, was Jefferson's statement that "to compel a man to furnish contributions of money for the propagation of opinions which he disbelieves, is sinful and tyrannical."

On the other hand, the dissent of a union minority should not foreclose united political action by the majority in support of or against candidates because of their positions on such religious-related questions as abortion (or, the Court could have added, evolution or aid to parochial schools). The solution, it said, was to be found in the case of *Railway Clerks v. Allen* (1963). There it had held that the Constitution required that such political expenditures be financed only from charges, dues, or assessments paid by employees who without coercion or fear of reprisal consent to such political use.

The net result of all this is that unions may finance support of or opposition to a candidate or to a referendum, but they may do this only to the proportional extent arrived at by excluding dissenters' dues or assessments from the sum total of the funds so used, and by refunding to the dissenters a portion of the union's funds in the proportion that the union's political expenditures bear to total union expenditures.

It may well be that the decision reached in the *Abood* case came about as a lowest-common-denominator compromise among the Court's members. Although there was no dissent from the disposition of the case, there was no unanimity with respect to its rationale; on the contrary, a majority could not be mustered in support of any single opinion. Powell (speaking for himself, Burger, and Blackmun), Rehnquist, and Stevens all found it necessary to submit separate opinions asserting their acceptance of the judgment in the case but not necessarily the reasoning supporting it. But until a better one can be brought forth, the *Abood* decision will have to do. It has the virtue of allowing the National Education Association, the American Federation of Teachers, and other unions to provide financial support to political candidates and at the same time entitle the dissident members of these organizations to get their money back.

CHAPTER 7

The Free Exercise
of Disfavored Religions

BACKGROUND IN HISTORY

The past decade has witnessed what might be called a crusade against newly formed unpopular religions, commonly called cults. The latter term is used in its derogatory rather than neutral sense and encompasses, among others, the Unification Church, the Church of Scientology, the Hare Krishna, the Worldwide Church of God, The Way Ministry, the Children of God, and Black Muslims. All of these and others not listed have, in one way or another, been the subject of criminal prosecution and civil litigation and all have invoked constitutional protection. (As this is written, the *New York Times* of June 24 and 30, July 11, and August 10, 1984, report an incident in Island Park, Vermont, in which the state police rounded up one hundred and twelve children whose parents are members of the Northeast Kingdom [of God] Community Church, a radical Christian group that is viewed by most townspeople as a cult because they deem it secretive, separate, and reclusive and given to dogmatic disciplining of its children. A local judge ordered their return for lack of any evidence as to a single act of abuse or neglect involving any of the children. The state's governor predicted that the case could end up in the United States Supreme Court.) An examination into the experiences of earlier unpopular faiths in their struggle for acceptance into the family of religions should be helpful to an understanding of the Burger Court's response to the constitutional claims of present-day cults.

In significant ways, the present often hysterical reaction on the part of millions of Americans to cults is reminiscent of the anti-witchcraft trials that were championed by Cotton Mather in Salem, Massachusetts, and which spread elsewhere in the colonies towards the end of the seventeenth century. In one Salem case, all twelve of the jurors later signed a statement admitting their error in handing down guilty verdicts. Of the defendants in others of the widespread trials (involving several hundred young women and "afflicted children"), nineteen were found guilty by juries and were hanged before hysteria passed into history.

Earlier in the century, Anne Hutchinson and her brother-in-law, the Reverend John Wainwright, were banished for heresy in preaching the covenant of grace rather than of works. So, too, was Roger Williams, a founder of the Baptist church in North America. (In the Sun Myung Moon tax fraud trial, related in part in Chapter 1, the government sought the banishment of the defendant through deportation but the trial judge refused to go that far in imposing sentence.)

Williams's sufferings because of religious prejudice were experienced by other Baptists, who during the "period of the Great Persecution" (1768 to 1774) were whipped, beaten, arrested, fined, and imprisoned, sometimes on bread and water. In 1774 James Madison, later to become the principal draftsman of the First Amendment, was moved to write to a friend:

> That diabolical hell-conceived principle of persecution rages among some . . . . This vexes me the worst of anything whatever. There are at this time in the adjacent county not less than five or six well-meaning men in close jail for publishing their religious sentiments, which in the main are very orthodox. I have neither patience to hear, talk, or think of anything relative to the matter; for I have squabbled and scolded, abused and ridiculed, so long about it to little purpose, that I am without common patience. So I must beg you to pity me, and pray for liberty of conscience to all.

Members of another religious cult, formally called the Society of Friends but then popularly and derisively known as the "Quakers" (just as adherents of the Unification Church are called "Moonies"), also suffered prosecutions and inevitable guilty verdicts (in a few cases even being put to death) because their beliefs were unacceptable to the general public. So, too, were the Catholics commonly and derogatively called "papists." Even Oliver Cromwell, an otherwise staunch defender of religious freedom, did not interpret that freedom to encompass "liberty to exercise the mass." Except in Maryland, where they constituted a majority, Catholics were widely subject to religious discrimination and group defamation. Thus, the General Court of Massachusetts decreed in 1647 that

> [n]o Jesuit or ecclesiastical person ordained by the pope or the see of Rome shall henceforth come into Massachusetts. Any person not freeing himself of suspicion shall be jailed, then banished. If taken a second time, he shall be put to death.

In 1689 a new charter was granted to the colony decreeing that "forever thereafter there shall be liberty of conscience allowed in the worship of God to all Christians (except papists)."

In the mid-nineteenth century, in an effort to effect congregational rather than individual (i.e., bishopric) control of Catholic church properties acquired through contributions and bequests in wills, incorporation statutes were enacted requiring lay representation in boards of directors empowered to make decisions with respect even to church properties used exclusively for religious purposes. At the same time, the Nativist or "Know-Nothing" Party stated its comprehensive purpose as "Anti-Romanism, Anti-Bedinism, Anti-Pope's Toeism, Anti-Nunneryism, Anti-Winking Virginism, Anti-Jesuitism, and Anti-the-whole-Sacredotal-Hierarchism with all its humbugging mummeries."

That this party was in tune with popular prejudice is evidenced by the fact that for a time it captured the legislatures in quite a number of states. In Massachusetts the Know-Nothing legislature appointed a "Nunnery Committee" to report on "such theological seminaries, boarding schools, academies, nunneries, convents, and other institutions of like character as they deem necessary." The appointment reflected a widespread belief that it was inconceivable that young women could voluntarily commit themselves to serve as nuns, but rather were the victims of physical or mental duress (what would later be called mind-control or coercive persuasion), a belief reflected today in a practically universal popular assumption with respect to cults. There was, indeed, strong condemnation of convents on the ground that unlawful means, such as kidnapping, were supposedly used to force young women into them.

This prejudice against Catholics endured well into the twentieth century. As late as 1929, in the wake of Alfred E. Smith's unsuccessful campaign for the presidency, Senator Tom Heflin of Alabama brought to the floor of the United States Senate a resolution seeking a vote on whether that body favored the American government or the Roman Catholic church. Although a Catholic (Roger Taney) could, with the consent of the Senate, be appointed Chief Justice of the United States Supreme Court in 1837, it was more than another century before one would be elected president.

Those to whom cults are an evil foreign import waging war against revered values in their false claim to be a "religion" would do well to read Sara Harris's book, "Father Divine." Born George Baker, the son of Georgia sharecroppers, "Father Divine" ultimately settled in the Harlem section of New York City. In many respects his career was similar to that of Moon, except that Moon was a non-white who came to the United

States from South Korea and Baker was a black born here. Both were considered by their followers to be in some respects divine (hence the name Father Divine), although perhaps not to the same degree. Originally, Baker took the name Major J. Divine, but later adopted the name Father Divine; to his followers he was literally God, like "our Father who art in Heaven."

Like Moon, Divine became the owner of many profit-making enterprises. He rode around in a Cadillac driven by his private chauffeur and wore custom made suits and the finest haberdashery, all of which were received as love offerings to God. Nevertheless, he paid no taxes and was never prosecuted for tax evasion for the simple reason that nothing was recorded in his name and all his many wants were taken care of by gifts from his worshippers. In short, the reason Divine (unlike Moon) was never prosecuted for income tax evasion was that, while his disciples, many of whom were wealthy, had incomes, he himself did not, or at least it could not be proven that he did.

Divine did have one encounter with the law; he was arrested for disturbing the peace, found guilty by a jury, and sentenced by an obviously hostile judge to prison for a year, the maximum term for the offence charged, this notwithstanding the jury's plea for clemency. Four days later, the judge, fifty years old and in apparent good health, died. Said Divine from his prison cell: "I hated to do it."

Father Divine (who died in 1965) made no contribution to constitutional law as it relates to the First Amendment. The same is not true with respect to Jehovah's Witnesses, who arose and flourished at about the same time as Divine. Jehovah's Witnesses, perhaps more than any other religious group in this century, were victims of religious prejudice, hatred, and fear—manifested in physical violence, hostile legislation, criminal prosecutions, and jury verdicts of guilt. Today in most parts of the nation the Witnesses are accepted in the family of "legitimate" faiths. But they reached this fortunate station only after suffering a period of trials and tribulations instigated with strong popular approval by government officials hostile to their beliefs and practices. New statutes were enacted and old ones resurrected to supply weapons to curb their activities and, when possible, completely to destroy their faith. All kinds of laws were used or attempted to be used for that purpose; laws against disturbing the peace, anti-peddling ordinances, laws forbidding the use of sound trucks, traffic regulations, tax revenue laws, and many others, were invoked against them.

America owes a great debt of gratitude to the Witnesses. Much of the current law relating to religious freedom resulted from the Witnesses' persistence in asserting their constitutional rights in the teeth of persecution and doggedly appealing adverse lower court verdicts to the Supreme Court. The sincerity, integrity, and self-sacrifice of Jehovah's Witnesses can hardly be questioned.

The same, however, cannot be said of the most unlikely of co-contributors to the development of constitutional protection of religious freedom, Guy W., Edna W., and Donald Ballard, organizers of what they called the "I Am" movement. (Today it would be called a cult.) In *United States v. Ballard* (1944) the Supreme Court was called upon to determine the constitutionality, under the First Amendment's Free Exercise Clause, of the validity of a guilty verdict handed down against them for using the mail to defraud. The indictments charged that they had falsely and fraudulently represented "that Guy W. Ballard . . . alias Saint Germain, Jesus, George Washington . . . had been selected and designated . . . as a divine messenger"; that the words of "ascended masters and of the divine entity Saint Germain" would be communicated to the world through the "I Am" movement; that the Ballards had supernatural powers to heal the incurably ill; and that they had in fact cured hundreds of afflicted persons. The indictments charged that the Ballards knew that these representations were false and made them solely for the purpose of obtaining for themselves the money of the credulous.

During the course of the trial there was testimony that the Ballards had represented that the teachings of the "I Am" movement had been dictated from Heaven to the Ballards, who took down and transcribed them, and that Jesus had shaken hands with them. The trial judge instructed the jury that they should not decide whether or not these statements were literally true but only whether the defendants honestly believed they were true.

The majority of the Supreme Court, in an opinion written by Douglas, agreed with the trial judge. Under the constitutional principles of the separation of church and state and religious freedom, he said, neither a jury nor any other organ of government had the competence to pass on whether certain alleged religious experiences actually occurred. The jury could no more constitutionally decide that Guy Ballard did not shake hands with Jesus than they could determine that Jesus did not walk on the sea. The opinion said:

> . . . Heresy trials are foreign to our Constitution. Men may believe what they cannot prove. They may not be put to the proof of their religious doctrines or beliefs. Religious experiences which are as real as life to some may be incomprehensible to others. Yet the fact that they may be beyond the ken of mortals does not mean that they can be made suspect before the

law. Many take their gospel from the New Testament. But it would hardly be supposed that they could be tried before a jury charged with the duty of determining whether those teachings contained false representations. The miracles of the New Testament, the Divinity of Christ, life after death, the power of prayer are deep in the religious convictions of many. If one could be sent to jail because a jury in a hostile environment found those teachings false, little indeed would be left of religious freedom. The religious view espoused by respondents might seem incredible, if not preposterous, to most people. But if those doctrines are subject to trial before a jury charged with finding their truth or falsity, then the same can be done with the religious beliefs of any sect. When the triers of fact undertake that task they enter a forbidden domain.

What the Court held, in effect, was that no agency of the secular state, including a jury, may pass judgment upon the factual reality of religious beliefs or religious experiences. On the other hand, it also held that it was constitutionally permissible to allow a jury to decide whether the Ballards themselves actually *believed* that what they recounted was true and, if the jury determined that they did not, they could convict them of using the mail to obtain money under false pretenses.

There were two dissenting opinions—one from what may be called the right, the other from the left. The former, by Chief Justice Harlan Stone, argued that if the Ballards obtained money from elderly or infirm persons by stating that through their spiritual powers they had cured hundreds of persons afflicted with diseases and ailments, the prosecution should be allowed to prove that no such cures had been effected. From the left, Jackson urged that the prosecution should not have been instituted in the first place. Few juries, he said, could find that the Ballards honestly believed in something that the jury felt was unbelievable.

The decision by the majority of the Court seems to have been a pragmatic compromise. Acceptance of Stone's approach would threaten the long-established legitimacy not only of Christian Science practitioners but also of all other teachers of the efficacy of prayers to heal physical ailments. Acceptance of Jackson's approach, on the other hand, would leave the aged and infirm at the mercy of charlatans.

The majority of the Court could not accept either approach; yet it may have felt uncomfortable with the compromise it had adopted, for logically it sanctioned prosecution for fraud not only of Elmer Gantry but at least theoretically of thousands of real-life ministers, priests, and rabbis who weekly preach the literal historicity of everything in the Bible even though they themselves do not believe it. Moreover, it required juries either to read the minds of defendants or to guess whether they were sincere in what they professed. It is a relatively simple matter for a judge or jury to determine whether a certain brick sold for a large sum of money is gold or lead and, if the latter, whether the defendant knew that fact when he made the sale; it is not so simple a matter to determine whether a solicitor of funds to build a spiritualist temple had actually communed with the dead and, if he did not, whether he honestly believed that he did.

Nevertheless, sincerity of belief has become the test for distinguishing between faith and fraud. Basically it is the way, imperfect as it may be, to ascertain whether an applicant for conscientious objection from the draft is entitled to it. At the same time, it has become the shield of innumerable charlatans who find it easy to extract money from persons only too willing to believe in supernatural relief from ills and anxieties when natural means have failed. Yet this may be a necessary price to pay for freedom of religion and a worthwhile one as well. Jackson stated the point eloquently in his dissenting opinion in the *Ballard* case:

> The chief wrong which false prophets do to their following is not financial. The collections aggregate a tempting total, but individual payments are not ruinous. I doubt if the vigilance of the law is equal to making money stick by over-credulous people. But the real harm is on the mental and spiritual plane. There are those who hunger and thirst after high values which they feel wanting in their humdrum lives. They live in mental confusion or moral anarchy and seek vaguely for truth and beauty and moral support. When they are deluded and then disillusioned, cynicism and confusion follow. The wrong of these things, as I see it, is not in the money the victims part with, half so much as in the mental and spiritual poison they get. But that is precisely the thing the Constitution put beyond the reach of the prosecutor, for the price of freedom of religion or of speech or of the press is that we must put up with, and even pay for, a good deal of rubbish.

THE CONTEMPORARY SCENE

The first encounter between government and faith that came to the Burger Court was in the prosecution of Muhammad Ali, discussed in an earlier chapter. It was shortly thereafter that the word "cults" came into common use to describe new groups such as the Unification Church and the Church of Scientology. Webster's Third New International Dictionary has several definitions for the word, the third, as "the rites, ceremonies and practices of a religion," giving as an example "reverence or ceremonial veneration paid to God or to the Virgin Mary or to the saints or to objects that symbolize or represent them," and the fourth, as a "religion regarded as unorthodox or spurious." It is the last word that justifies the use of the term "cults" in this chapter.

Webster to the contrary notwithstanding, today's anti-cultists have refused to use the term "religion" when speaking of cults; they use it only if it is preceded by "spurious" or "pretended" or similar synonyms indicating that they are not a religion, even an unpopular one. The reason for this lies in the fact that anti-cultists are not prepared to accept the relevance of the First Amendment, which guarantees the rights of the most unorthodox of religions. Cult leaders, they assert, are no more practitioners of religion than astrologers are of astronomy, quacks of medicine, or alchemists of chemistry. Cultists may no more justly use the term "Reverend" than other pretenders have the right to call themselves "Doctor" or "Professor."

Prosecuting attorneys or lawyers bringing civil suits against cults generally follow the same policy. Moon was rarely called Reverend Moon by those who opposed him. Cult leaders, they assert, claim and persuade their dupes to believe that they are divine or at the very least have unique characteristics that enable them to perform miracles and to communicate with the Divinity in ways not shared by other believers, but this obviously false claim does not make it a religion.

Today, kidnapping and measures called "deprogramming," aimed at restoring their children to the faith of their fathers or even to no faith at all, are resorted to by parents whose children join cults, so much so that a class of professional "deprogrammers" has evolved. Their justification is predicated upon the maxim that fire must be met by fire: even if victims of cultism are not physically kidnapped, the same result is achieved through brainwashing and therefore must be met by deprogramming. On occasion, however, "deprogrammers" have been sued for damages and even prosecuted and convicted by juries for kidnapping. In some instances, too, a jury may hand down a substantial verdict in a civil case. The *New York Times* of December 2, 1983, reported that in one case a federal jury returned a verdict for fifty thousand dollars against Ted Patrick, probably the most prominent of "deprogrammers," in a suit not by a teenager but a thirty-one-year-old convert to the Divine Light Mission. It appears that the American conscience will often not tolerate illegal use of force against religious dissidents—at least not where other measures such as successful civil suits against rather that by cultists resulting in substantial jury verdicts or criminal prosecutions for tax fraud or other wrongs are available.

A ninety-eight page article by Richard Delgado, entitled "Religious Totalism: Gentle and Ungentle Persuasion Under the First Amendment," in the November 1977 issue of the *Southern California Law Review*, justifies resort to law as a means to curb cults in their utilization of high-pressure, harmful, and deceptive tactics in recruiting and indoctrinating young members. (The tenor of the article is reflected by the statement in footnote 174 that "Krishna couples don't believe in intercourse except to have children." If this is a symptom of cultism, then Catholicism, fundamentalist Protestantism, and Orthodox Judaism with respect to couples no longer capable of bearing children are suspect.)

The article is replete with fear-inducing words and phrases, some new and some borrowed from other contexts. Among them are "mind control," "behavior control technology," "brainwashing," and "coercive persuasion." (The last term would seem to be self-contradictory, such as "true myths" or "humane torture.") The cults asserted to be guilty of "gentle and ungentle persuasion" are, in the order in which they appear in the article, Moon's Unification Church, Children of God, New Testament Missionary Fellowship, Transcendental Meditation, Hare Krishna, Love Family, Divine Light Mission, Founding Church of Scientology, Church of Armageddon, The Way, and the Alamo Christian Foundation.

Delgado recognizes that some accepted religious groups (and some nonreligious ones, such as officer training schools and executive training institutes) engage in thought-control processes. Jesuits and other religious training institutions, he writes, may isolate the seminarian from the rest of the world at various stages of the training period but this does not constitute "physiological depletion." He cites a Jesuit priest who stated that the seminarians are afforded adequate opportunities for rest, reflection, and recreation; they eat well, "at times too well."

This, of course, is correct in what it says, but it is not all that is relevant in an impartial scholarly study of cultism. Also relevant would be a consideration or at least mention of Cistercians of the Stricter Observance, more commonly known as Trappists. They have turned over to the church not only a part but all of their earthly possessions. Their whole life, not merely the training period, is one of strict seclusion from the world. Working hours are devoted to worship, labor, and study. There is no recreation, no meat is eaten by the healthy, and strict silence is observed except under unusual circumstances. It is not unfair to suggest that were the Trappists not part of the Catholic church but the creation of a Moon or an L. Ron Hubbard (originator of the Church of Scientology), they would be condemned by anti-cultists as one of the most horrendous of cults.

The cultural difference between the popular fear-hatred response to cults and the affectionate good humor that accompanies the depiction of

Trappists in cinema lies in the reality that the latter are part of the Catholic religion and therefore obviously could not be a cult. The same is true with respect to Hasidism, no less a part of acceptable Judaism than Trappists are of Catholicism. A long, respectful report, with large size photographs, of a ritual marriage between children of two Hasidic sects in the June 11, 1984, issue of the New York Times testifies to this.

A somewhat different picture of Hasidism is presented by the following report in the September 11, 1981, issue of the New York Times:

> A warrant for the arrest of a Brooklyn rabbi was issued today after he failed to show up in State Supreme Court here to tell what he knows about the disappearance of a 13-year-old girl.
>
> Justice Paul Kelly signed the arrest warrant, which orders Rabbi M. Premock and his wife, who was unidentified, to appear in court Monday.
>
> The 13-year-old girl, Rivkah Abrams, apparently ran away from her Amity Harbor, L.I., home on Aug. 26, the day after she returned from an upstate summer camp operated by a Hasidic sect.
>
> Her father, Yisroel Abrams, has charged that his daughter was "brain-washed" by members of the sect. He said he had evidence that she went to Rabbi Premock's home in Brooklyn's Borough Park section the night she disappeared. Mr. Abrams contended that the religious group was harboring his daughter—with her consent—because it disapproved of her religious training.

(It should be noted that while the report uses the word "sect" rather than "cult," it does refer to "brainwash[ing]," a standard term in cultology.)

Four years before this incident, Rabbi Arthur J. Lelyveld, then president of the Central Conference of American (Reform) Rabbis and earlier president of the American Jewish Congress, delivered a sermon in his temple citing the similarities between cults and some Hasidic groups. The similarities, as reported in the April 1, 1977, issue of the National Jewish Post, included the authority of a charismatic leader, the irrationality and medievalism of their stance, the deliberate driving of a wedge between parents and children, and the removal of the cult follower from society's mainstream.

Nor is modern Islam without its cults. Within the past century a sect has arisen and continues to flourish all over the world, including the United States, which had it not achieved acceptance within the Islamic religion would certainly have become a cult in the realm of American jurisprudence. This sect, called the Ahmadiyya, was established by Mirza Ghulam Ahmad, who claimed to be the promised Messiah coming in the spirit of Jesus and with his power to perform miracles.

There can be little doubt that many of the horrendous incidents related in the Delgado article and in the books, articles, news reports, and government investigations relating to cultism, both before and after the article was published, are factually true. But it is fairly certain that many are not or at least not fully true. Practically all the firsthand evidence against cults comes from hostile sources, primarily penitent ex-cultists. Monetary and other tangible benefits, such as favorable news stories, can be the reward for penance and confession. Since cross-examination is not likely in hearings by legislative committees, and suits for libel or prosecutions for perjury are almost certain of failure, testimony given in such hearings must be taken with some degree of caution. Finally, in the prosecution for tax evasion brought against Moon, *amicus curiae* briefs in his support were submitted to the Supreme Court not only by civil liberties organizations but by many religious organizations. It seems unlikely that the latter would do so if they believed that the published anti-cult evidence was a true indictment of cultism.

LEGISLATIVE EFFORTS

In one sense the accounts of cruelties inflicted by cults is irrelevant to the issue of constitutionality. No new laws are needed to impose criminal procedures or authorize civil lawsuits by victims of cults. Ever since the first anti-Mormon law criminalizing polygamy was upheld in the 1878 case of *Reynolds v. United States* it has been the law of the land that the Free Exercise Clause does not preclude governmental action against practices that violate basic American values.

In 1978, mass suicide of adults and homicide of children (whose parents gave them cyanide-laced Kool-Aid to drink) occurred at Jonestown, Guyana. Had the event happened within the United States it would obviously have been subject to criminal and civil response without need of judicial determination. And this would be so whether or not the People's Temple Full Gospel Church (originally affiliated with the Disciples of Christ) had remained a religion or had become a cult under the charismatic leadership of miracle-performing Jim Jones.

The difficulty in relying only upon existing laws in efforts to eradicate cultism lies in the fact that most cult leaders, or at least those financially able to engage top-ranked law firms, do not violate—or cannot easily be proved to have violated—criminal or civil laws that would land them in jail or subject them to million-dollar verdicts in lawsuits. Hence, the expressed need to enact new laws to meet the problem, even if no consideration were to be given to the political benefit that might incur to the legislators who introduce them or the prosecutors who enforce them.

California's effort in the legislative arena will be considered later in this chapter in the discussion of the Worldwide Church of God litigation, as will Minnesota's mandatory reporting law, invalidated in *Larson v. Valente*. Here it need only be noted that the statutes could only inconvenience rather than destroy cults. What was needed was an effective and constitutionally acceptable statute that could seriously injure or, hopefully, eradicate cultism.

New York's legislature thought it had found a solution in a bill introduced in 1980 and again in 1981. The first was vetoed by then Governor Hugh L. Carey on the grounds of unconstitutionality and the second, which sought to overcome that difficulty, was equally unsuccessful and was vetoed on the same grounds by Governor Mario M. Cuomo. In neither case was the legislature able to override the veto.

The purpose of these measures was to protect gullible victims from "the evils of coercive persuasion" and to accord parents legal means to regain custody of their children who had been so coercively persuaded. To achieve this end, the courts would be empowered to appoint temporary guardians of persons sixteen years or older (presumably because existing law provided adequate means to regain custody of children below that age) who were under the control of what are commonly called cults, although that word itself was not used in the bills. Coercive persuasion would be indicated by efforts on the part of the cult leaders to deprive the victims of ability to make independent decisions or act in a voluntary manner, and would do this by isolation, control of information and channels of communication, physical debilitation, intense peer pressure, lack of physical or mental privacy, abnormally long work schedules or continued performance of repetitious tasks, and other similar methods.

The measure, if enacted, would have empowered courts to appoint temporary guardians until a final decision was reached, during which period the courts could place the victim in the custody of his family and subject him to such psychological, psychiatric, and medical treatment (i.e., deprogramming) as was deemed appropriate so long as it was effected without physical force except for purpose of restraint or emergency.

Perhaps inadvertently, and to save space, the measure used the phrase "treating the temporary conservatee as if he were an incompetent." This can only mean that a cultist could be deprived not only of his property but also of his liberty if the court was persuaded that he might be a victim of cultism. In *Addington v. Texas* (1979) the Supreme Court held that a person, even if adjudicated mentally incompetent, could not constitutionally be deprived of his liberty in the absence of any evidence that he might be a risk to his own or any other person's life or safety. The New York measure contained no such condition.

In 1982 the New Jersey legislature voted in favor of a measure basically the same as the New York bill. In an apparent effort to avoid the serious injury that might result from an unfounded proceeding against an individual, the bill asserted that the subject of the proceeding must not be deprived of any right with respect to civil service employment or eligibility for state-issued licenses or permits. If, however, he sought a job in the private sector, in many cases a broadly worded questionnaire, hardly unusual, would require disclosure of the guardianship proceeding. It cannot be doubted that many a prospective employer would reject an alleged cultist without, of course, admitting that he did so because of the proceeding authorized by the legislature. And a cautious employer might do so even if the proceeding was dismissed by a court as unfounded. With so many unemployed prospects available, why take a chance?

There were other substantial problems relating to the measure. It allowed a proceeding to be instituted by an *older* brother or sister. Thus, a thirty-year-old plaintiff could resort to the procedure against a sibling of twenty-eight but not the latter against the former, and this notwithstanding the Fourteenth Amendment's Equal Protection Clause. Moreover, a section of the measure allowed the respondent to waive his right to the final hearing required by the bill. But if he was so incompetent as to justify a guardianship order against him, it would seem that the interests of justice would mandate a full hearing and one with assigned counsel. In any event, Governor Thomas H. Kean vetoed the measure.

REVEREND MOON AND THE UNIFICATION CHURCH

This brings us to contemporary judicial responses to the use of law as an instrument in the continuing war against disfavored religions.

In the period following World War II, politically ambitious legislators, prosecuting attorneys, tax revenue and other administrative officials, and even judges quickly came to recognize that there was pay dirt in anti-Communism; one of them even achieved the presidency by exploiting it. Today, with the supply of domestic Communists practically exhausted, anti-cultism can serve the same purpose, although of course to a much lesser degree.

For a number of reasons the religion created by Reverend Sun Myung

Moon, which helped serve this purpose, merits separate consideration. It is by far the most prominent cult and its leader is an alien from South Korea, presumably unable to speak the English language and thus requiring an interpreter in his dealings with the government. (Moses, too, had difficulty with oral communication and needed his brother, Aaron, to enable him to communicate with Pharaoh [Exodus 4:10; 7:2].)

Moon presented no threat to America's political-economic system. His abomination of Communism and commitment to capitalism matched those of President Reagan. Monies expended in the unsuccessful defense of his tax evasion prosecution may have exceeded those in any criminal prosecution against an individual in American history but it is unlikely that any one seriously charged that these monies came from Moscow and that Moon was a secret agent of the Soviet Union.

With respect to the number and diversity of organizations submitting or joining in *amicus curiae* briefs in support of a defendant in a criminal proceeding, the Moon appeal from his tax evasion conviction discussed in Chapter 1 is probably unprecedented. Among those submitting briefs in what ordinarily would be considered a run-of-the-mill tax evasion case were: the National Council of Churches of Christ in the U.S.A.; the Presbyterian Church (USA); the American Baptist Church in the U.S.A.; the African Methodist Episcopal Church; the National Association of Evangelicals; the Christian Legal Society; the American and New York Civil Liberties Union; the Southern Christian Leadership Conference (organized by Martin Luther King); the National Conference of Black Mayors; the National Bar Association (an organization of black lawyers); the Catholic League for Religion and Civil Rights; Church of Jesus Christ of Latter-Day Saints (Mormon Church); the Center for Judicial Studies; the Freeman Institute; the National Emergency Civil Liberties Committee; the American Association of Christian Schools; and the Institute for the Study of American Religions, a scholarly institution that had never before submitted an *amicus curiae* brief.

Other *amicus curiae* briefs in support of Moon were submitted by Orrin G. Hatch, Chairman of the Subcommittee on the Constitution of the United States, Senate Committee on the Judiciary; one brief on behalf of Catholic Bishop Ernest L. Unterkoefler, Catholics Clare Boothe Luce, Eugene J. McCarthy, Robert Destro, and a coalition of Catholic laymen; and one jointly submitted by three states—Hawaii, Oregon, and Rhode Island. The grounds for reversal set forth in these briefs varied. Among them were the unconstitutional imposition of a jury trial upon an unwilling defendant; impermissibility of government dictating the manner in which churches handle their internal funding and use their own funds;

the widespread practice, particularly among low-income churches, of depositing church funds, obviously exempt from taxation, in the name of their pastor; the equally widespread practice (as in the Catholic church) of holding church property in the name of the local bishop; and the danger to free exercise rights in allowing courts to define the content of religious belief even contrary to the good faith profession of the believers as to what they themselves believe.

Conspicuous by their absence were those major national organizations that frequently file *amicus curiae* briefs in litigation involving the Establishment and Free Exercise clauses of the First Amendment: the Joint Baptist Committee on Public Affairs, Americans United for Separation of Church and State, and the Synagogue Council of America. The reason for the abstention on the part of the first two organizations may be only a matter of conjecture but there is no doubt as to the Synagogue Council. The hate-fear syndrome in relation to cults that affect most Americans is shared even more intensely by all Jewish organizations, secular as well as religious, and by the great majority of their members, motivated by a fear of what cultism could do to Jewish children. (There were, however, no serious efforts on the part of Jewish anti-cultists to induce submission of briefs urging affirmance of the conviction.)

Intervention or nonintervention really did not matter one way or another; with no recorded dissent, the Supreme Court in 1984 refused to review Moon's conviction. The ultimate consequence may turn out to be equally or even more unwelcome to those Protestant and Catholic religious groups that submitted *amicus curiae* briefs and to the Jewish groups that did not. The trial judge rejected a government proposal that Moon, who was not an American citizen, be deported but did impose a sentence of eighteen months imprisonment. It may be assumed that with time off for good behavior the actual period of penal service may be as little as six months. That, however, may be enough to justify a claim to martyrdom, and martyrdom both before and after Jesus Christ has had the effect contrary to what the anti-cultists seek to achieve; instead of destroying a hated new creed, it enhances its potential for survival and growth.

Stripped of all constitutional questions, it is not easy to quarrel with the Supreme Court's refusal to set aside the jury's determination. A reading of the lengthy trial record and the manifest efforts on the part of the trial judge to assure fairness of trial (he went so far as to forbid use of the derogatory term "Moonies") may well lead to the conclusion that Moon was guilty of the crime with which he was charged. The problem with the government's action of prosecuting him lay in the reality of selective prosecution; as has been noted in the first chapter of this book, the trial judge acknowledged this reality but determined that it did not affect the validity of Moon's conviction. What constitutes impermissible selective prosecution is now before the Supreme Court in the cases of *United States v. Wayte* and *United States v. Schmucker,* discussed earlier in this book.

However the *Wayte* and *Schmucker* cases are decided, the fundamental issue will remain: Is it fair to use the taxing power, assigned to the federal government in Article I, Section 8, of the Constitution in order that it might raise revenue, as a means to punish an unpopular religious leader or group? As Jehovah's Witnesses can testify, the Unification Church is not the first and, in view of the government's success in the *Moon* case, will not be the last instance of attempted utilization of tax laws to punish hated religious groups; as will be seen later in this chapter, the Church of Scientology can testify to that.

The Unification Church fared considerably better in the case of *Larson v. Valente,* decided two years before the Court's rejection of the *Moon* case. (The full title of the case as originally brought before the Court was *Valente and the Holy Spirit Association for the Unification of World Christianity v. Larson and Spanner.* Valente was a follower of the Unification Church and the latter two were the State Commissioner of Securities and the Attorney General of Minnesota.) The suit was brought for an injunction against enforcement because of unconstitutionality of a 1978 Minnesota amendment to its Charitable Solicitation Act that was clearly aimed at the Unification Church and only incidentally other cults. The act, as initially adopted in 1961, was designed to protect both the public generally and the beneficiaries of bona fide charities against fraudulent practices in the solicitation of contributions for purportedly charitable purposes. It required charitable organizations to register with the state's department of commerce before soliciting contributions and thereafter to submit annual detailed reports of receipts, expenditures, and financial transactions in which they were involved. Should a report indicate that a particular organization expended more than thirty percent of its income for management or fund-raising costs, the registration would be cancelled and further fund raising forbidden.

In 1973 the churches were able to obtain an amendment exempting from the registration requirement groups serving a "bona fide religious purpose." The trouble with this effort was that many cults, and particularly the Unification Church, claimed to be bona fide religious organizations and were recognized as such by the United States Internal Revenue Service. More important, during the period between 1973 and 1975 the State of Minnesota itself recognized the Unification Church to be a bona fide religious organization and therefore exempt from the reporting requirement. So in 1978 ingenious legislators, having no doubt that the Unification Church should not be allowed to mulct innocent people, conceived of a way to make it difficult though perhaps not impossible for the Unification Church to do so.

Accordingly, they introduced a measure that would limit the exemption from required registration and reporting to religious organizations that solicited "substantially more than half of the contributions it received . . . from persons who have a right to vote as members of the organization." But before the measure was enacted, some legislator realized that it would require registration by such noncongregational religions as the Catholic church. This was not what the legislature had in mind, so before the measure was put to a vote it was amended to delete the right-to-vote phrase, thereby limiting the exemption to churches that solicited from their own members (irrespective of their right to vote) more than half of all the contributions they ultimately received.

Unfortunately, this too had its problems. As drafted, there was nothing that prevented Unification Church solicitors from according on-the-spot membership to anyone who made a contribution. So the state legislators added a sentence reading: "the term 'members' shall not include those persons who are granted a membership upon making a contribution as a result of a solicitation."

It is difficult to avoid the conclusion that these machinations had effective cooperation from the state attorney general's staff. Barely had the "fifty percent rule" amendment been approved by the governor than a member of the staff sent a letter to the Unification Church (and to no one else) reading in part:

> From the nature of your solicitation it appears that Holy Spirit Association for the Unification of World Christianity must complete a Charitable Organization Registration Statement and submit it to the Minnesota Department of Commerce. The Charitable Organization Registration Statement must be accompanied with a financial statement for the fiscal year last ended.
>
> I am enclosing the proper forms and an information sheet for your use. Please be advised that the proper forms must be on file with the Department of Commerce by September 30, 1978, or we will consider taking legal action to ensure your compliance.

This was too much for Powell. He broke away from the inevitable dissents of White, Rehnquist, Burger, and O'Connor and joined in Brennan's opinion, thereby making it the majority's decision. Since the *Everson* case, Brennan said, the Court had adhered to the principle that no state could pass laws that preferred some religions such as those passing the "fifty per cent" tests as against those (like the Unification Church) that did not. While there might be instances in which some compelling government interest would justify preferential treatment, the challenged statute was not shown to be one of them. The argument that members of a religious organization could and would exercise supervision and control to prevent misuse if their contributions exceeded fifty percent failed to explain the exemption of the Catholic church as against the nonexemption of the Unification Church. What this amounted to, he said, is impermissible "religious gerrymandering," similar to drawing election district lines to favor some parties over others.

Moreover, while the statute might pass the purpose aspect of the Establishment Clause test, it could not do the same with respect to the effect and entanglement criteria; as to the former because its primary effect was to inhibit the religion of the Unification Church, and the latter because it engendered a risk of politicizing religion, "as evidenced by the continuing debate respecting birth control and abortion." (As will be seen in the next chapter, the risk of politicizing religion did not deter the Court from upholding a statute that forbade federal financing of abortion for the poor.)

Brennan's majority opinion invoked not only the Establishment Clause but also the Free Exercise Clause. "The constitutional [i.e., Establishment] prohibition of denominational preferences," he said, "is inexorably connected with the continuing vitality of the Free Exercise Clause." He quoted in support of this assertion Madison's statement that "Security for civil rights must be the same as that for religious rights: it consists in one case in a multiplicity of interests and in the other in a multiplicity of sects."

The dissenting opinions, one by White for himself and Rehnquist and the other by Rehnquist for all four dissenters, did not respond to the constitutional issues in the majority opinion but argued that the lower court's decision in favor of the Unification Church should be set aside on what were basically technical grounds, such as the Unification Church's lack of standing to sue.

OTHER ASIAN CULTS: HARE KRISHNA

Notwithstanding its origin in South Korea, the Unification Church deems itself to be a Christian church: it all started when Moon, at the age of sixteen, received a vision in which Jesus Christ appeared to him and commissioned him to restore God's Kingdom on earth. Until the Supreme Court rules to the contrary, the church has a constitutional right to designate itself as Christian and use the term Reverend with respect to Moon even though he seems to have been self-ordained. Most other cults originating in Asia, however, do not identify themselves as Christian. Among these is the International Society for Krishna Consciousness (ISKCON).

ISKCON members are popularly known as Hare Krishnas and the sect is an offspring of Hinduism. Members are often found at airports and at railroad and bus terminals, where they approach people and request donations, usually in exchange for a carnation, lapel pin, or book about the group's teachings. Traditionally, they wear orange robes and their heads are shaved, they beat drums, shake tambourines, and engage in rhythmic chanting.

Heffron v. International Society for Krishna Consciousness (ISKCON) (1981) involved a state law authorizing the Minnesota Agriculture Society, a public corporation, to operate a fair on state-owned property and to promulgate rules for its governance. One of the rules issued by the Agriculture Society made it a misdemeanor to sell or distribute any merchandise, including written or printed material, except from a "duly licensed location."

Although the rule did not prevent organizational representatives from walking about the state-owned fair grounds and communicating with fair patrons in face-to-face discussions (the First Amendment free speech guarantee would hardly sanction that), it did require exhibitors to conduct sales, distribution, and fund solicitation operations from booths rented from the Agriculture Society.

ISKCON brought suit challenging the rule, maintaining that it would suppress the religious ritual of Sankirtan, which enjoins its members to go into all public places to distribute or sell religious literature and to solicit donations for the support of the Krishna religion.

In his majority opinion, White stated that, although the fair grounds were publicly owned property, established First Amendment free speech principles permitted reasonable government restrictions with respect to the time, place, and manner of communication so long as alternative unrestricted forums were available. ISKCON could sell its materials on public streets outside the fair grounds, and even on the fair grounds its members could merge with the crowd and orally propagate their faith, so long as they sold their religious materials only from the booth they rented. Were ISKCON permitted to sell their materials while mingling with the crowd, the same right would have to be accorded to other religious and social political and charitable organizations such as the Church of Christ, Abortion Rights Council, American Association of Retired Persons, Independent Republicans of Minnesota, Save Our Unwanted Life, Inc., Christian Education Services, and many others who had rented space at the 1978 fair.

> ISKCON . . . and its ritual of Sankirtan [said White] have no special claim to First Amendment protection as compared to that of other religions who also distribute literature and solicit funds. None of our cases suggest that the inclusion of peripatetic solicitation as part of a church ritual entitles church members to solicitation rights in a public forum superior to those of members of other religious groups that raise money but do not purport to ritualize the process.

In their complaint the plaintiffs alleged that the state's action violated both the Free Exercise and Free Speech clauses but for some unexplained reason in their brief and in oral argument their counsel stated that they rested their case solely upon their general right of free speech. Except for the two quoted sentences, the majority opinion treated the controversy as a free speech case and decided it against the plaintiffs on free speech principles. Brennan, in his dissenting opinion, stated that he was therefore "somewhat puzzled by the Court's treatment of the Sankirtan issue"; there was certainly ample precedent for consideration under the Free Exercise Clause. Before the Court in *Cantwell v. Connecticut* (1940) held for the first time that the Free Exercise Clause was applicable to the states, cases involving Jehovah's Witnesses were decided under the Free Speech Clause.

True enough, in the flag salute case, *West Virginia State Board of Education v. Barnette,* decided three years after the *Cantwell* decision, Jackson's majority opinion was predicated on the free speech rather than free exercise guarantee. Nevertheless, after 1940 it was no longer necessary to invoke the free speech claim, and the *ISKCON* case was basically one in the arena of free exercise; withdraw religion from it and the controversy makes no sense. ISKCON was not distributing free copies of the Communist Manifesto but of the Bhagavad Gita, a holy book of divine origin as ancient as the New Testament, and they were doing so because their religion required them to. Yet if White had considered the controversy as a free exercise case, he may well have been wrong in stating that none of the Supreme Court's cases justified the preferred treatment claimed by ISKCON.

There were ample precedents to this effect. During the Prohibition period Congress authorized the purchase of wine to be used for sacramental purposes but denied that privilege to those whose religion did not mandate such use. In *Wisconsin v. Yoder* (1972) the Amish were accorded preferential treatment with respect to compulsory school attendance by virtue of the Free Exercise Clause. In *Sherbert v. Verner* (1963) Seventh Day Adventists received the same preferential treatment in the administration of unemployment compensation laws. In *Thomas v. Review Board* (1981) similar preferential treatment was accorded to a Jehovah's Witness who had been denied unemployment compensation benefits for refusing on religious grounds to accept a job requiring work in a plant manufacturing weapons for war. And, finally, in the case of *In re Jennision* (1963) the Court ruled in effect that a person who for reasons of religious conscience refused to serve upon juries could not constitutionally be punished, thus according preferential treatment as against those not so inhibited.

Considered in the light of these decisions, it is difficult to justify the Court's five to four ruling against ISKCON. It may be suggested, however, that even if counsel for ISKCON had retained the free exercise claim, it is unlikely that the outcome would have been different; White indicated as much in the quoted paragraph from his opinion. All the withdrawal did was to relieve him of the need to justify the decision under free exercise grounds. He certainly had the ingenuity necessary to accomplish that task were that necessary.

One further comment on ISKCON and its treatment is relevant here. The disfavored faiths or pseudo-faiths, uniformly called cults, such as the Unification Church, the Church of Scientology, and the Worldwide Church of God, are newly formed. ISKCON, on the other hand, is almost as old as Christianity. It has nevertheless been considered and treated as a cult by legislatures, law-enforcing attorneys, and the public in general. It is therefore appropriately included in this chapter on disfavored religions, for that is what ISKCON is.

OTHER ASIAN CULTS: TRANSCENDENTAL MEDITATION

Although *Malnak v. Yogi*, decided by the Federal Court of Appeals in 1979, was not appealed to the Supreme Court, it merits reference here as another of the Asian cult cases relating to the Religion Clauses of the First Amendment. This case, however, differs from the others dealt with in this chapter in that, unlike them, the constitutional issue involved related not to the Free Exercise Clause but to the Establishment Clause.

Challenged in it was the teaching of the "Science of Creative Intelligence" and the propagation of its technique of "Transcendental Meditation" (SCI/TM) in New Jersey's public high schools. The plaintiffs in the case were taxpayers and parents; the defendants, the Maharishi Mahesh Yogi, a native of India, and the public school educational authorities, a rare instance in which government and cult were on the same side in a lawsuit. The course was offered under the title "Science of Creative Intelligence." However, unlike Christian Science and the Church of Scientology, which are claimed by their believers and practitioners to be religions, protagonists of the Science of Creative Intelligence assert that it is not a religion and therefore may constitutionally be introduced into the curriculum of public schools.

Transcendental Meditation is a technique in which the meditator contemplates a meaningless sound aid called a "mantra." The Science of Creative Intelligence is a theory, devised or promulgated by Maharishi, which purports to explain what occurs within a meditator's mind during meditation and posits that thought develops until the mind reaches the entity or "field of life," called the "field of pure creative intelligence."

The course, with the textbook designed for it, was offered as an elective in five New Jersey high schools and was taught four or five days a week. The teachers were neither selected nor paid by the school authorities but were trained and supplied by the World Plan for Creative Intelligence. According to the textbook, during TM the meditator experiences directly the field of "restful alertness" in which the mind is infused with creativity that "refines" it and the nervous system so that the expanded perceptions experienced during TM will carry over into conscious thoughts and activities. The textbook was replete with statements that creative intelligence is "the basis of life" and "the source, course and goal of all existence."

Students who registered for the SCI/TM course participated individually in a ceremony called the "puja" conducted off public school premises on a Sunday. The student was asked to bring a clean white handkerchief, a few flowers, and three or four pieces of fruit. These items were placed on a table in front of which the student stood while the teacher sang a chant in Sanskrit. Every student was required to sign a document promising never to reveal his or her mantra.

Scientific research, the promoters of SCI/TM assert in a brochure entitled "Fundamentals of Prayers," verifies their claim that the course "will improve the quality of life by allowing everyone to develop his full potential of mind and body and thereby to spontaneously contribute his maximum to progress and enjoy fulfillment in life." The brochure presents data, published in such respected journals as *Scientific American, Amer-*

ican Journal of Psychology, American Journal of Psychiatry, The Lancet, and *New England Journal of Medicine,* among many others, purporting to indicate that SCI/TM increases sociological, ecological, and physiological adaptability and improvement.

After a long and strongly contested trial, the trial court reached a decision, affirmed by the Court of Appeals, that although New Jersey's association with SCI/TM met the secular purpose aspect of the purpose-effect-entanglement principle, it failed to pass muster under the effect aspect. Creative Intelligence, both courts held, was clearly a religion and its introduction into the public school system constituted an impermissible advancement of religion. It therefore violated the Establishment Clause and its teaching had to be enjoined. For some unexplained reason neither the State of New Jersey nor Maharishi chose to appeal to the United States Supreme Court.

OTHER ASIAN CULTS: DIVINE LIGHT MISSION

Brief mention should also be made of another and considerably less notorious cult that originated in India, the Divine Light Mission. Its leader, Guru Maharaj Ji, came to the United States in 1971 and was treated by his followers as a divine being. He made Denver his national and international headquarters and for a time caused considerable interest among hippies and college youths. However, most converts dropped out after a short period of experimentation, perhaps because his doctrines prescribed celibacy and vegetarianism and forbade indulgence in alcohol, tobacco, and drugs.

Ji quickly Americanized his life. He adopted a fashionable hairstyle, wore Western clothing, and enjoyed a luxurious lifestyle complete with mansion, limousines, and hippie vocabulary. After a while, Ji himself was no longer referred to as Lord of the Universe and, although in the late seventies he was once again regarded as a quasi-divine personality, the movement itself did not reach its earlier size and wealth.

Since the tribulations of Ji or the Divine Light Mission never reached the Supreme Court, further attention to it in this book is not warranted. It is treated here along with Moon's Unification Church, ISKCON, and Transcendental Meditation because it manifests the general public assumption that cultism is not American but is an import from the Far East. However, as will be indicated in the balance of this chapter, the dominance of Far Eastern cultism is not reflected in the relevant litigation that has reached the Burger Court.

AMERICAN CULTS: FOUNDING CHURCH OF SCIENTOLOGY

There are a number of reasons that explain why most Americans regard cultism as something alien to our culture. One is that by far the most affluent of all cult leaders, Reverend Moon, came from the Far East. Another is the fact that the cult most visibly recognizable is ISKCON, whose faithful wear distinctive and patently non-American clothes. (So, too, do the Amish and Jewish Hasidim.) And the third is the natural inclination to identify what is hated and feared with what is alien to our native culture.

Nevertheless, by far the majority of cult cases reaching the courts could properly bear the label "made in America." Of these, the major litigant, either as plaintiff or as defendant, has been the Church of Scientology. Its origin and its entrance into the Valhalla of divinities are perhaps unique. It is the creation of L. Ron Hubbard, although he did, hardly convincingly, claim kinship between his theories and those espoused by Eastern religions, especially Hinduism and Buddhism.

Hubbard was born in Nebraska in 1911 and has been a world traveler most of his life. After service as a naval officer in World War II he entered into the field of science fiction and achieved modest fame before he created the technique he called "Dianetics." Resort to it, he claimed, could help cure a host of personal problems, physical as well as psychological. His article on the subject appeared in, of all places, the May 1950 issue of *Astounding Science Fiction*. It proved so popular that he expanded it into a book, *Dianetics: The Modern Science of Mental Health*, which in a short time became a best seller.

The Dianetics movement quickly spread but then a strange and what could perhaps seem to be an unprecedented evolution took place. In 1952 Hubbard created Scientology, a new therapeutic system that incorporated notions of reincarnation, extraterrestrial life, and ultimately spiritual elements, and declared it to be a religion.

Out of this came the Founding Church of Scientology, predicated upon what could hardly be considered a novel belief in healing through faith, for such beliefs are basic elements in the religions founded by Moses, Jesus Christ, and Mary Baker Eddy, to name but a few. Nor was it the only new religion that created a unique theological terminology, with words such as "Dianetics," "thetans," "clean," "engrams," "auditing," and "Scientology" itself, just as the Science of Creative Intelligence had its "Transcendental Meditation," "mantra," "field of life," and "field of pure creative intelligence."

The beliefs of Scientology center around the spirit or "thetan" that resides within the physical body of every human being. Its adherents believe that the spirit is immortal and that it receives a new body upon the death of the body in which it earlier resided. They also believe that in the course of its various lives the spirit is inhibited by "detrimental aberrations" or "engrams," which result from misdeeds or unpleasant experiences. The objective of Scientology is to counteract this burden through "processing," also called "auditing." This objective, which is the principal practice of Scientology, attempts to make the person being audited, called a "preclear," aware of these aberrations and engrams and thus reduce the burdens and inhibitions affecting his spirit. Processing is performed by ministers or persons studying to become ministers and is done in individual sessions with an auditor processing a single preclear through the use of a Hubbard Electro-Meter of "E-Meter." The E-Meter is an instrument that indicates changes in electrical resistance in the preclear's body; changes in such resistance are viewed as an index of the activity of the spirit.

The test of religion under the Free Exercise Clause is the sincerity of its believers and, at least as far as the Internal Revenue Service was concerned, the Founding Church of Scientology passed that test as indicated by the fact that it received and has retained its tax-exempt status. This does not mean that state taxing authorities may not reach a contrary conclusion; many do not. Thus, for example, in *Missouri Church of Scientology v. State Tax Commission* (1978) the Supreme Court dismissed an appeal from a decision that denied state tax exemption to the church on the ground that it was not a "religion" within the meaning of the state's tax exemption provision since, among other reasons, it did not embody "a belief in the Supreme Being." Only Stevens dissented from the dismissal, which was based on the conclusion that the appeal did not present a substantial federal question meriting consideration by the Court.

Federal recognition with respect to tax exemption does not necessarily preclude other governmental actions, federal as well as state, aimed at destroying cults if possible or, if not, at least placing obstacles in their missionary efforts. *Founding Church of Scientology v. United States* (1969) illustrates this. In that case, the federal government, acting under the Food, Drug and Cosmetics Act, obtained a decree of condemnation and destruction in relation to the E-Meter and related literature. The government did not challenge the church's claim that it was a religion, nor that use of E-Meters for "auditing" or "processing" was a sacramental act. This it considered immaterial, since the First Amendment protects only religious *beliefs; action* in the name of religion was subject to legal regulation under the same standards and to the same degree as it would be if entirely secular in purpose. For its part, the church argued that auditing or processing was a central practice of their religion, akin to confession in the Catholic church, and therefore exempt from regulation or prohibition. In a decision, which over Douglas's lone dissent the Supreme Court refused to review, the Court of Appeals held that the positions of both parties were erroneous.

The correct test, said the Court of Appeals, was the one promulgated in the *Ballard* decision. What the church preached and taught was subject to judicial action if the beliefs asserted to be religious were not held in good faith by those asserting them and if the forms of religious organization were created for the sole purpose of cloaking a secular enterprise with the legal protection of religion. The claim of the Founding Church of Scientology that it was a bona fide religion was not challenged by the government. Nevertheless, to protect human life and safety, adulterated foods, drugs, or devices may well be condemned even if used in bona fide religious practices, and the claim of religious freedom would not necessarily prevent government action.

At the conclusion of its opinion the Court of Appeals summarized what it held and did not hold substantially as follows:

1. Since the government did not offer any evidence to controvert that of the church, the latter must be held to be a bona fide religion.

2. For the same reason, auditing is a religious practice.

3. The *Ballard* doctrine precluded judicial determination that the E-Meter and "auditing" literature constitute "false or misleading labeling" in violation of the Food, Drug and Cosmetics Act.

4. It was still open to the government to prove that the beliefs asserted to be religious were not held in good faith by those asserting them and that the Church of Scientology was established "for the sole purpose of cloaking a secular enterprise with the legal protection of religion."

5. Even if Scientology was a religion, not all literature published by it was religious doctrine immune from the act.

6. Public health laws in general may have application to a bona fide religion, since adulterated foods, drugs, or devices in religious practices can be condemned under the act for misbranding or failure to provide adequate directions for safe use.

7. Finally, no holding was made concerning the extent of Congress' power to deal generally with the making of false claims deemed injurious to the public health or welfare, even if such claims are made by religions.

(In *Swann v. Pack* [1975], a case not appealed to the Supreme Court, Tennessee's highest court ruled that the pastor and elders of the Holiness Church of God in Jesus Name could be forbidden to handle poisonous snakes or consume strychnine even though the doctrine of the church impelled such action.)

Government institutions, such as tax collecting agencies or legislative bodies, can resort to law as a means to curb cults, but astute private attorneys and their clients can also resort to it as a possible source of substantial monetary gains. *Christofferson v. Church of Scientology* (1982) attests to this.

Christofferson, a liberated former member of the church, brought a suit on the claim that the church enticed her into membership. She had become involved with the Church of Scientology through a friend who was taking vocational courses from the church's mission in Portland, Oregon. Deciding to take communication courses, and upon being told that only members of the church were eligible to register, she applied and was accepted as a member. Thereafter she worked as a provisional staff member and resided at a church-owned educational institution. After two months' residence she was asked to leave until she could convince her mother to stop opposing her involvement in Scientology. She thereupon took up residence with other Scientologists and got a job as a waitress.

Upon return to her parents' house for a visit, she was locked up and "deprogrammed." The effort proved exceptionally effective; not only did she terminate her relationship with the church but became active in anti-Scientology and participated in "deprogramming" others who had become Scientologists. Moreover, her suit against the church was won handsomely. The jury handed down a verdict in her favor in the sum of two million, three thousand dollars—three thousand dollars representing tuition she had paid and two million dollars as punitive damages.

The Oregon Supreme Court did not reverse the judgment because the amount of the jury's verdict, including the award for punitive damages, was unconstitutionally excessive and unreasonable. Yet by its name the concept of punitive damages in any civil suit would seem strange to nonlawyers; if a defendant is to be punished for wrongdoing, the proof of guilt should be beyond a reasonable doubt, rather than merely by a preponderance of the evidence as in civil suits, and the trial should be subject to other limitations applicable to criminal proceedings. Moreover, the Eighth Amendment forbids the imposition of excessive fines, and imposition of one in an amount sixty-six times as large as the sum mulcted from Christofferson would seem to be excessive.

In its appeal the church argued that the imposition of any punitive damages was unconstitutional because it would violate protection of both freedom of speech and religion. The church did not, however, argue the question of excessiveness of the two-million-dollar award and the Court naturally did not consider or pass upon that question; it ruled only that imposition of punitive damages was of itself not unconstitutional. It did, however, order a new jury trial, which could conceivably result either in a verdict for the church or one against it but in an amount substantially lower than that imposed in the first trial and accepted by the lower court. If the jury did not do so, the issue of excessiveness could probably be litigated at the trial and the trial judge could decrease the amount or eliminate it altogether.

The Court ordered a new trial because it deemed the trial judge's instructions to the jury to be erroneous. He directed it to examine each misrepresentation allegedly made by the church or its agents and decide whether each was religious or was held out to Christofferson as religious in nature. What the judge should have done was to instruct the jury to decide whether, even though the church was a religious organization, it offered the instruction services on a wholly nonreligious basis.

Assuming that a jury of nonlawyers could really understand the difference between the instructions that were given and those that should have been given, it is highly unlikely that it would have made any difference. The reality of the situation was that the defendant was a detested and feared cult (at least some parents on the jury would think, if not say, "My God, this could happen to me!"); the two-million-dollar verdict for punitive damages attests to this.

In any event, neither the church nor Christofferson was happy with the decision, and each called upon the United States Supreme Court to reverse it and either reinstate the trial judge's decision (as Christofferson wanted) or throw the whole case out of court (as the church wanted). The Court did neither and the controversy was returned to the lower court for a new trial.

AMERICAN CULTS: WORLDWIDE CHURCH OF GOD

Three times, during its 1979–1980 term, the Supreme Court refused to review a takeover by the State of California not only of all the properties and assets of the Worldwide Church of God but also of its function in engaging and dismissing personnel, including clergymen conducting religious services.

Imagine, if you can, Madalyn Murray O'Hair, accompanied by a court marshall, entering a Catholic church during Sunday mass, informing the priest that he was discharged, and personally taking over his sacred duties. Impossible? Of course, but only because Catholicism is not considered a cult, as was the Worldwide Church of God in the eyes of the California attorney general. It is doubtful that many of the millions of Americans who for fifty years listened first to the radio and later also to the television sermons of Herbert W. Armstrong, founder and spiritual leader of the church, considered it to be anything other than a Christian church.

What, then, made the Worldwide Church of God a cult? After all, cults do not usually use radio and television as an instrument to spread their faith. Earlier in this chapter reference was made to Madison's letter complaining about the jailing of men who published "religious sentiments, which in the main [were] very orthodox." True enough, Armstrong's church did differ in some respects from conventional Protestantism. For example, it declared Saturday rather than Sunday to be the divinely ordained Sabbath (a convert to the faith, Bobby Fischer, world-renowned chess champion, refused to compete in matches on Saturdays) but so did other non-cult faiths such as those of the Jews, Seventh Day Adventists, and Seventh Day Baptists.

The transformation of Armstrong's Radio Church of God into the theology and ecclesiastical structure of the Worldwide Church of God and then to the unwelcome status of a cult engaged in a bitter struggle for survival came about by coincidence of two unforeseeable events. The first was a disagreement between Armstrong and his son, Garner Ted, which led to the expulsion of the latter and his later establishment of his own Church of God, International. The other was the tragedy at Jonestown, which sparked an almost hysterical fear of cultism.

Richard Nixon, a Californian, ultimately achieved the presidency through his crusade against Communism. Perhaps California's attorney general, George Deukmejian, was motivated at least in part by a hope that anti-cultism would serve the same purpose now that domestic Communism was realistically no longer a significant producer of fear and hate. In any event, Deukmajian, a Republican, was elected governor in 1982, a year in which Republican candidates for governorships did not do well.

The Worldwide Church of God was not the only cult subjected to investigation by Deukmajian. In all, twelve groups, including the Synanon Foundation and the Faith Center Church, were targeted for investigation. But at that time the most newsworthy of them was by far the one aimed at the Worldwide Church of God. Only the Worldwide Church of God was the subject of a takeover effort and it was the only one that instituted proceedings to terminate the investigation.

In *Worldwide Church of God v. Superior Court* the Supreme Court thrice rejected appeals based upon claims that the state's action violated the Religion Clauses of the First Amendment and the Fourth Amendment's ban on unreasonable searches and seizures, but the California legislature brought an end to the investigation. In June 1980 it enacted a law withdrawing from the attorney general power to conduct investigations (except in criminal cases) of religious organizations. Although the measure provided that its effective date was to be June 1, 1981, so that the investigations of the Worldwide Church of God and other cults could continue during that period, Deukmajian publicly announced that he was dropping all the pending investigations, including that of the Synanon Foundation, thus making unnecessary any further appeals to the Supreme Court.

AMERICAN CULTS: SYNANON FOUNDATION

Notwithstanding Deukmajian's generosity, the Synanon Foundation, a drug rehabilitation program that became a religious cult, is not yet out of trouble with government authorities. Once praised by many for its program of treating heroin addicts, and accorded tax exemption as a religious organization, it came to be called a cult after it adopted a communal type of organization, accepted addicts as permanent members, and later evolved into a paramilitary structure. The degeneration reached its nadir when its founder, Charles Dederich, warned in a 1977 speech: "Don't mess with us. You can get killed. Physically dead."

That Dederich was in earnest is indicated when an attorney, who had won a three-hundred-thousand-dollar settlement against Synanon, was bitten by a rattlesnake placed in his mailbox. (Dederich and two other members of Synanon were convicted of conspiracy to murder.) Later a producer for NBC received repeated threats following the broadcast of a not quite friendly report on the cult.

These were but two of a series of instances in which opponents or investigators of Synanon were threatened and intimidated. The situation reached a point where the Internal Revenue Service could no longer ignore it and accordingly revoked Synanon's tax-exempt status that it had received in 1960 as a rehabilitation and religious association. The government, defending the revocation, contended that exemption was not warranted because Synanon's earnings in a variety of fund raising businesses were diverted to private use and because its policy of "terror and violence" did not conform to the requirement that a tax-exempt organization "must serve a public benefit." In February 1984 the Federal District Court in Washington, D.C., dismissed Synanon's suit to regain its tax-exempt status. In his decision Judge Charles B. Richey determined that Synanon's officers had engaged in "willful, systematic and intensive destruction and alteration of tapes" needed to assess Synanon's right to exemption.

In the chronicle of history the Synanon experience may be unique. Historically, the progress of disfavored faiths has been upward towards acceptability in the family of religions; with the Synanons, it was the reverse—from religion to cult. In the latter role, it has joined the chamber of horrors and has become oft-invoked evidence supporting enactment of anti-cult legislation.

AMERICAN CULTS: BLACK MUSLIMS

The Black Muslim faith has been partly considered in the section of Chapter 5 that deals with prisons but it merits further consideration here. It did not originate in prisons, nor are prisoners the only blacks who have embraced the faith. Muhammad Ali claimed exemption from military service not only as a conscientious objector but also as a minister of that faith and only the former aspect was considered by the Supreme Court. Ali is not the only prominent black athlete who has embraced the Black Muslim faith and adopted a Muslim sounding name; so too did Kareem Abdul-Jabbar, the basketball star. Among black nonathletes who adopted an Islamic name upon joining the faith is Abdul Akbar Muhammad, righthand man to Louis Farrakhan, who brought so much trouble to Jesse Jackson, Walter Mondale, American Jews, and the Democratic Party.

Notwithstanding its name (it is also called by some of its adherents the Nation of Islam) and its acceptance of some Islamic commandments, e.g., prayer five times daily and prohibition of smoking, drinking, gambling, and taking narcotics, the faith of Black Muslims is basically American. It was founded in 1930 by Wali Farad, a resident of Detroit, who claimed to be "Allah in person." Four years later he disappeared mysteriously and leadership of the group was taken over by Elijah Poole, a resident of Georgia, who adopted the name of Elijah Mahammad and called himself the "Messenger of Allah." He was imprisoned during World War II and it may have been there that the Black Muslim faith really took root.

Why an emulated foreign faith should become so popular among blacks in the United States is a matter of speculation. A reasonable assumption rests upon the unfriendly treatment they suffered from the established Protestant, Catholic, and Jewish religions. The consequence was resort to black variations of Christianity, such as Jehovah's Witnesses and the churches of Father Divine and Jim Jones. (There were even efforts by some blacks to find refuge in Judaism, resulting in the formation of B'nai Israel and similar minute groups, no more welcome within Jewry than within Christianity.) Jehovah's Witnesses have achieved recognition as a religion; Father Divine's and Jim Jones's efforts have proved unsuccessful. Black Muslims have not yet made it but seem,to be on the way.

Black Muslims have been particularly successful in prisons and their efforts have resulted in litigation that has reached the courts, including the Supreme Court. *Cooper v. Pate* was one of the cases that did. There, the prosecuting attorney, in an unsuccessful effort to justify a warden's denial of a prisoner's request for permission to purchase certain Islamic religious publications, introduced evidence seeking to show that the "Black Muslim Movement despite its pretext of a religious facade, is an organization that outside of prison walls, has for its object the overthrow of the white race, and inside prison walls, has an impressive history of inciting riots and violence." The Supreme Court ruled to the contrary; it held that prison authorities cannot constitutionally deny prisoners permission to purchase certain religious publications and deny other privileges enjoyed by other prisoners.

Cooper v. Pate was decided in 1964, before Burger was appointed to the Supreme Court in 1969, but it was not long thereafter that it too was faced with claims by Black Muslims of discriminatory treatment in prisons. In *Knuckles v. Prasse* (1971) it refused, over Douglas's dissent, to review a decision that prison authorities could constitutionally forbid prisoners to wear Black Muslim medallions, censor Black Muslim publications, and monitor collective worship services with visiting Muslim ministers to make sure that the latter did not urge defiance of prison authorities.

The progress of the Black Muslims' efforts to be recognized as a bona fide religion rather than a cult was manifested by the 1976 decision in the case of *Finney v. Hutto.* There the District Court ruled that Black Muslim prison inmates of an Arkansas prison were entitled to the same privileges in the area of religious worship, including visits by clergymen, as were accorded inmates adhering to generally recognized faiths. The District Court's ruling that the wardens' treatment of Black Muslim prisoners with respect to solitary confinement, daily meals of fewer than one thousand calories, overcrowding, and inadequate toilet facilities violated the Eighth Amendment's ban on cruel and unusual punishment was appealed. The prison authorities prudently decided not to contest the religious worship issue.

SUMMARY

1. The word "cult," acceptable as it might be in the arena of sociology, contemporary literature, drama, and popular impressions, is not a legal term, at least not within the scope of constitutional law. It can be suggested, only half facetiously, that a cult is something that if you like it, it is a religion; if you don't care one way or another about it, it is a sect; but if you fear and hate it, it is a cult.

Since there is no legal definition of what constitutes a "cult," the term should perhaps not be used in lawsuits. It is pejorative rather than neutral and is employed only by its adversaries; at the Moon trial, the prosecuting attorney, the presiding judge, and (obviously) defense counsel carefully avoided use of the term.

2. Historically, what is new is the name. At some time or another within the past three centuries disfavored religions that would today be called cults encompassed among others Catholics, Baptists, Jews, Quakers, Mormons, and Jehovah's Witnesses. Once they achieved popular acceptability they were no longer cults but respected members of the family of religions. Groups that fail to achieve that enviable status (and the great majority, including the "I Am" movement and believers in the divinity of Father Divine) pass away and become only footnotes in books on the history of religion. In short, survivability may be the best test of non-cultism.

3. The faiths, I Am, Jehovah's Witnesses, Father Divine, Scientology, Worldwide Church of God, Black Muslims, Jim Jones's Peoples Temple, and the Alamo Christian Foundation (discussed in Chapter 6), among many others, were American born; the notion that all or most cults are recent imports from the Far East is erroneous.

4. Erroneous too is the assumption that all cult leaders are inordinately rich and have acquired their wealth through mulcting trusting victims. Those who do are the exceptions rather than the rule, and become newsworthy at least in part because of that fact.

5. Use of the term "Science," as in Christian Science, Church of Scientology, and Science of the Creative Intelligence-Transcendental Meditation, neither precludes nor establishes the applicability of the Religion Clauses of the First Amendment.

6. Recognition of a group as a religion does not necessarily immunize it from government action, criminal or civil. While the Free Exercise Clause extends beyond merely freedom to believe and encompasses freedom to act in accordance with belief, it does not preclude, among many others, prosecution for tax evasion, perjury, or endangering human life.

Religion must yield to governmental police power to protect public health and safety. Inducing homicide of children, as in the Jim Jones incident, is not protected by the Free Exercise Clause.

7. Permissible action against cultists must be governmental; anti-cultists may not take the law into their own hands. Kidnapping and "deprogramming" of alleged victims of cultist "mind control" are constitutionally subject to criminal prosecution or civil lawsuits.

8. Some cults attribute a degree of divinity to the founder. The cults of Father Divine and Sun Myung Moon are examples. (Of course, so too do Christians with respect to Jesus.) Most, perhaps, do not, but all attribute some unique personal relationship between the founder and the divinity (as do Jews with respect to Moses). That relationship enables them to engage in two-way communication rather than the exclusive one-way communication that is the basis of all prayer.

9. The leader's ability to perform miracles is another attribute often present among cultists; Father Divine is an example. It is also found in Catholicism and Hasidic Judaism. (With respect to the former, canonization or beatification requires proof of two miracles, or in certain instances, four. The continuing prevalence of belief in miracles among Hasidic Jews is attested to by a satirical Yiddish ditty composed by some anonymous enemy of Hasidism: "The *rebbe* [Hasidic term for rabbi] performs miracles. I myself have seen it. He goes into the water and comes out wet.")

10. Since the *Ballard* decision, the protagonists' sincerity has been the test that distinguishes constitutionally protected religion from unprotected cultism. Its presence or absence is a question of fact to be decided by the jury rather than by the judge (except where both parties waive trial by jury).

11. Finally, on the whole, American courts have treated cults well and have recognized and enforced their rights under the Religion Clauses of the First Amendment. Even the judge who sentenced Moon to prison for tax evasion refused to order his deportation as urged by the government, although the eighteen-month prison sentence might, under the circumstances, be considered to be excessive.

CHAPTER

8

Religion and the Family

POPULATION CONTROL: CONTRACEPTION

The bitter struggle revolving about abortion and to a lesser extent contraception reflects another instance in which the Reagan-Catholic-fundamentalist (e.g., Moral Majority, Orthodox Jewish) coalition has been so prominent in recent years. Here, as in the case of aid to parochial schools, Reagan's position appears somewhat anomalous. He won the 1980 election in large measure because of his assault upon excessive taxation resulting from wasteful expenditures of public funds and his promise to reduce the national budget in all domestic areas (i.e., excluding those relating to defense against the Soviet Union). Yet his pro-parochial school aid and anti-abortion efforts would, if successful, adversely affect efforts to reduce taxes since success would necessarily increase expenditures in both areas.

With respect to school aid, this is obvious, but it is no less true where birth control through contraception or abortion is involved. Well-to-do and even middle-income parents can afford contraception devices and, where necessary, can finance their daughter's trip to Sweden or some other country where abortions are licit. This option is not open to the poor, with the unavoidable consequence of increased welfare rolls at taxpayers' expense. As will be indicated shortly, this reality, ignored by Reagan, was recognized by many state legislatures and other government officials.

The contraception issue had faced the Supreme Court before Burger became Chief Justice and Reagan became president. In the 1965 case of *Griswold v. Connecticut* the Court was called upon to adjudicate the constitutionality of a Connecticut law forbidding what was euphemistically called "birth control."

Contraception was deemed sinful by many Protestant leaders long before 1930, when Pope Pius XI issued an encyclical against the practice, citing in its support Genesis 38:9. It is also noteworthy that since Talmudic times Orthodox Judaism, relying on the same Biblical verse, has forbidden contraception, at least on the part of the man. The Court, in the *Griswold* case (in an opinion by Douglas), sought to meet the constitutional problem by finding within the Bill of Rights a previously unrecognized protected right of marital privacy that forbade government intrusion into domestic bedrooms. In its opinion it emphasized, by using italics, that the defendants, the Planned Parenthood League and a professor at Yale Medical School, prescribed devices only to *"married persons."*

However, this effort proved inadequate since unwanted pregnancies are not visited exclusively upon married couples. In *Eisenstadt v. Baird* (1972) the Burger Court, relying upon the Equal Protection Clause of the Fourteenth Amendment, ruled that unmarried persons could likewise not be denied access to contraceptive material. Finally, in *Carey v. Population Services International* (1977) it ruled unconstitutional a New York law forbidding the sale of contraceptives to minors under sixteen under all circumstances and to persons over that age by anyone other than a licensed pharmacist.

Reality impelled the Court's contraception decisions. At a conference on October 18, 1983, the director general of the United Nations Food and Agriculture Organization cited extreme population growth as one of the reasons for catastrophic food shortages in twenty-two African countries. According to the *New York Times* of July 11, 1984, the World Bank (officially, the International Bank for Reconstruction and Development) reported that the earth's population might double to ten billion by the year 2050. The United States government, in its program of aid to underdeveloped countries, had already established the policy of not only sanctioning birth control but also of affirmatively financing it. It did this because it recognized that limitations on population expansion had to be resorted to lest ultimately everyone would starve, thus verifying T. S. Eliot's prophecy that the world would end not with the bang of nuclear explosion but with the whimper of universal starvation. (The August 17, 1984, issue of the *National Catholic Reporter* quotes Robert McNamara, former World Bank president, as saying: "Short of thermonuclear war itself, population growth is the gravest issue that faces the world over the decades ahead.")

Reagan did not agree. A draft position paper prepared by administration officials described population growth as a "natural phenomenon" that might in fact stimulate economic growth. The paper cited the United

States as an example of a country where this had occurred, blandly ignoring the reality that contraceptive birth control is practiced by almost all married couples in this country. (The most notable exceptions are surprisingly not Catholics, and this notwithstanding the continued condemnation of the Holy See, but some, though by no means all, Protestant fundamentalists and Orthodox Jews.) To Reagan, the localized crisis of population growth was evidence of too much government control and planning and suggested that the United States might reduce financing for population programs.

POPULATION CONTROL: ABORTION

Reagan did not go that far. The administration's position was a rejection of "compulsion or coercion in family planning programs" but not of uncoercive programs. Abortion, however, was a different matter. In an unqualified statement the United States warned that it would no longer "contribute directly or indirectly to family programs funded by governments that advocate abortion as an instrument of population control." (The word "directly" was obviously used to avoid the device of financing abortions through non-World Bank funds and using the World Bank funds to finance contraceptive birth control.)

The United States was more successful in this than in contraceptive birth control. As reported in the August 12, 1984, issue of the *New York Times,* the United Nations International Conference adopted a recommendation that abortion "in no way should be promoted" as a family planning method. According to the report, the Vatican had urged adoption of a recommendation that "abortion should be excluded as a method of family planning, rather than being merely not promoted." According to the *Times* report, adoption of the resolution, even though so limited, was viewed as a victory for the United States and the Vatican.

In the United States, allowing unfettered access to contraception, and even sanctioning use of tax-raised funds to finance it as many states did, proved inadequate to meet the overpopulation problem. The poor were continuing to have too many babies and the fathers, if known (laws in some states compelled naming them) and could be found, were often too poor to support them.

When governor of California, Reagan, like other governors, was confronted with the budgetary burden of unwanted pregnancies. A committee appointed by him to recommend means to cope with the problem of growing welfare rolls considered the enactment of a law mandating forfeiture for adoption of all a woman's illegitimate children after the second. The measure, however, deemed too Draconian for public acceptance, was rejected by the legislature.

American conscience could not accept allowing unaffordable babies, once born, to die for want of food and shelter. Prevention by contraception having proved ineffective, abortion was the only remaining alternative, at least until the medical profession could come up with some other means to ease the taxpayer's burden. The apparently unsurmountable obstacle lay in the reality that, unlike anti-contraception statutes, those forbidding abortion had not, in a large majority of states, been repealed or left unenforced.

The constitutionality of anti-abortion laws was passed upon by the Burger Court in the 1973 landmark case of *Roe v. Wade* and companion case of *Doe v. Bolton.* The Court held that most laws criminalizing abortions violated the Due Process Clause in the Fifth and Fourteenth amendments. For the first trimester of pregnancy, it held, abortion was a woman's absolute right. For the second trimester, a state could regulate abortion procedures in a way reasonably related to maternal health. For the stage subsequent to viability (i.e., the third trimester), a state could, if it chose, forbid abortions except where necessary to preserve the life or health of the mother.

There are a number of significant and to some extent surprising aspects relating to these cases. In the first place, it is not the usual practice for a court to give legal advice to parties in a lawsuit. Usually, it restricts itself to deciding whether or not a challenged statute is constitutional; it does not offer advice to legislators as to how other statutes with specific procedures relating to the different trimesters could be drafted without violating the Constitution.

Second, the Court's opinion was written by Blackmun with the concurrence of Burger and Powell, all three Nixon appointees. Concurring, too, were Brennan and Stewart, who were appointees of another Republican president, Eisenhower. The only concurring justice not appointed by a Republican president was Marshall, a Johnson appointee. The two dissenters, White and Rehnquist, were appointed respectively by President Kennedy, a Democrat, and Nixon, a Republican. One would not ordinarily expect so radical, almost revolutionary, a decision to be handed down by a Court, seven of whose nine members were appointed by presidents belonging to the presumably conservative party.

Finally, and most unexpectedly, this conservative Court reached its conclusion by expanding the Bill of Rights. This was not really unprecedented. In 1925, a Court, six of whose nine members had been appointed by Republican presidents, handed down a decision (written by a Harding appointee) in the case of *Gitlow v. New York* based upon the premise that freedom of speech and of the press—which are protected by the First Amendment from abridgment by Congress—are among the fundamental personal rights and "liberties" protected by the Due Process Clause of the Fourteenth Amendment from impairment by the states. From this dictum came the series of Supreme Court decisions holding, with only slight exceptions, that all rights protected under the Bill of Rights against national impairment were equally protected against state impairments. The *Gitlow* decision was one of the great landmarks in the American history of freedom and liberty, and to the majority in America who do not consider abortion to be murder but rather a woman's inherent right, the holding in *Roe v. Wade* is in the same class.

It is therefore not surprising that the Court struggled long in disposing of this case. It was first argued in December of 1971, reargued in October of 1972, decided in January of 1973, and reaffirmed by denying a motion for a rehearing in February of 1973. It was one of the most significant decisions in the arena of church-state relations handed down by the Burger Court (the other was *Lemon v. Kurtzman*), and this notwith-standing the Court's initial refusal to recognize the church-state issue; instead it decided the case on a right not mentioned in the Constitution, that of personal (rather than only marital) privacy, written into the Constitution a year earlier in the *Eisenstadt* case. Blackmun sought to trace this back to the 1891 case of *Union Pacific Railway Company v. Botsford.* There the Court held that a woman in a suit for personal injuries could not constitutionally be required to subject herself to a surgical examination before trial even though it be made in a "manner not to expose the person of the plaintiff in any indelicate manner." The Court's ruling, applicable to male as well as female plaintiffs, has long since been overruled, although it is still generally the practice to allow the plaintiff to opt for a doctor of his of her own sex. This right, Blackmun said, was to be found in the Fifth and Fourteenth amendments, which provide that no person shall "be deprived of life, liberty, or property without due process of law."

The Due Process Clause, however, guarantees not only "liberty" but also "life." If what the Court and pro-choice advocates call a fetus and anti-abortionists an unborn child is a person, would not abortion deprive him or her of life without due process of law? The "person" in the womb had not committed a crime, and certainly not one warranting capital punishment. And even if abortion were deemed necessary to preserve the woman's life so that the plea of self-defense could be asserted, would not the same Due Process Clause require a trial by jury after an indictment on a charge warranting the death penalty? Would not the "person" have a right to counsel and protection against compelled self-incrimination and unlawful searches and seizures?

Undoubtedly recognizing these difficulties, the Court resorted to what appears to be the only available response—a determination that a fetus is not a "person" within the purview of the Constitution. Nevertheless, the state has an important legitimate interest in "potential" life and could therefore proscribe abortion after viability (i.e., the last trimester when the fetus has the capability of meaningful life outside the mother's womb) unless continued pregnancy endangered the woman's life.

What is most significant about the Court's opinion, at least in relevance to this book, is not what it said but what it did not say. Although urged to do so in some of the briefs presented to it, the Court refused to decide whether or not anti-abortion laws violated the First Amendment's prohibition of laws respecting an establishment of religion or prohibiting its free exercise. In his opinion, Blackmun did note that religious training was one of the several factors likely to influence one's views about abortion; and in the historical preface he did mention the Christian theology and canon law that fixed the point of "animation," or the beginning of life, forty days for a male and eighty days for a female. More than that the opinion noted that Jews, Catholics, and Protestants had differing views on when life begins and therefore on the legitimacy of abortion. But beyond that, Blackmun did not go; he made no mention, for example, of the claim that anti-abortion laws constituted impermissible aid to those religions that judged abortions to be sinful.

Yet ignoring the religious aspects of the abortion controversy was like playing Hamlet, if not without the Dane, then without the Dane's father; the ghost of religion simply would not disappear. The forty/eighty "animation" concept is no longer part of Catholic theology, having been replaced by the doctrine that human life begins at conception. Abortion was therefore even more sinful than contraception, since the latter prevents human life from coming into existence, while the former destroys it after it has achieved that status. Unlike other controversial decisions, there is little dissent on this issue from organized Catholicism; liberal Catholic voices, such as those of the editors of *America, Commonweal,* and the *National Catholic Reporter,* assailed the Court and its decision, although not as intensely as the priests and bishops. To most of them, abortion was murder.

The only exceptions have been two small unaffiliated groups known as Catholics for a Free Choice and more recently the National Coalition of

American Nuns. The latter group expressed its opposition to abortion but asserted that responsibility in this matter rested not with government but with those personally involved. (As reported in the *New York Times* of May 28, 1982, it stated: "It is paradoxical to us that the same leaders who are currently demanding that women bring their babies to term are simultaneously voting to cut off food stamps, child nutrition programs and related benefits essential for the health and well-being of our children.")

Views such as these were rare. Justice Blackmun reported that ten years after the *Roe* decision was announced, he continued to receive thousands of protesting letters, many calling him a murderer, a butcher, a Pontius Pilate, and the equivalent of Nazi overseers of genocide *(New York Times,* January 18, 1983).

It should not be assumed that the Catholic church was alone in assailing the Court's decision; the Lutheran Missouri Synod, the Mormon church, and Orthodox Judaism, among others, were non-Catholic creeds that adjudged abortion to be sinful. Indeed, so had Protestantism and Judaism generally before the spectre of famine and overpopulation came on the world scene. However, by large majorities American Protestantism and Judaism today support the *Roe* decision. (Surprising as it may seem, so too do Catholic laymen, although not by large majorities.) Moreover, many deeply resent what they deem to be the efforts of the Catholic church to impose upon all its own theology not merely by persuasion but by the coercive arm of the law.

What disturbs many of them even more is the position taken by President Reagan on the subject of population control, particularly in light of his efforts to simultaneously reduce expenditures for relief of the millions of undernourished children in the United States and of the even many more starving children in Third World countries. Despite this, Reagan expressed opposition to the *Roe v. Wade* decision and support of a constitutional amendment to overrule it.

Laws seeking to overcome or limit as far as possible *Roe v. Wade* and *Doe v. Bolton* have been enacted in more than a few states. Typical was a Missouri law, held in large part unconstitutional in *Planned Parenthood of Central Missouri v. Danforth* (1976), which required, among other things, the written consent to the abortion on the part of the woman's spouse or, in the case of an unmarried woman under eighteen, of a parent, unless in either case a licensed physician certified that the abortion was necessary to preserve the mother's life. The statute also required the physician to preserve the life and health of the fetus at whatever stage of pregnancy and imposed criminal (manslaughter) and civil liabilities upon a physician who failed to take measures necessary to sustain its life.

Anti-abortionists were more successful in *Harris v. McRae* (1980). This was a suit challenging the constitutionality of the so-called Hyde Amendment (tacked on as a rider to the annual appropriation bill financing the Medicaid program) forbidding financing of abortion procedures "except where the life of the mother would be endangered if the fetus were carried to term; or except for such medical procedures necessary for the victims of rape or incest, when such rape or incest has been reported promptly to a law enforcement agency or public health service."

An attorney's application to be appointed counsel for Children Unborn and Born Alive, a motion by the Legal Defense Fund for Unborn Children to file an *amicus curiae* brief, and a motion by some members of the House of Representatives to participate in the argument in support of constitutionality were made to the Court and all were denied. Their efforts, however, proved to be unnecessary. Reversing the lower court decision, the Supreme Court upheld the validity of the Hyde Amendment. While, said the Court in an opinion by Stewart, it had upheld the right of a woman to choose abortion rather than birth, it did not thereby hold that the government had to pay for the procedure, and the result that the poor could not avail themselves of a privilege open to the wealthy and middle classes did not give rise to a government obligation to equalize the situation. Therefore, exclusion of abortion did not violate the equal protection guarantee in the Due Process Clause of the Fourteenth Amendment.

In the *Harris* case, the Court for the first time addressed itself to the assertion that limitations on abortion violated the Establishment and Free Exercise clauses of the First Amendment. Both contentions were presented in the brief of the plaintiff, a Medicaid recipient (represented by counsel for the American Civil Liberties Union), and an *amicus curiae* brief submitted on behalf of a number of Protestant and Jewish organizations (and also Catholics for a Free Choice), including among others the United Methodist Church, the Church of the Brethren, the Disciples of Christ, and the Union of American Hebrew Congregations.

With respect to the Establishment Clause, the briefs asserted that the purpose and effect of the law was to advance the religion of the Catholic church and the other religions that deemed abortion sinful, that it entangled government in political divisions along religious lines, and that it preferred those religions that deem abortions sinful over those that do not. Also asserted was the claim that the Hyde rider violated the Free Exercise Clause in that it impinged upon the freedom of those whose faiths mandated medically or economically necessary abortions even in absence of clear danger to the woman's life.

Stewart made short shrift of these contentions. The statute, he said, was not unconstitutional simply because it "happens to coincide or harmonize with the tenets of some or all religions. That the Judaeo-Christian religions oppose stealing does not mean that a State or the Federal Government may not, consistent with the Establishment Clause, enact laws prohibiting larceny."

Although the Court divided by the expected five to four division, none of the dissenting opinions by Brennan, Marshall, Blackmun, and Stevens expressed any disagreement with Stewart's disposition of religious contentions. Yet this reasoning leaves much to be desired. It just doesn't "happen" that restrictions on abortion coincide with the tenets of some religions; if they did not coincide, it is hardly likely that the statute would have been enacted. Moreover, stealing is also a punishable offense in atheistic countries such as the Soviet Union and was so before the Judaeo-Christian religions came on the scene. The millions of devoutly religious Protestants and Jews who oppose anti-abortion laws could justly feel offended by the implication that they would sanction stealing were it not a statutory offense. Did the Supreme Court itself in *Roe v. Wade* sanction larceny as long as it was committed within a specified trimester?

The Court was slightly more charitable with respect to the Free Exercise Clause. It did not declare it untenable but ruled that the claim had not been raised by Cora McRae or any of the other individual plaintiffs, who therefore apparently did not feel that their religious beliefs had been violated. The co-plaintiffs (officers of the women's division of a Protestant church) the Court held had no standing to raise the issue since they did not allege that they were then pregnant, or expected to become pregnant, or were eligible recipients of Medicaid.

Those who on the basis of the *McRae* decision hopefully awaited further Supreme Court acceptance of substantial limitations on permissible abortions were disappointed when, in 1983, the Court announced its decision in the case of *City of Akron v. Akron Center for Reproductive Health, Inc.* An ordinance in that city required all abortions after the first trimester of pregnancy to be performed in a hospital; prohibited physicians to perform abortions on an unmarried minor under fifteen without the consent of one of her parents; required the physician to inform his patient of, among other things, the emotional complications that might result from abortion; prohibited a physician to perform an abortion until twenty-four hours after the pregnant woman requested it; and required physicians to ensure that fetal remains were disposed of in a "humane and sanitary manner." For all practical purposes the Court, in an opinion by

Powell and over the dissents of O'Connor, White, and Rehnquist, declared the entire law unenforceable as a legislative effort to nullify a constitutionally protected right.

This is the situation as it is today and it is unsatisfactory to all. The Catholic church is unhappy since the Court sanctions abortions that can be financed by pregnant women or their families, notwithstanding the fact that abortion is murder. It is unsatisfactory to the many Protestants and Jews who consider the denial of Medicaid financing for abortions a consequence of Catholic church political pressure upon Congress and the president. It is unsatisfactory to the growing number of state and municipal officials who recognize that it would be less costly to finance abortions than to increase the relief rolls and, for the same reason, it is unsatisfactory to the taxpayers (including probably a majority of Catholics) ultimately called upon to pay the costs of caring for the unwanted children of women with low or no income.

As of now, the status is that of a standoff. Resolutions have been and continue to be introduced in Congress calling for a constitutional amendment aimed at outlawing all abortions except those proved to be necessary to preserve the woman's life. President Reagan has often expressed support for such an amendment and has urged members of Congress to approve it. Senator Helms and Congressman Hyde are seeking to obtain the votes necessary for its adoption, or at the least to obtain roll call votes on the proposal so that the dissenters may face the wrath of the Catholic church when the next election day comes around. Congressional leaders have, as of now, succeeded in avoiding a roll call for votes but they may not always be able to do so. Prediction is a dangerous endeavor, but probabilities point in the direction of non-action by Congress with respect to further statutory restrictions or constitutional amendments. In the long run, recognition of reality will prevail. Until such time as ever-increasing population growth can be curtailed through some other method, abortion, like contraception, will be allowed. After all, it is preferable to the alternative of limiting overpopulation by means of a nuclear war.

DIVORCE AND ANNULMENT OF MARRIAGE

Two cases, one that reached the Supreme Court and another that probably will, raise the question whether a state can constitutionally bar access to a divorce court by reason, directly or indirectly, of the parties' religion. The first, *Avitzur v. Avitzur,* is considered here; discussion of the second, *Doe v. Goodman,* will follow.

The *Avitzur* case involved a New York couple who were members of the Conservative branch of Judaism and had been married by a Conservative rabbi. That branch, like the Orthodox, requires that in order for a legally divorced couple to remarry, the husband must place a *get* (bill of divorcement) into the hands of the wife. Until he does so, neither he nor she is permitted to marry a third person, although a husband may in certain circumstances place the *get* into the hands of a rabbinically appointed substitute. (Reform Judaism deems divorce, unlike marriage, to be a purely secular act and thus does not require rabbinic intervention.)

It occasionally happens that the husband will refuse to participate in the *get* procedure, thereby leaving the wife in the status of an *agunah* (literally, one who is anchored) ineligible to remarry. Should she nevertheless do so in a civil marriage, or a marriage ceremony performed by a Reform rabbi, *halakhah* (Talmudic law) deems her to be an adulteress and her offspring illegitimate .

To meet the problem that arises when a husband will not physically place a *get* in the wife's hand as required by *halakhah* or a wife will not receive it, the Conservative rabbinate has altered the text of the *ketubah* (marriage contract) placed into the wife's hands during the marriage ceremony by adding a paragraph to it. As originally drafted in 1953, the proposed paragraph read as follows:

> In the event either party obtains a civil divorce from the other which is valid under the laws of the state in which the parties resided immediately prior to the divorce, each party to the marriage consents to the preparation and delivery of the *get* at the request of the other party, and if either party should refuse to give his or her consent and to take the necessary steps to prepare and deliver such a *get,* they shall have the right to submit the matter to the national *Beth Din* [rabbinic tribunal] for arbitration. The national *Beth Din* shall have the power to fix and determine the amount of money to be paid by the party refusing to consent. . . .

Some of the rabbis, however, deemed it not quite tactful to make provision for divorce while bride and groom were still under the *hupah* (marriage canopy). Accordingly, the proposed *ketubah* was revised and ultimately adopted. So revised it reads as follows:

> And in solemn assent to their mutual responsibilities and love, the bridegroom and bride have declared: as evidence of our desire to enable each other to live in accordance with the Jewish law of marriage throughout our lifetime, we, the bride and bridegroom, attach our signatures to this *ketubah,* and hereby agree to recognize the *Beth Din* of the Rabbinical As-

sembly and the Jewish Theological Seminary of America, or its duly appointed representatives, as having authority to counsel us in the light of Jewish tradition which requires husband and wife to give to each other complete love and devotion, and to summon either party at the request of the other, in order to enable the party so requesting to live in accordance with the standard of the Jewish law of marriage throughout his or her lifetime. We authorize the *Beth Din* to impose such terms of compensation as it may see fit to the failure to respond to its summons or to carry out its decision.

So that there might be no claim by the parties that they did not know what they were promising, since the *ketubah* though read vocally under the *hupah* is written in Aramaic and is not signed by either the groom or the bride, the Conservative marriage ritual now requires that the *ketubah,* as altered, be accompanied by an English translation and be signed by both bride and groom as well as by two witnesses.

After a few years, the Avitzur marriage, at which the revised *ketubah* was read, broke up and the wife sought a divorce. The husband consented but only on the condition that he would be the plaintiff in the proceeding based on the ground of cruel and inhumane treatment. However, after the legal divorce was obtained, the husband refused to appear before a *Beth Din* appointed in accordance with the *get* provision. The wife thereupon brought an action to enforce the provision and by a vote of four to three New York's highest court held it to be enforceable to the extent that it required the husband to appear before the *Beth Din.* The rationale for the ruling was that the provision was no more than a contractual agreement to submit to arbitration and could be enforced as such.

In 1983, the United States Supreme Court denied the husband's petition for a writ of certiorari. Since, as is usually the case, no opinion was handed down, one can only speculate as to the reason for the denial. A probable explanation lies in the fact that the challenged decision did not effect a final determination of the controversy, since it arose before a trial took place and the trial judge expressly stated that "it would be inappropriate at this junction to resolve the controversy on mere submission" (i.e., without a trial). What this means is that it may be constitutional to require the husband to appear before the rabbinic tribunal but not necessarily to comply with any decision it should hand down.

It was therefore possible for the husband to appear before the rabbinic tribunal and keep his hands clasped behind his back. Should the tribunal impose a penalty and the wife seek to enforce it, there would be a serious question whether under our Constitution a secular court can force payment of a penalty imposed by a rabbinic tribunal for a person's refusal to perform an act that is nonexistent anywhere other than in Orthodox and Conservative Judaism. Only the Supreme Court can give the definitive answer and it is not likely to do so in the *Avitzur* case. The reason for this is that ten months have passed and the wife has taken no action to bring the case to trial, notwithstanding the husband's continued refusal to appear before the rabbinic tribunal. Her inaction may well be a decision by her to abandon the controversy rather than having again to go to the United States Supreme Court for a final determination.

The constitutional issue may, however, reach the Supreme Court in the pending case of *Doe v. Goodman,* now before the United States District Court in New York. That case does not involve an agreement between the husband and wife but rather a law enacted by the New York legislature in 1983, probably because Orthodox *halakhah* does not sanction the Conservative rabbinate's variation in the traditional *ketubah.*

The Orthodox rabbinate was able to prevail upon the New York legislature to enact, and Governor Mario Cuomo to approve, a measure that could meet the problem of the *agunah.* It provides that a person seeking a civil divorce or annulment must allege in the complaint that "he or she has taken . . . all steps solely within his or her power to remove any barrier to the defendant's remarriage." The term "barrier" is defined as including "any religious or conscientious restraint or inhibition imposed on a party to a marriage, under the principles of the denomination of the clergyman or minister who has solemnized the marriage, by reason of the other party's commission or withholding of any voluntary act."

The law specifically excludes from its operation marriages solemnized by clergymen "of a religious denomination which has authority to annul or dissolve a marriage under the rules of such denomination." Although the statute does not identify the intended "religious denomination" it obviously refers to Catholicism, which does not permit remarriage after a divorce and sanctions a second marriage only if it takes place after the first has been annulled or dissolved with the approval of the Holy See.

Finally, the law provides that a divorce may not be granted if the clergyman who solemnized the marriage files a statement in court that, to his or her knowledge, the plaintiff had not taken all steps religiously necessary to remove the barriers to the defendant's remarriage.

Obviously, the purpose of the statute is to resolve the problem of the *agunah* without affecting Catholic marriages but through careless draftsmanship and an obvious desire not to mention the words "Jewish" or "Catholic" the draftsmen and the legislators seemed to have forgotten that Protestants too may be divorced and may wish to remarry. Except in rare cases this would not matter since, like Reform Judaism, Protestantism does not have a ritual divorce procedure and Protestants would therefore be able to make the necessary sworn statement without further ado.

But to all rules there is an exception and in this case the exception involved a woman who, for the purpose of the litigation, felt it wise to use the name "Jane Doe." She had been married by a minister of the Pentecostal Christian denomination and therefore could not obtain the (uncontested) divorce decree she sought without making the sworn statement required by the law, which, as a matter of conscience or otherwise, she obdurately refused to do. Hence, the suit against Goodman, the official in charge of handling divorce decrees, for a court order requiring him to issue the desired divorce decree.

It is hardly unusual for a defendant's lawyer in a civil suit to invoke all conceivable technicalities that might dispose of the litigation without the necessity of justifying the particular act that gave rise to the suit. An attorney representing government, national, state, or local, stands in a different position, at least where the constitutionality of a law is being challenged. This is so particularly in a case where taxpayers would be unaffected no matter how the court decides. In such a situation it would seem that the public would be best served if the question of constitutionality were resolved as expeditiously as possible.

In *Doe v. Goodman,* New York State's attorney general did not exercise this option. Instead he insisted that the Federal District Court did not have jurisdiction to decide the constitutionality question because the clerk to whom the divorce decrees were presented for the judge's signature—a pure formality in uncontested divorce cases—refused to pass it on to the judge because it lacked the necessary sworn statement that there were no religious barriers to the defendant's remarriage. Perhaps the attorney general was not too confident of a favorable decision in the federal court in which the suit was brought and hoped that Jane Doe would sign the necessary affidavit rather than engage in protracted litigation.

If "Jane Doe's" conscience or obstinancy does not yield, the controversy may end up in the Supreme Court. If it does, it is difficult to see how the Court can do otherwise than rule the law to be unconstitutional for any of a number of reasons.

With respect to the Establishment Clause, it would seem to violate each prong of the purpose-effect-entanglement ban. If the purpose of the law is not the advancement of Orthodox and Conservative *halakhah* it is difficult to see what purpose it can have, and the same is true with respect to effect. Nor can entanglement in religion be disregarded. Suppose there is a conflict as to whether the religious divorce obtained by the plaintiff really complied with the relevant religious law; a *get* acceptable to Conservative rabbis might not be acceptable to an Orthodox spouse. Determination of the controversy by a secular court cannot but constitute forbidden entanglement.

The Free Exercise Clause is also pertinent. How can a law withholding access to a secular court unless a religious act is first performed, even if its performance would violate the individual's religious conscience, be anything but an abridgment of free exercise? It is no answer that by engaging in a religious marriage the plaintiff voluntarily agreed to participate in a religious divorce should the occasion arise. Assuming that the plaintiff was aware of the statute when he participated in the religious marriage—an assumption highly unlikely except in marriages of lawyers whose practice is largely in the area of matrimonial relations—and by knowing that he implicitly agreed to be bound by it, the guarantee of religious freedom encompasses the right to change one's religion or even to become an atheist.

The free speech guarantee is also implicated. In *West Virginia State Board of Education v. Barnette* (1943) the Supreme Court ruled that saluting the flag is a form of symbolic speech, and refusal to salute a form of silence, both of which are protected by the free speech guarantee. It follows from this that placing a *get* in the wife's hands, as is required by Talmudic law, is a form of speech and refusal to do so the equivalent of silence, and therefore in both cases is protected by the Free Speech Clause.

Finally, the New York law is vulnerable to attack under the Fourteenth Amendment's equal protection guarantee. As noted, Catholicism does not permit remarriage after a divorce and the only way a second marriage can be licit is if it takes place after the first has been annulled by the Holy See. Few Catholics can afford the expense of a papal annulment or wish to suffer the long delay in this procedure, even if they assume that the pope would give the necessary approval. (England, it should be remembered, became a Protestant country in large measure because the pope would not approve the dissolution of Henry VIII's marriage so that he could marry Anne Boleyn.) Catholics in the New York legislature refused to accept the *agunah* bill if it applied to Catholic couples, one or both of whom wanted to marry other persons. Accordingly, a provision stating in effect that the law was not to be applied to Catholic marriages was included in the measure. (It does not even require that the parties make an effort to have their marriage annulled or dissolved by the Holy See.) Why should a Jew be required to appear before a rabbi if a Catholic is not required to appear before a priest? That is hardly equality within the purview of the Fourteenth Amendment's Equal Protection Clause. (It also amounts to "religious gerrymandering," forbidden by the Establishment Clause.)

There is one aspect of the *agunah* problem that an American legislature, no matter how pliant, cannot solve. As noted, in Jewish law the term *agunah* applies not only to the wife of an uncooperative husband but also to one whose husband has disappeared and therefore cannot place a *get* in her hands even if, as in most cases, he would be willing to do so. Secular law has met the problem by enacting statutes (they used to be called Enoch Arden laws) that create a presumption of the death of one who has been unheard from for a certain period of time, generally seven years, but a shorter period if the husband was a soldier missing in action or was involved in an accident likely to have caused death, such as an explosion in an arms factory.

With respect to this *agunah* problem, the secular law can do nothing, since it cannot compel an unwilling wife to marry again. To some extent, but far from completely, rabbinic law has sought to meet the problem. Thus, for example, it provides that a wife may remarry on the basis of testimony by a witness who saw the husband sink in a lake (but not a sea or ocean) and remain underwater long enough that he could not still be alive.

The crux of the whole matter can be summarized briefly. One cannot but be sympathetic to the plight of the *agunah*. If her husband refuses to give her a *get* or is missing in action in war she can never remarry, even if she was only twenty years old when her marital life was terminated either by secular divorce or by the husband's disappearance in military action. Nevertheless, it is religious law that imposed the barrier against remarriage and it is in religious law that a solution must be found. As will be seen in the next chapter, for more than a century the Supreme Court has refused to allow secular courts to become entangled in religious controversies. This is sound policy in a nontheocratic democracy and should not be compromised because of religion's inability to solve its own problems.

RELIGION IN THE UPBRINGING OF CHILDREN

In the United States the role, if any, that religion should play in the upbringing of children is a matter within the judgment of their parents, and their right to exercise that judgment is protected by the Free Exercise Clause of the First Amendment. This right, however, is subject to what lawyers call *parens patriae*, which means the power and indeed duty of the state to act as a substitute parent itself or to compel the natural parents to take such action as is reasonably necessary to protect the health and welfare of their children.

Thus, in the exercise of its powers as *parens patriae*, a state may constitutionally authorize a hospital to perform a medically necessary blood transfusion notwithstanding the protests of the child's parents, who as Jehovah's Witnesses, deem the procedure violative of the Biblical prohibition against consuming blood. In the same capacity, it can require Christian Scientists to provide necessary medical treatment for their children though they deem that sinful. The same rationale justifies compulsory vaccination and the fluoridation of water supplies. And so too states can enforce compulsory school attendance laws and laws forbidding child labor even where compliance would violate the religious conscience of the parents.

Intrusion upon parental authority is of course not unlimited. At some point the free exercise rights of parent and child must prevail over the state's role as *parens patriae* and its interest in an educated community. Thus parents have a constitutional right to send their children to nonpublic, including parochial, schools to receive the secular instruction required by law. Moreover, in *Wisconsin v. Yoder,* discussed in Chapter 3, the Court indicated that the turning point with respect to compulsory attendance is the child's fourteenth birthday or completion of elementary schooling (it is not quite clear which) and compulsory school attendance beyond that age may violate the Free Exercise Clause.

RELIGION IN CHILD CUSTODY PROCEEDINGS

Court struggles between parents for custody of children upon termination of a marriage by divorce or annulment is almost always a sorrowful experience in the life of the child. The sorrow is intensified when, in cases of interreligious marriages, the parents are unable to agree on the faith in which the child should be raised.

Consistent with a policy of nonintervention in purely matrimonial disputes, the Supreme Court has been reluctant to hear cases involving the upbringing of children, even where they might involve bona fide controversies under the Religion Clauses of the First Amendment. This long-standing policy of abstention has been adhered to by the Burger Court, as indicated by the case of *Johnson v. Johnson* (1978).

Several years after their marriage, the Johnsons became converts to the

Jehovah's Witnesses' faith and both were baptized into the congregation. However, a few years later, the husband became disenchanted with the religion and was excommunicated or "disfellowshipped" from the congregation for willfully smoking cigarettes. The consequence was an uncontested divorce but a strongly contested dispute as to the custody of the two children of the marriage, one seven and the other five years old.

The heart of the husband's case was the claim that if he were denied custody he would have virtually no input in their lives because of his disfellowshipped status. The reason for this is that a disfellowshipped member of Jehovah's Witnesses is believed to have come or was in danger of coming under satanic control and members of the congregation therefore would not associate with him. He testified that since the conversion his wife had not taught the children such simple tasks as counting money, washing themselves, and helping to clean around the house. He testified further that his wife would not allow the children to celebrate holidays and birthdays or to join such organizations as the Brownies and, finally, that she did not believe in college for the children.

For her part the wife testified to incompatibility, evidenced by her husband's threats of suicide, his unsuccessful suicide attempt, and his capacity for violence when frustrated.

On this testimony and the testimony of a psychologist and a court-appointed social worker, the judge concluded that both parents were fit *(sic)* to have custody of the children. Nevertheless he awarded physical custody to the wife on the basis of what is called the "tender year presumption," which means that all things being equal a mother of young children should generally be given custody.

On appeal, Alaska's highest court ruled that the wife's continued membership in Jehovah's Witnesses could not be used as ground for awarding custody to her husband. To do so, said the Court, would violate her right to freedom of religion. Accordingly, the lower court's decision was set aside and the case sent back to it for determination of custody but without applying either the sexual discriminatory tender years presumption or the wife's religious beliefs and associations.

The United States Supreme Court denied the husband's petition for certiorari without stating any reason for the denial, nor did any member of the Court dissent from its denial. A reasonable explanation for the Court's action lies in the fact that Alaska's high court's decision did not finally adjudge the controversy, since it had sent the case back for ultimate trial determination.

Presumably, on the retrial the Alaska court will maintain its ruling that the wife's membership in the Jehovah's Witnesses sect did not disqualify her from being granted custody. A second appeal to the United States Supreme Court might then be accepted for determination. If so, the Court will be faced with a difficult choice, a choice which it had not previously found it necessary to make: in the scale of constitutional values, which shall prevail—the right of a parent to determine the upbringing of children or the court's duty to protect the interest of children from the trials and tribulations of growing up in a community that despises and fears cults?

Jehovah's Witnesses is a faith which, though still disfavored in many parts of the country, has generally achieved the status of a bona fide religion. Suppose, however, the controversy involved a creed almost universally deemed to be a cult, such as the Unification Church or the Church of Scientology or Hare Krishna. Can a judge who states in his opinion that he would have granted custody to one parent constitutionally give it to the other only because of the former's membership in a cult? Would it matter that the particular cult involved has, at least for income tax exemption purposes, been recognized as a bona fide religion?

Generally the question of cultism in relation to the custody of children arises when a marriage is terminated by divorce, separation, the death of one parent, or even in cases where both parents have joined a cult and suit for custody is brought by grandparents who are associated with a conventional religion or perhaps no religion at all. In these cases the only acceptable standard is the best interests of the child, measured by purely secular standards. It would seem that in deciding this question the family judge may and should consider cultism as one but not the only factor.

It follows from this that the court in the *Johnson* case was incorrect in ruling that consideration of cult membership in determining custody would violate the First Amendment's free exercise guarantee. As has been noted, the Supreme Court has ruled in cases involving blood transfusion, child labor, and medical care, among others, that the religious freedom claims had to yield to the child's best interest.

The only acceptable standard is the best interests of the child, measured by purely secular standards. In situations in which both parents (or a surviving parent when one has died) join a particular cult, that fact alone may not justify a withdrawal of custody from the parent or parents. On the other hand, where the marriage is terminated by divorce or annulment, the divorce court judge may reasonably determine that the child's best interest dictates award of custody to the parent associated with a conventional faith or perhaps even with none at all.

Problems also arise in the more usual situation of interreligious marriages relating to generally accepted faiths, and the solution is even more difficult. The applicable standard is still the child's best interest, and that term refers to interests in this life rather than the life that comes after death. This means, and most courts have so held, that they are in no way bound by the parties' prenuptial agreement—an obligation required by Catholic ecclesiastical law—that the couple's children shall be brought up in the faith of one parent or the other. On the other hand, it does not mean religion is always irrelevant in determining best interest. In applying the best interest criterion, the judge may give weight to the fact that when a child has been brought up in one religion, a change in religious up-bringing may have a traumatic effect. It is not uncommon in custody controversies for the trial judge to question the child, though not in the presence of either or both parents, before deciding which parent should be granted custody.

RELIGION IN ADOPTION

In adoption, as in divorce proceedings, the child's best interest is the criterion for granting or denying the requisite judicial approval. There is, however, one significant difference between the two situations. In one the parties have a parental relationship that began at birth and continues for life. In the other there may have been no relationship at all, as in the case of foundlings, or a terminated relationship upon judicial approval of the adoption. Logic would therefore dictate that in adoption cases the religion of the mother or her preference should play no role in judicial determination of best interests.

On the face of it, this procedure would seem to be entirely consistent with American concepts as to the status of religion in a democratic society committed to the separation of church and state. No person is born into a religion. Entrance into or exit from a religion is a matter entirely of individual choice. When a person is an infant the choice is made by the parents but is subject to change upon attainment of maturity. Then or later, the child makes the decision, even if an unpopular religion or a cult is the choice.

When the child is a foundling, or shortly after birth is turned over by the parent or parents to an institution for possible adoption, the child has no religion and does not acquire one until it is adopted and thereby achieves the status of children generally. In cases where the father is unknown or has abandoned both mother and child, he certainly cannot morally claim a right to participate in the mother's decision to place the child for adoption. Moreover, even the mother should not exercise any parental right after placing the child for adoption. A child is not a chattel subject to a lien even if held by the mother.

Nevertheless, many states have adopted what are generally called religious protection laws. (Whether so intended or not, that term itself signifies a purpose of protecting religion rather than protecting only the welfare of the child.) These provide that wherever practicable or wherever possible, judicial approval of an adoption shall be given only where the child (even if but a few months old) and would-be parents are of the same religious faith.

In the 1972 case of *Dickens v. Ernesto* the Supreme Court had an opportunity to pass upon the constitutionality of religious protection laws. A county department of social services in New York refused to accept an application for adoption approval made by Robert and Ann Dickens because in the interview with the assigned caseworker the husband stated that he was an atheist and his wife said that she no longer had any religious affiliation. The practice of the department when interviewing the natural mother placing a child for adoption was to inquire as to her religious preference for the child. She could opt for her own religion, another religion, or no religion at all. The director of the department testified that in her sixteen years of service no mother ever opted for no religion, although some would indicate that they had no preference among the religions (Catholic, Protestant, and Jewish). In the case of children whose parents were unknown (foundlings) and there was no evidence with respect to the child's religion, the department would take "the first good home that comes along, whether Catholic, Protestant or Jewish." In light of this and the state's religious protection law, the department said that there was no point accepting the applications of persons with no religious affiliation. (In reality, the department had adopted a rotating system: one for Protestant applications, the second for Catholic, and the third for Jewish.)

The Dickenses appealed to a state court, which ordered the department to process the application. In the first place, it ruled, the department had no authority to limit placement of foundlings to couples of the three major faiths or of any faith, but had to offer them to the first suitable applicants, even if they had no religious affiliation. Moreover, the state's religious protection law did not make religious diversity an absolute bar to adoption; while religion was an important factor to be considered, it was the best interests of the child that determined whether a particular placement should be made, even if it should be contrary to the expressed wishes of the natural mother.

The Dickenses were unsatisfied and sought an appeal to the Supreme

Court on the ground that all religious protection laws should be declared unconstitutional and that under the Establishment Clause religion may not be considered even as one of the many factors in determining where a child should be placed for adoption or whether an adoption should be approved. However, the Supreme Court, with only Douglas dissenting, rejected the Dickens's appeal for lack of any substantial federal question.

Measured by the suggestion set forth in this chapter, neither the Dickens's nor the New York courts' interpretation of the Establishment Clause is quite correct. The clause does not bar consideration of religion in adoption proceedings if it is relevant to a secular determination of best interests, as would be the case if the child had been reared in a particular religion before being placed for adoption, so that a change in religion might have traumatic consequences. On the other hand, if the child had been placed for adoption shortly after birth, so that the religion of the mother would have no significance for the child, the courts' view that religion fixed by parentage at birth can be an important factor in adoption proceedings would seem to be inconsistent with the mandate of neutrality set forth in the *Everson* case.

CHAPTER 9

Inter- and Intra-church Disputes

HISTORIC BACKGROUND

As recorded in Biblical history, the first death occurred when there were only four persons in the entire universe and it came as the result of a religious conflict. Cain killed Abel because he was a rival for the favor of the Lord. Since then, more blood has been shed in religious conflict than in any other cause, including that of nationalism, although the two became intertwined as soon as enough people had been created to form two nations.

The Cain-Abel homicide reflected one of two types of religious conflict, that which occurs within one religion. The other, which came about as soon as enough people had been created for the purpose, involves believers in different faiths. The first is generally designated as intra-religious or intra-church; the second, as interreligious or inter-faith. Many examples of both can be found in Biblical history, but for our purpose one of each will suffice.

The first is illustrated by the unsuccessful rebellion of Korah, Dathan, and Abiram against the Aaronic priesthood established by Moses (Numbers 16). The second deals with Elijah and his response to the Baalist rebellion during the reign of Ahab (1 Kings 18). In both instances the penalty for unsuccessful revolt against the established religion was death. In the first and other Biblical revolts, execution was directly by God through fire, earth-swallowing, and other miraculous means; in the second and in all post-Biblical rebellions against the Biblical God, through the sword wielded by the state at the direction of His priests (for example, the Crusades; the Inquisition; the wars of Islam; the Near East wars of Muslim Arabs against Jews and Jews against Muslim Arabs; and in Lebanon of Jews and Christians against Muslim Arabs, of Shiites against Sunnis, Druse against Muslims, and some Christians against other

Christians).

Not that there were no cries for peace among the nations of the world. Isaiah spoke of the day when the Lord's temple would be a house of prayer for all the nations (56:7). He pictured God as blessing all peoples as equally his children. He pictured God as saying, "Blessed be Egypt My people and Assyria the work of My hands and Israel My inheritance" (19:23).

Amos expressed the same thought: "Are ye not as the children of the Ethiopian unto Me, O children of Israel, saith the Lord. Have I not brought up Israel out of the Land of Egypt and the Philistines from Caphor and Aram from Kir?" (9:7). Three prophets, Isaiah (2:4), Joel (3:10), and Micah (4:3), all spoke of the day when there would no longer be any wars, when (in Isaiah's words) people "shall beat their swords into plowshares, and their spears into pruninghooks: nation shall not lift up sword against nation, neither shall they learn war any more" (2:4). (Translated into present-day terms: when nations both of the NATO and Warsaw Pact constituencies convert their nuclear armaments into instruments of peaceful energy.)

Alas, this was not to be. Jeremiah in exile preached that because of their inequities, people would say "Peace, peace, when there is no peace" (6:14) and, half a millenium later, the Son of God preached that He "came not to send peace, but a sword" (Matthew 10:34).

It should be noted that although the Hebrew word *shalom,* used by the prophets, is translated in the King James version of the Old Testament as peace, it has two other related meanings: one, that of individual well-being, and the other of domestic tranquility. Thus, with respect to the former, the full verse of the quotation from Jeremiah reads: "They have healed also the hurt of the daughter of my people slightly, saying Peace, Peace, when there is no peace." So too, the universal Hebrew equivalent of hello are the words *shalom aleikhem,* generally translated as peace be unto you, actually meaning well-being unto you.

The second meaning, that of domestic tranquility, is the one that is most relevant to the subject of this chapter. It is manifested in the letter of Roger Williams to the Town of Providence, referred to earlier in this book. In it he asserted that a ship captain acts legitimately in commanding that "justice, peace and sobriety" be exercised by all on the ship but illegitimately if he seeks to force participation by crews or passengers in prayers or worship.

This alternative meaning is echoed in Voltaire's statement: "If there were one religion in England, its despotism would be terrible; if there were only two they would destroy each other; but there are thirty, and therefore they live in peace and happiness."

Just about the same time, Madison and his colleagues were drafting a constitution to form a more perfect union that would, among other things, insure domestic tranquility partly by prohibiting religious tests for public office and shortly thereafter by an amendment forbidding Congress to make any law respecting an establishment of religion or prohibiting the free exercise thereof.

INTER-CHURCH DISPUTES

Interreligious conflicts (those between defenders of different deities) did not end with the final victory of Jehovah over Baal. They extended to the time when the Macabbeans warred against the forces of Antiochus Epiphaneus, who sought to impose idolatry upon the worshippers of Jehovah. Later, the temple was destroyed in a war between the Hebrews and the Romans that came about, at least in part, because of the Hebrews' refusal to further offer sacrifices for the well-being of the Roman emperor.

In the Western Hemisphere considerable blood was shed in efforts to impose Christianity upon the obstinate heathen redskins. And as late as the twentieth century, victorious General Douglas MacArthur imposed upon the Japanese the American principle of church-state separation, destroying governmental *shinto* and compelling Emperor Hirohito to disavow his own divinity (an act hardly consistent with religious freedom).

Americans who are committed to religious freedom can be proud of the clerical response to the still ongoing war against unfavored religions called cults. The subject has been treated earlier in this book and need not be repeated. What is relevant here is the fact that in all other chapters in the story of interreligious conflict, it has been the churches rather than the faithful who have instigated wars of religion against religion while today the situation with respect to cults is exactly the reverse; the instigators, abetted by ambitious politicians, are the adherents of the accepted faiths.

Indeed, not only have the clergy refrained from joining the anti-cult crusade, but instead they have actively participated in the constitutional efforts against it. In the *Worldwide Church of God* case, practically all the major religious organizations, speaking through their clergy, joined in an *amici curiae* brief in defense of the church. In the *Moon* case, the Jewish organizations, rabbinic and congregational, refused to join Christian churches in Moon's defense but they refrained from actively participating in support of the prosecution through submission of an *amicus curiae* brief. They defended their position of nonparticipation on the claim that the cults were not really religions but only pseudo-religions established to mulct the innocent, in the same category as clairvoyants and astrologers.

In short, what can be said with respect to constitutional law conflicts of churches against churches today is that there aren't any.

INTRA-CHURCH DISPUTES: SCHISMS

Normally, when husband and wife split and do not agree as to division of their properties, or partners dispute about the management of their business, or stockholders vie with one another to control a corporation, the controversy is not likely to reach the courts as a church-state or religious freedom controversy. Where, however, the assets fought for are church-owned bank accounts, church-owned buildings, and sometimes even church-owned commercial enterprises, the split, generally called a schism, may well wind up in the Supreme Court as First Amendment problems arising under either or both of the Establishment and Free Exercise clauses.

Surprisingly, however, the 1872 case of *Watson v. Jones,* the starting point of Supreme Court constitutional law relating to church schisms, was decided under neither of these provisions but rather under what the Supreme Court deemed to be the appropriate but new common (decisional, as contrasted with constitutional or legislative) law principles. Before the Court handed down its decision in that case, the state and federal courts usually resorted to what was called the departure-from-doctrine test in determining these property disputes, a procedure long used in England as part of the common law then applicable in such cases. In these suits the contesting parties presented testimony by experts in the particular religion involved, and on that basis the court would decide whether the Mother Church had substantially departed from the basic doctrine of the particular religion as fixed by its founders. If the answer was yes, the property went to or remained that of the local church; if not, it remained or became the property of the Mother Church.

Watson v. Jones, involving a church building in Louisville,Kentucky, brought an end to the departure-from-doctrine test as it was until then applied in the federal courts. The case involved the question whether slavery was permissible under the doctrines upon which Presbyterianism was founded. In 1845 the General Assembly of the Presbyterian Church, its highest body, declared that slavery was not sinful; however, in 1861 it reversed itself and ruled that it was. The consequence was a schism, with the Northerners retaining the title United Presbyterian Church in the United States of America and the Southerners calling themselves the Presbyterian Church in the United States.

In *Watson v. Jones* the Louisville Presbytery, supported by the State Synod, condemned the decree of the General Assembly as schismatical and heretical. The congregants of the Walnut Street church in Louisville, splitting down the middle, found themselves in the federal court, with each faction claiming that it represented true Presbyterian doctrine and therefore legally entitled to possession of the church building.

In those days, when a case came to a federal court because the contestants resided in different states, the court decided the suit in accordance with common law principles as it judged them to be. This would have required the court in Kentucky to examine Presbyterian doctrine from the 1647 Westminster Confession to the time of the trial in order to determine which faction represented the true faith and which was heretical.

In England, the Court said in *Watson v. Jones,* laws "existed upon the statute-book hampering the free exercise of religious belief and worship in many most oppressive forms, and though Protestant dissenters were less burdened than Catholics and Jews, there did not exist that full, entire and practical freedom for all forms of religious belief and practice which lies at the foundation of our political principles."

In this country [the Court continued in words often quoted by American courts] the full and free right to entertain any religious belief, to practice any religious principle, and to teach any religious doctrine which does not violate the laws of morality and property, and which does not infringe personal rights, is conceded to all. The law knows no heresy, and is committed to the support of no dogma, the establishment of no sect. The right to organize voluntary religious associations to assist in the expression and dissemination of any religious doctrine, and to create tribunals for the decision of controverted questions of faith within the association, and for the ecclesiastical government of all the individual members, congregations, and officers within the general association, is unquestioned. All who unite themselves to such a body do so with an implied consent to this government, and are bound to submit to it. But it would be a vain consent and would lead to the total subversion of such religious bodies, if any one aggrieved by one of their decisions could appeal to the secular courts and have them reversed. It is of the essence of these religious unions, and of their right to establish tribunals for the decisions of questions arising among themselves, that those decisions should be binding in all cases of ecclesiastical cognizance, subject only to such appeals as the organism itself provides for.

Yet the courts cannot wash their hands of intra-church controversies; some impartial tribunal had to decide which faction should have possession of the church and its assets, else the issue would be decided by physical force. Judicial intervention is unavoidable, but it must be kept to a minimum and may not in any event encompass theological determinations. All that a court can and should do is to accept the determination of the appropriate ecclesiastical tribunal as to which faction represents the true faith and direct its marshals to enforce that tribunal's ruling.

In reaching this decision, *Watson v. Jones* held a court must determine whether the structure of the national church is hierarchical or congregational. In the former, such as the Catholic church, the courts must abide by the decision of the highest ecclesiastical body having authority in the area in which the local church is situated. If the structure is congregational, such as in Baptist, Congregational, or Jewish faiths, the court must abide by the decision arrived at by a majority of the members in the local congregation. Since the polity of Presbyterianism was hierarchical, ownership of the Walnut Street church was vested in the General Assembly rather than in a majority of the local congregation.

Some judicial or legislative intervention beyond determining the relevant church polity often cannot be avoided. In an hierarchical church structure the courts have to determine which is the highest ecclesiastical authority having jurisdiction over a particular controversy, for example, priest, bishop, cardinal, or pope, with respect to a local Catholic church. When the controversy involves a Baptist church or Jewish synagogue, the court must intervene to the extent of determining whether a quorum was present at the meeting in which the decision on property ownership was made by majority vote and the meeting complied with due process of law requirements, e.g., whether the congregants were given adequate prior notice and the votes were honestly counted.

Two comments are relevant with respect to the decision in *Watson v. Jones*. First, in concluding its opinion the Court stated that it had withheld issuing its decision for a year after the case was argued in "the hope, that since civil commotion [euphemistic synonym for Civil War] which evidently lay at the foundation of the trouble, has passed away, that charity, which is so large an element in the faith of both parties, and which by one of the apostles of that religion, is said to be the greatest of all virtues, would have brought about a reconciliation. But we have been disappointed."

So much so that the Court's reporter found it necessary to add the following footnote to the opinion:

> To assist the reader, as far as possible, in a controversy and case perplexed by a multitude of names, to keep in his mind a distinct conception of who were on one side and who on the other, the Reporter, all through his statement of the case, has put the names of those who were on one side (and which for mere convenience may be distinguished as the pro-slavery or conservative side), in *italic* letter; and those on the other in Roman.

The second comment relates to the First Amendment Religion Clauses. The opinion does not mention the Establishment Clause but does predicate its decision on the spirit of the Free Exercise Clause, which, it said, required that secular court intervention be kept at a minimum in order to secure the latter right. Just two years less than a century later, the Court, in the *Walz* case, manifested the same spirit, now become a mandate, of minimum intervention by reason of the entanglement prohibition in the Establishment Clause.

In 1952 the Supreme Court, in the case of *Kedroff v. St. Nicholas Cathedral,* was again faced with the task of passing upon an intra-church dispute but, unlike the *Watson v. Jones* case, this time it was Communism rather than slavery that triggered the schism. The specific issue was the rightful ownership of St. Nicholas Cathedral in New York City. The contestants were the Russian Orthodox Church in Moscow (the Mother Church) and the Russian Church in America. The latter had been established in 1925 by a number of American churches to serve the faithful until such time as conditions in Russia would allow free and independent action by the Patriarchate in Moscow, the highest authority in the church structure.

In 1945, after World War II had effected a period, short as it was, of friendly relations between the United States and the Soviet Union, a metropolitan or bishop was sent by the Moscow Patriarchate to take over as Archbishop of America and as such he obtained possession of the cathedral. The New York legislature would have none of this and quickly passed a law that declared that the Russian Church in America was the legally recognized church. It was thus entitled to control of all church assets within the state, together with the power to select its archbishop and other officials, free from any control on the part of the Moscow Patriarchate.

By the time the *Kedroff* case came to the Supreme Court it had already established that both the Free Exercise Clause and the Establishment Clause were applicable to the states to the same extent as to the federal government. The New York statute, the Court held, violated both aspects of the First Amendment. Although the amendment was not applicable to the states when *Watson v. Jones* was decided, the opinion in that case, it said, radiated a spirit of freedom for religious organizations with independence from secular control or manipulation and a power to decide for themselves, free from state interference, matters of church government as well as those of faith and doctrine.

The Russian Orthodox Church was a hierarchical church headed by the Moscow Patriarchate and it was therefore within its power to determine who had rightful control of the New York church's assets, and this notwithstanding the fact that the New York church had incorporated itself under the state's statute. In short, the First Amendment mandated that New York recognize true ownership in the Mother Church in Moscow.

Justice Robert Jackson, the only dissenter from Stanley Reed's opinion in this case, could not see how the First Amendment required New York to "yield to the authority of a foreign and unfriendly state masquerading as a spiritual institution."

Inasmuch as President Franklin Roosevelt had recognized the Soviet Union and exchanged ambassadors with it (as Reagan was later to do with the Holy See), it would seem that, notwithstanding Jackson's disagreement, the New York legislature and the United States Supreme Court were required to accept the rules of law applicable to our relations with all foreign political entities, including rules dealing with recognition of established church polity. Yet it is not quite that easy to see how the First Amendment compels us to recognize the property rights of a church whose highest judicatory resides in a nation based upon the Marxist principle that religion is the enemy of the people and should therefore be eradicated as soon as it was feasible to do so.

There is an interesting sequel to the Court's decision. At the time *Watson v. Jones* was decided there existed a rule, established in the 1842 case of *Swift v. Tyson,* that in determining the applicable common law in a suit brought by a citizen of one state against a citizen of another state a federal court was not required to accept a state court's construction of the applicable common law. Instead, on the assumption that father knows best, the federal courts would decide that question for it. In the 1938 case of *Erie Railroad v. Tompkins,* however, the newly established New Deal Court put an end to that rule. *Swift v. Tyson,* it said, was wrongly decided and was no longer to be followed; rather, the federal courts would apply the appropriate decisions of the states' own courts on the contested subjects.

Acting on that principle, New York's highest court, in the case of *Kreshik v. St. Nicholas Cathedral* (1960), held that while New York's statute was invalid, New York's common law nevertheless required a determination in favor of the Russian Church in America.

This was not the first time that gambit had been essayed but it proved no more effective than its predecessor. In the case of *National Association for the Advancement of Colored People (NAACP) v. Alabama,* the Supreme Court, in 1958, held that the state's effort to destroy the NAACP was unconstitutional whether it was made by its legislative rather than its judicial branch or *vice versa.* The same principle, the Court said, was applicable in the *Kreshik* case and the effort was equally constitutionally impermissible.

In 1969, shortly before Burger's appointment as Chief Justice, the Supreme Court found itself again called upon to referee a controversy within the Presbyterian church, this time one that was both sociopolitical and theological. Two local Presbyterian churches in Savannah, Georgia, had serious grievances against the General Assembly, complaining of its:

> . . . ordaining of women as ministers and ruling elders, making pronouncements and recommendations concerning civil, economic, social and political matters, giving support to the removal of Bible reading and prayers by children in the public schools, adopting certain Sunday School literature and teaching neo-orthodoxy alien to the Confession of Faith and Catechism, as originally adopted by the general church, and causing all members to remain in the National Council of Churches of Christ and willingly accepting its leadership which advocated practices such as the subverting of parental authority, civil disobedience and intermeddling in civil affairs.

If that were not enough, they also charged that the General Assembly "made pronouncements in matters relating to international issues such as the Vietnam conflict and disseminated publications denying the Holy Trinity and violating the moral and ethical standards of the faith."

Deciding that there was no hope of reconciliation with the Mother Church, the two congregations voted to withdraw from it and to reconstitute the local churches as an autonomous Presbyterian organization. The Mother Church responded by directing the Presbytery of Savannah to take over the local churches' properties and administer their use until new local memberships loyal to the Mother Church could take over. The local churches' countermove was to bring a lawsuit in a state court to vindicate their right to keep the properties as the true representatives of authentic Presbyterianism.

Under Georgia law the right to property used by local churches was determined by a civil court jury's decision as to whether the Mother Church had fundamentally or substantially abandoned the tenets and doctrines upon which it was originally founded and which were held and practiced at the time the local churches affiliated with it. Accordingly, a trial was held and, hardly surprising, the jury decided in favor of the local churches. The case ultimately reached the Supreme Court under the title *Presbyterian Church in the United States v. Mary Elizabeth Hull Memorial Presbyterian Church.*

In its opinion by Brennan the Court held unconstitutional the so-called departure-from-doctrine rule. Under that rule it was the trial court or jury that had the power and duty to determine whether challenged action departed substantially from prior church doctrine as it (the trial court or jury), rather than the Mother Church, interpreted the meaning of that doctrine. If it decided that there had been a substantial departure, it then had to go on to determine whether the issue on which the Mother Church departed held a place of such importance in the traditional theology as to require that the trust conferred by the local church upon the general church be terminated. The departure-from-doctrine principle, he said, violated the First Amendment's Religion Clauses. That amendment's values were plainly jeopardized when ownership of church property was made to turn on the resolution by civil courts of controversies over religious doctrine and practice.

The role of civil courts, as prescribed by the First Amendment, he continued, was strictly limited. It could decide whether the decision of the Mother Church resulted from fraud, collusion, or arbitrariness, but not whether the Mother Church violated the departure-from-doctrine principle.

What realistically may be the crux of Brennan's opinion is the statement that if "civil courts undertake to resolve such controversies in order to adjudicate the property dispute, the hazards are ever present of inhibiting the free development of religious doctrine." This means that a person who joins a church must realize that its present position on religious, civil, economic, social, and political issues, such as, for example, Bible reading and prayer recitation in the public schools, may make a 180 degree turn from for it to against it, and if so there is nothing civil courts can do about it.

In his concurring opinion, Harlan stated that he did not understand Brennan's opinion as going further than rejecting the departure-from-doctrine approach if it necessarily requires the civilian courts to weigh the significance and meaning of disputed religious doctrine. He did not read it as going further to hold that the Constitution forbids civilian courts from enforcing a deed or will that clearly and expressly lays down conditions limiting a religious organization's use of the property which is granted. If, "for example, the donor expressly gives his church some money on the condition that the church never ordain a woman as a minister or elder, or never amend certain specified articles of the Confession of Faith, he is entitled to his money back if the condition is not fulfilled. In such a case, the church should not be permitted to keep the property simply because church authorities have determined that the doctrinal innovation is justified by the faith's basic principles."

The Burger Court's first encounter with intra-church controversies relating to property ownership came in *Maryland and Virginia Eldership of the Churches of God v. The Church of God at Sharpsburg, Inc.* (1970). That case involved a church property dispute between the Mother Church, represented by the General Eldership of the Churches of God, and two secessionist local churches.

In a short *per curium* (unsigned) opinion, the Court upheld the Maryland court's decision, which had relied upon provisions of state statutes relating to the holding of property by religious corporations. The statute provided that, in determining ownership and right to control church property, the Maryland court could rely upon language in the deeds conveying the properties to the local church corporations upon the terms of the charter of the corporations and upon the relevant provisions in the constitution of the Mother Church.

The Mother Church had argued that the statute, as applied, deprived it of property in violation of the First Amendment. However, the Court said, this contention was fallacious since the Maryland court's resolution of the dispute involved no inquiry into religious doctrine. Accordingly, the Mother Church's appeal had to be dismissed for lack of a substantial federal question.

Brennan, for himseslf, Douglas, and Marshall, felt it necessary to issue a concurring opinion that stated that there were three constitutional approaches toward resolving intra-church disputes relating to the ownership and control of church property. One was the *Watson v. Jones* method of judicial intervention limited to identifying the highest judicatory body and enforcing its determination.

The second was resort to neutral principles of law generally applicable to all property disputes. Under this approach, civil courts could determine ownership by studying express provisions in deeds or general corporation laws or decisions, provided these did not require the civil courts to resolve doctrinal issues, e.g., as would necessarily be the case in applying the departure-from-doctrine rule.

The third possible approach could be the enactment of new special statutes governing church property arrangements. These were constitutional as long as they left control of ecclesiastical polity as well as doctrine to church-governing bodies.

The next significant case involving intra-church disputes coming to the Supreme Court was *Serbian Eastern Orthodox Diocese for the United States v. Milivojevich* (1976). Challenged in it was an Illinois state court decision that ruled arbitrary and therefore unconstitutional the action of the Serbian Mother Church in removing the defendant Dionisije, who had initially been appointed by it to serve as Bishop for the American-Canadian Diocese. The ground for his removal was his refusal to comply with a decision by the Mother Church dividing the diocese into three geographic sections and restricting his jurisdiction to one of them.

In the suit, Dionisije claimed that the action of the pro-Communist Mother Church was arbitrary in that it did not follow its own laws and procedures in defrocking him. Illinois' highest court ruled in his favor on the ground that, while he had initially been validly suspended, the same could not be said of the Mother Church's arbitrary refusal, in violation of church law, to try him within a year after his suspension began.

The Supreme Court, in an opinion by Brennan, reversed the Illinois court decision on the ground that the First Amendment permits hierarchical religious organizations to establish their own rules and regulations for internal discipline and government and to create tribunals for adjudicating disputes over these matters. A civil court, he said, has no power to set aside an intra-church resolution of a dispute because it deems it arbitrary and not in conformity with legal proceedings in secular tribunals; the Constitution requires civil courts to accept as binding these ecclesiastical decisions.

As of this writing, the most recent Supreme Court opinion relating to church schisms was that in the case of *Jones v. Wolf* (1979). By a majority vote, the congregants of a local Presbyterian church in Macon, Georgia, decided to separate from the Presbyterian Church in the United States, and the state courts were called upon to decide which faction should retain ownership and control of the building and other assets of the local church. By a five-to-four vote the Supreme Court ruled that a state was not bound by the hierarchical-congregational dualism first set forth in *Watson v. Jones*. It could constitutionally adopt what had been called a "neutral principles of law" analysis involving consideration of the deeds by which the church acquired the contested property, state statutes governing the holding of church property, the local church's charter, and the general church's constitution. This rule, said Blackmun for the majority, did not violate the First Amendment, since a state could constitutionally adopt any one of various approaches for settling church property disputes so long as it involved no consideration of doctrinal matters, such as those relating to the ritual and liturgy of worship or to tenets of faith.

The primary advantages of this neutral-principles approach, Blackmun said, were first, that it was completely secular in operation and yet was flexible enough to accommodate all forms of religious organizations and polity and, second, that the method relied exclusively on objective, well-established concepts of trust and property law familiar to lawyers and judges.

The dissenting opinion, written by Powell and joined in by Burger, Stewart, and White, urged that the test set forth in *Watson v. Jones* had served the nation well for more than a century and should not be tampered with.

Several comments may be made regarding this decision. First, the trinity of fraud-collusion-arbitrariness first announced in the 1929 case of *Gonzalez v. Roman Catholic Archbishop of Manila,* shortly to be discussed more fully, had become an unchallenged but unconfirmed fraud-collusion duality in the *Serbian Eastern Orthodox* opinion. Citing that opinion, Blackmun stated in *Jones v. Wolf*:

> There is no suggestion in this case that the decision of the [church] commission was the product of "fraud" or "collusion." In the absence of such circumstances, "the First and Fourteenth Amendments mandate that civil courts shall not disturb the decisions of the highest ecclesiastical tribunal within a church of hierarchical polity, but must accept such decisions as binding on them, in their application to the religious issues of doctrine or polity before them."

The *Gonzalez* opinion was written by Louis Brandeis, who with Oliver Wendell Holmes were for a time the solitary liberal pair in a conservative court, to be followed later by Black and Douglas, who in turn were followed by Brennan and Marshall. That Brandeis and Brennan should reach opposing positions on the fraud-collusion-arbitrariness issue suggests Rehnquist's quip in the *Serbian Eastern Orthodox* case: "Will the real liberal stand up." Second, it represents a rare though not unprecedented instance in which Rehnquist joined with Brennan and Marshall in a church-state case. Third, one can debate which rule better serves the democratic values underlying our Constitution: recognizing and enforcing the majority vote in a church, whether it be designated congregation or hierarchical, or avoiding impingement upon the constitutionally protected rights of church self-rule to the fullest feasible extent, even if it results in minority control. Finally, the wound feared to have been inflicted by the Court upon *Jones v. Wolf* is considerably less deep than a well and not so wide as a church door. All that church authorities need do is to enter into an agreement in writing with a congregation seeking to join the Mother Church family that the congregation abide by the decisions of the Mother Church in matters relating to ownership and supervisory control of property acquired by the local church. The congregation will then have the option of accepting or rejecting membership on those terms, but is that not what democracy, religious freedom, and church-state separation are all about?

NON-SCHISMATIC DISPUTES

The cases discussed in the preceding section of this chapter all dealt with intra-church schisms and involved competing claims to ownership of church assets. However the courts might decide the conflict, there were now to be two separate and independent churches where before there was only one. The three cases considered in this section deal with controversies in what were single ecclesiastical entities before the suits started and remained such after the final court decisions were handed down.

The earliest of these cases was *Gonzalez v. Roman Catholic Archbishop of Manila*, decided in 1929 when the Philippine Islands were still an American territory and the decisions of its highest court were appealable to the United States Supreme Court. In that case the latter court appeared to have qualified somewhat the broad scope of its decision in *Watson v. Jones*. The *Gonzalez* case involved a dispute relating to a testimonial bequest to the Archbishop of Manila of income to finance the service of a Catholic church chaplain in celebrating sixty masses annually on behalf of the souls of the deceased and her family. The will provided that a named great-grandson of the donor was to be appointed by the archbishop as chaplain and thereafter the post was to descend to the nearest relative of the preceding appointed chaplain.

The chaplaincy was founded in 1820 and continued until 1912, when the nearest relative, the plaintiff in the suit, turned out to be a boy of twelve. The then archbishop refused to appoint him (and pay to his guardian the cumulated income of the chaplaincy, then amounting to some eighty-six thousand dollars) not because of his age but because he had not begun the required course in theology. Canon law in force when the chaplaincy was first established under the will did not require attendance at the course and the Philippine trial court ruled that enforcing it against the plaintiff would violate the constitutional ban on laws impairing the obligations of existing contracts. The Philippines' highest court reversed the decision and the would-be chaplain, through his guardian, appealed to the United States Supreme Court.

"In the absence of fraud, collusion, or arbitrariness," the Court said in affirming the dismissal of the complaint, "the decisions of the proper church tribunals on matters purely ecclesiastical, though affecting civil rights, are accepted in litigation before the secular courts as conclusive, because the parties in interest made them so by contract or otherwise." Since there was not even a suggestion that in ruling against the claimant the Archbishop of Manila exercised his authority arbitrarily (or that there was any fraud or collusion in the controversy), the Philippine court's decision in his favor was affirmed.

The second non-schismatic instance dealt with the First Amendment question raised in the cases of *Granfield v. Catholic University* and *Broderick v. Catholic University*. Those involved lawsuits by two members of religious orders who were dissatisfied with refusal on the part of the church to pay them the same salaries received by nonclerical members of the university's law school.

In both cases the Court of Appeals, in decisions that the Supreme Court refused to review, avoided passing upon the question whether preferential treatment favoring nonclerics over clerics violated either the Establishment or Free Exercise clauses of the First Amendment. It held that secular courts had no jurisdiction to determine the dispute within a church, notwithstanding the claims that its actions violated the First Amendment.

These cases also did not involve church schisms. The plaintiffs had no intention to leave the church, nor were they expelled from it. (Their cases were decided three years before the Court handed down its decision in *Jones v. Wolf.*)

The most recent non-schismatic dispute to reach the Supreme Court was in the case of *Struemph v. McAuliffe*. There, five years after *Jones v. Wolf* was decided, it refused to review a Court of Appeals decision which could reasonably be considered to be inconsistent with the principles set forth in that case. The *Struemph* case differs from the others treated in this section, or for that matter in the preceding section in that the controversy did not concern conflicting claims to church funds and properties but to matters of art and sentimentality.

Specifically, the problem arose by reason of a difference of opinion between the congregation and the priest over whether there should be only one altar or three in the church. He demanded removal of two of the altars, including the original main altar, and the retention of only the altar of sacrifice so that the other two should not "distract from the liturgic unity and centrality of the one altar of sacrifice." The congregation, on the other hand, insisted that all three altars be retained (one had been donated by the father of one of the plaintiffs).

At one point during the controversy a truck and a crew accompanied by the pastor arrived at the church for the purpose of removing two of the altars. At this point some six or eight parishioners arrived at the scene and sought to block the path of the pastor and the crew. Tempers flared and heated words were exchanged. To a police officer who arrived at the scene, violence seemed imminent and was averted only by the withdrawal of the pastor and the crew.

Thereafter, the arena of controversy was removed to a courtroom by reason of a suit against the local bishop (who had approved if not commanded the priest's action) for an injunction against the removal of the main and side altars and the relocation of the altar of sacrifice. The trial judge ruled in favor of the parishioners, stating as a conclusion of law that the First Amendment did not require a state to accord "automatic deference to religious authority in resolving church property disputes." As a means of adjudicating a church property dispute, he said, a state court was constitutionally mandated to adopt a "neutral principles of law" analysis. Although the initial deed of the property was to the archbishop and his successors, it nevertheless created a trust for the benefit of the parishioners and in a controversy between them the latter must prevail. This, said the judge, is what *Jones v. Wolf* mandated.

Had the judge prevailed it is obvious that the formula initiated in *Watson v. Jones* would disappear and all intra-church controversies between priest and parishioners would be determined by a majority vote of the latter.

The appeals court did not agree. *Jones v. Wolf*, it said in a decision that the Supreme Court refused to review, was not intended to bring to an end the rule of deference to determinations of clerical authorities within the Roman Catholic church. It certainly was not intended to mean that even where there is no actual schism within the church the courts may disregard the hierarchical structure of the church in determining control of church property. This was particularly so where, unlike *Watson v. Jones* and subsequent schism cases, title to and control of church property was vested not in the congregation but in the bishop.

In other words, *Struemph v. McAuliffe* illustrated what was suggested earlier—that is, that any effort to democratize a polity relating to hierarchical control can be constitutionally vitiated by placing formal title to the church building and assets in the name of the bishop rather than the congregation.

CHAPTER

10

Religion and the Welfare
of the Community

WELFARE AND THE POLICE POWER

The Preamble to the Constitution adopted in 1787 set forth six purposes that impelled establishment of a new government: to form a more "perfect" (i.e., more effective) union, establish justice, insure domestic tranquility, provide for the common defense, promote the general welfare, and secure the blessings of liberty.

As written, the Constitution did comparatively little to secure the blessings of liberty: it guaranteed the privilege of the writ of habeas corpus, undoubtedly a major instrument in securing liberty; it guaranteed the right to trial by jury in criminal cases; it forbade bills of attainder and ex post facto laws; and it banned religious tests for public office.

That was not enough for the libertarians, and it was only the assurances by Jefferson and Madison that a Bill of Rights would be added that prevailed upon enough reluctant states to ratify the Constitution. Beginning with the 1925 decision of *Gitlow v. New York*, the Supreme Court, in a series of cases, made practically all of the Bill of Rights applicable to actions by states—legislative, executive, and judicial.

The general welfare provision had a different life history; indeed, it apparently died soon after birth. Notwithstanding its inclusion in the Preamble, the Supreme Court has consistently ruled, in effect, that with respect to promoting the general welfare "We the People" refers to them as citizens acting through their state legislatures rather than through Congress. Legislation by states aimed at promoting that end is referred to as an exercise of their police power. That term, however, extends beyond keeping the peace; it encompasses what is considered general welfare legislation, such as that which secures the prosperity, morals, and health of the people.

Nevertheless, in *Champion v. Ames* (1903) the Supreme Court ruled

275

that Congress could constitutionally assist state legislatures in the exercise of their police power by use of its own power under Article I, Section 8, to regulate commerce among the states. It therefore could make it a federal crime to carry lottery tickets into a state forbidding their sale with the purpose of selling them there.

This specific application of the rule in *Champion v. Ames* is pretty much a symbol of times past. Too many states resort to multimillion-dollar lottery prizes and too many churches resort to bingo for the common purpose of meeting their budgets for many states to outlaw these fund-raising devices. The rule itself, however, has survived and has flourished. Thus, for example, the power of Congress to aid education rests upon Article I, Section 8, of the Constitution, which authorizes it to lay taxes and spend the proceeds, and the Commerce Clause, which in the same section justifies Congress' power to forbid religious discrimination in employment. Congress has also used other powers as the basis for legislation relating to religion, as, for example, the war power to authorize employment of chaplains. And, as discussed below, the status of the government as a purchaser of products authorizes it to limit purchases to livestock that has been slaughtered by humane methods, thereby achieving a purpose that would ordinarily be deemed within the scope of the states' police power.

HUMANE TREATMENT OF ANIMALS

That the states' police power encompasses protection of animals from human cruelty is hardly open to doubt. In many states, legislation authorizes the designation of the American Society for the Prevention of Cruelty to Animals (ASPCA) as a government agent with power to issue summons to court in the enforcement of laws forbidding the infliction of needless pain to animals.

On the not unreasonable assumption that death is the ultimate cruelty, logic would seem to justify laws forbidding the killing of animals for human consumption, thus making vegetarians of us all (and, as reward, extending our own longevity). Human appetite does not allow for this—it does not allow even a ban on hunting as a sport—but human conscience can compel the killing of animals in the least painful way.

Senator Hubert Humphrey was apparently the first member of Congress to see it that way. He could have invoked the Commerce Clause to achieve that end by means of a law forbidding the transportation across state lines of animals that had been slaughtered in an inhumane way. For some unexplained reason, he did not go that far but limited his proposal substantially to forbid purchase, by the federal government for its own use, of meat and meat products from animals slaughtered by an inhumane method. In several states, such as New Jersey and Connecticut, bills patterned after the Humphrey measure were not so limited and, in exercising the states' police power, sought to impose penalties of fines and imprisonment upon all slaughterers violating the proposed laws irrespective of who the purchasers were.

Only two methods of slaughtering and handling of livestock were declared in the federal act to be humane. Section 2 of the Humane Slaughter Act reads as follows:

No method of slaughtering or handling in connection with slaughtering shall be deemed to comply with the public policy of the United States unless it is humane. Either of the following two methods of slaughtering and handling are hereby found to be humane:

(a) in the case of cattle, calves, horses, mules, sheep, swine, and other livestock, all animals are rendered insensible to pain by a single blow or gunshot or an electrical, chemical or other means that is rapid and effective, before being shackled, hoisted, thrown, cast, or cut; or

(b) by slaughtering in accordance with the ritual requirements of the Jewish faith or any other religious faith that prescribes a method of slaughter whereby the animal suffers loss of consciousness by anemia of the brain caused by the simultaneous and instantaneous severance of the carotid arteries with a sharp instrument.

Section 3 reads in part as follows:

The public policy declared in this chapter shall be taken into consideration by all agencies of the Federal Government in connection with all procurement and price support programs and operations. . . .

Section 4 (c) provides:

Handling in connection with such slaughtering which necessarily accompanies the method of slaughter described in subsection (b) of this section shall be deemed to comply with the public policy specified by this section.

Our concern here relates to subdivision (b) but one comment with respect to subdivision (a) also has some relevance here. The Eighth Amendment forbids cruel punishments and the Supreme Court has accepted as constitutionally permissible execution by hanging (although it is by no means certain that it would do so today), firing squads, electrocution, and, most recently, lethal injections. It may safely be assumed that the Supreme Court would not tolerate execution by a sledge hammer blow upon the head, even if it were a "single blow." Even with respect to death by "gunshot," execution is generally by a firing squad rather than a single individual to assure instant death with a minimum degree of pain. Why then does the Humane Slaughter Act allow slaughtering of animals by rendering them "insensible to pain by a single blow" ("stunning" is the term usually used in the trade)? And what happens if a single blow or gunshot proves insufficient to achieve death? In military practice the latter problem is avoided by resorting to firing squads on the assumption that at least one of the bullets will be effective in terminating life instantaneously. But the statute does not require it; when you go hunting, you don't bring along seven companions so that you can shoot simultaneously at the same bird or rabbit.

Perhaps the answer might be suggested by La Rochefoucauld's definition of hypocrisy as the homage vice pays to virtue. Putting it more charitably, and somewhat more realistically, exemption of the comparatively inexpensive method of fatal stunning or shooting is the price that had to be paid to win the vote of senators and representatives from cattle farm and meat producing areas and to avoid the disfavor of the anti-gun control lobbies.

Jones v. Butts, which reached the Supreme Court in 1974, was a suit by nine taxpayers and consumers of meat seeking an injunction against the Jewish method of slaughter. It related to subdivision (b) and involved both the establishment and free exercise mandates of the First Amendment and could have also been considered under the Equal Protection Clause. An understanding of the case requires some explanation of the phrase "ritual requirements of the Jewish faith" (the Hebrew term is *shehitah*).

The term "Jewish faith" is what the courts call "overbroad." Reform Judaism does not mandate any particular method for the killing of animals for human consumption other than that it be done with the minimum amount of pain that is practicable. Its association with the defense in the lawsuit was based on two considerations: that the religious freedom of all Jews—Orthodox, Conservative, or Reform—be protected and, second, that any defamation of Jews for engaging in inhumane slaughtering practices be judicially declared to be false.

The Pentateuch (Mosaic law) forbids the consumption of certain animals, such as horses, mules, or swine, and the Talmud (called the Oral Law) requires that the slaughter of permissibly edible animals be done in a way that would result in the minimum amount of pain. That Judaism is concerned with the avoidance of pain to the greatest extent possible in the slaughtering process was established by the expert evidence, presented at legislative hearings before the act was adopted, that *shehitah* may well be the most humane practical method of slaughtering. The trial court stated in its opinion in the *Jones v. Butts* case that the Jewish organizations had "made a persuasive showing that Jewish ritual slaughter, as a fundamental aspect of Jewish practice, was historically related to considerations in times when such concerns were practically non-existent." Further evidence that *shehitah* is humane could be found in the fact that the ASPCA supports it as such. But perhaps the most conclusive evidence on this point can be found in the fact that the plaintiffs in *Jones v. Butts* did not challenge the *shehitah* itself, but only the shackling and hoisting that precedes "the simultaneous and instantaneous severance of the carotid arteries with a sharp instrument."

To paraphrase Shakespeare, there is nothing humane or inhumane but declaring makes it so. Subdivision (a) of Section 2 declares it to be humane to kill by a blow with a hammer or by gunshot; *ergo,* that must be humane; so, too, with respect to the shackling and hoisting of the animal that precedes *shehitah* (i.e., the instantaneous severance of the carotid arteries).

Would not a law that permits killing by a blow or gunshot but bars *shehitah* violate the Equal Protection Clause? The three-judge District Court in *Jones v. Butts* did not find it necessary to consider that aspect. Instead it rejected the plaintiffs' claim that the challenged statute violated the Establishment Clause in that its purpose was religious. It also held that the fact that the statute coincided with the tenets of the Jewish religion did not violate the effect aspect of the Establishment Clause. Congress, the Court said, considered ample and persuasive the evidence that the Jewish ritual method of slaughter, including the handling preparatory to such slaughter by shackling and hoisting, was humane.

The Court noted too that exemption of Sabbatarians in Sunday closing laws and of conscientious objectors in selective service draft laws had been upheld as constitutional by the Supreme Court. It rejected the contention that the plaintiffs' rights under the Free Exercise Clause were violated because they were forced "knowingly or unknowingly" to eat ritually slaughtered meat, and in some cases were compelled by their conscience to cease eating meat altogether, since they could not be sure that the animal had not been slaughtered by *shehitah*. This, said the Court, could hardly be judged to be a violation of the Free Exercise Clause, since they made no claim that eating meat resulting from ritual slaughter violated any religion of their own. Ethical principles against eating such meat do not justify a claim under the Free Exercise Clause.

In sum, without any dissent, the District Court concluded that in making it possible for those who wish to eat ritually acceptable meat, Congress neither established the Jewish faith nor interfered with the practice of any other.

The plaintiffs appealed the decision to the Supreme Court. The Court did not merely dismiss the appeal; instead, it affirmed the judgment of the District Court, thus making it a judgment of its own.

One amusing—or perhaps not so amusing—aspect of the suit is noteworthy. Paragraph 2 of the plaintiffs' complaint reads:

> Since the livestock animals now and hereafter awaiting slaughter in the United States are real parties in interest, and since they cannot speak for themselves, Miss Jones also sues here as next friend and guardian on their behalf.

Why the self-appointed friend and guardian did not fulfill her obligation to challenge not merely the method of slaughtering but the slaughtering itself, the complaint does not say. Nor does the complaint say, at the very least, why the plaintiffs did not challenge Section 2 (a) of the act, which permits slaughter by "a single blow or gunshot."

Perhaps—and this is what makes this postscript not amusing at all—the answer may be found in Footnote 7 of the District Court's opinion:

> Certain members of the orthodox Jewish community were alarmed with respect to the implications of the proposed legislation both with regard to the possible restriction of pre-slaughter handling and to the possibility of anti-Semitic propaganda which had accompanied similar legislation in other countries.

It is important to note that the Supreme Court's affirmance did not mean constitutional protection of all methods of preparation for *shehitah*. Section 2 (a) forbids the use of shackling and hoisting as a preparatory step in non-kosher slaughter. Congress could have but elected not to enact a law requiring the same preparatory restriction with respect to *shehitah*. Conclusive evidence that Jewish religious law does not mandate it is evidenced by the fact that in Israel the practice is forbidden, and this with the approval of the Israel Rabbinate.

Why then do not the American Orthodox and Conservative rabbis do the same? The reason given by them is that shackling and hoisting is the most economical method of preparation for *shehitah* and that alternative methods (such as the use of a casting pen in which the animal is rotated until it is lying on its back and then slaughtered) would be too costly to enable lower-income Jews to consume meat to the extent they desire. Why the Rabbinate in Israel, which has its own share of low-income Jews, does not allow shackling and hoisting, is not stated.

ZONING LAWS AND RELIGION

At first glance, zoning laws present a most ingenious paradox to purist champions of laissez faire capitalism. On the one hand, they seem clearly to violate the constitutional prohibition against deprivation of property without due process of law. To the purists, government has no right to forbid owners to use their own properties in otherwise lawful endeavors that are most likely to produce maximum profits, and this without the just compensation required under the Fifth Amendment when private property is taken for public use. On the other hand, the owners of these properties do not relish invasion of their suburban residential districts by (other) capitalists seeking maximum profits.

Since no one has yet conceived of a means to have one's cake and eat it too, the wealthy have accepted enactment of zoning laws that protect the sanctity of their residential areas even though opportunities for higher profits would have to be sacrificed. The urban working class has been quite content with this solution, since it lessens both the time and cost of reaching the industrial or commercial enterprises where they work.

Constitutional permissibility for zoning laws (established by the Supreme Court's 1926 decision in the case of *Village of Euclid v. Ambler Realty Co.)* is based upon the police power, which is reserved to the states by virtue of the provision in the Tenth Amendment that powers not delegated to the federal government are reserved to the states, and by the language of the Fourteenth Amendment, which forbids deprivation of property (including how it is used) only if it is without due process of law. Since the opportunity accorded to property owners to present their positions to legislatures and zoning boards constitutes due process, it is constitutionally permissible for states to impose restraints upon an owner's use of his own property.

Restraints, however, must be confined within the limits of the police power; that is, they must be necessary to protect or promote the public health, safety, morals, and general welfare. Over the years, the Supreme Court has maintained a fairly consistent policy of according wide discretion to legislatures and zoning authorities with respect to both the original fixing of zoning lines and the granting or withholding of requests for variances (uses which otherwise would not be permissible). So long as all interested persons were given adequate notice and opportunity to be heard the Court generally refrained from accepting a challenge from either proponents or opponents concerning a particular zoning ordinance or variance.

The reticence is understandable when First Amendment clauses, particularly the Free Exercise and Establishment clauses, are not relevant to the determination of constitutionality. Suppose, however, a zoning board is faced with a request for a variance made by Orthodox Jewish residents that would permit erection of a synagogue in a particular zone limited exclusively to residential one family houses. Since Orthodox Judaism forbids traveling on the Sabbath other than on foot, does not denial of a variance to permit building of a synagogue violate the Free Exercise Clause? On the other hand, does not granting a variance violate the Establishment Clause by preferring Orthodox Judasim over other religions?

The extent to which some state courts will impose claimed free exercise restrictions on zoning boards, and the Supreme Court will be reluctant to review them, is indicated in its 1976 denial of a petition for certiorari in the case of *Incorporated Village of Roslyn Harbor v. Jewish Reconstruction Synagogue.* There New York's highest court ruled in violation of the clause a zoning board's denial of a variance (exception) that would have allowed a congregation to use as a synagogue a residence purchased for that purpose.

In that case, a village ordinance required a setback of one hundred feet for permissible religious institutional use, whereas the purchased house was only twenty-nine feet from the property line. The plot purchased by the congregation was large enough to have allowed a one-hundred-foot setback (one hundred and seventy-seven feet from the nearest residence) but the congregation claimed financial inability to erect a new building or to move the purchased residence. Objection to the granting of a variance was made by four residents who did not relish having a synagogue so close to their homes.

New York's highest court held that to enforce the ordinance against a congregation not able to afford either erecting a new building or moving the old one would be tantamount to a denial of use in violation of the Free Exercise Clause. Nor was it material that only four percent of the congregation's family members resided in the village. Even potential traffic hazards by reason of the fact that the nonresident congregants would have to drive through the village was not determinative.

We have not said that a consideration of the surrounding area and potential traffic hazards are [the Court said] unrelated to the public health, safety or welfare when religious structures are involved; [but] they are outweighed by the constitutional prohibition against the abridgment of the free exercise of religion and by the public benefit and welfare which is itself an attribute of religious worship in a community. If the community can, consistent with this policy, both comply with the constitutional requirement and, at the same time, avoid or minimize, insofar as practicable, traffic hazards or other potential detriments bearing a substantial relation to the health, safety and welfare of the community, there is no barrier to its doing so. Nevertheless, . . . where an irreconcilable conflict exists between the right to erect a religious structure and the potential hazards of traffic or diminution in value, the latter must yield to the former.

What would seem to be a directly contrary result can be found in the Supreme Court's denial of a petition for certiorari in the case of *Lakewood, Ohio, Congregation of Jehovah's Witnesses, Inc. v. City of Lakewood* (1984). That case involved a challenge under the Free Exercise and Due Process clauses of the Constitution to a municipal ordinance excluding church buildings in nearly ninety percent of an area set aside for single-family residences.

The practical effect of the prohibition, the Witnesses claimed, was to exclude them from building a church in the district (since the allowable ten percent had already been exhausted) through enforcement of an ordinance that did not bear a substantial relation to public health, safety, morals, or general welfare.

The congregation had worshipped in the business section of the community on one of the city's two main commercial thoroughfares since 1947. In 1972, desiring to erect a larger and more attractive Kingdom Hall (house of worship) with more off-street parking, it purchased a lot in a residential area. A year later, but before the congregation applied for a permit, the city council enacted an ordinance which, unlike its predecessor, made no exception for churches. Accordingly, the congregation's application to build its church in that area was denied.

The congregation had a membership of slightly over one hundred. On Sunday mornings about one hundred and ten people attended services, on Tuesday evenings about fifty came to Bible school, and on Thursday evenings eighty to ninety people attended theocratic services. The congregation did not use its Kingdom Hall at any other time; it held no social activities (and certainly not bingo) in its building and did not lend its facilities to other groups.

In its defense against the congregation's suit, the city attempted to show that the Kingdom Hall would create a traffic hazard (on Sunday mornings and Tuesday and Thursday evenings) and that the city's general ban on the building of churches in residential districts was reasonable inasmuch as other denominations used their church buildings for a variety of social and community activities and allowing more use would greatly increase the noise and traffic in the neighborhood.

The zoning board had the power to grant variances but refused to do so, and both the Federal District Court and the Court of Appeals upheld its right to refuse. They rejected the church's claim that the denial of a variance infringed upon the congregation's free exercise rights in precluding public worship in ninety percent of the city, including all of its single-family residential areas.

In its brief to the courts, counsel for the congregation quoted Deuteronomy 31:12:

> Congregate the people, the men and the women and the little ones and your alien resident who is within your gates, in order that they may listen and in order that they may learn, as they must fear Jehovah your God and take care to carry out all the words of this law.

The lower courts were not persuaded.

> The Congregation's "religious observance" [the Court of Appeals said] is the construction of a church building in a residential district. In contrast to prior cases, the activity has no religious or ritualistic significance for the Jehovah's Witnesses. There is no evidence that the construction of a Kingdom Hall is a ritual, a "fundamental tenet," or a "cardinal principle" of its faith. At most the Congregation can claim that its freedom to worship is tangentially related to worshipping in its own structure. However, building and owning a church is a desirable accessory of worship, not a fundamental tenet of the Congregation's religious beliefs. The zoning ordinance does not prevent the Congregation from practicing its faith through worship whether the worship be in homes, schools, other churches, or meeting halls throughout the city. The ordinance prohibits the purely secular act of building anything other than a home in a residential district . . . . Despite the ordinance's financial and aesthetical imposition on the Congregation, we hold that the Congregation's freedom of religion, as protected by the Free Exercise Clause, has not been infringed.

Nor, the Court of Appeals concluded, did the ordinance violate the Due Process Clause. In creating exclusive residential districts to control traffic congestion and off-street parking in secluded residential areas, the city was legitimately and rationally exercising "its police power to preserve a quiet place where yards [were] wide, people few, and motor vehicles restricted."

As in *Incorporated Village of Roslyn Harbor v. Jewish Reconstruction Synagogue,* the Supreme Court denied a petition for certiorari (eleven years after the first application for a variance). Superficial appearances to the contrary, there is a consistency in its disposition of most (not all, as will shortly be seen in the discussion of *Larkin v. Grendel's Den)* zoning law cases. The common underlying principle is that the Court will not interfere with a state's exercise of its police power in cases involving zoning laws, whether by its highest court (as in the synagogue case) or its legislature (as in the Kingdom Hall case).

Before considering the *Grendel's Den* case, *City of Evanston v. Lubavitch Chabad House of Illinois* merits noting. There a Hasidic Jewish group was denied a permit to use a building owned by them as a religious sanctuary for Jewish students at nearby Northwestern University. Services that were to be provided in the building would include rabbinical counseling, group discussions, and worship service on the Sabbath and Jewish holidays. Also a number of sleep-in accommodations on the Sabbath and Jewish holidays would be provided for Orthodox Jewish students who did not reside within walking distance of the property and did not travel on those days.

Close by was Canterbury House, an Episcopalian facility that had year-round boarders and in which worship services and meals were available. A nearby Lutheran House held Sunday night dinners. Hillel Foundation, which conducted Jewish worship services for students who were not as strictly Orthodox as the Lubavitch group, had applied for and received a special use permit to allow it to operate a synagogue and furnish rabbinical counseling at another nearby building but decided not to acquire it.

It is difficult to avoid the conclusion that, were it not for the fact that the applicants for a permit were Hasidic, the application would have been granted. In any event, in upholding the Lubavitch group's right to a special use permit, the Illinois court held that denial violated the Free Exercise Clause and ordered issuance of a permit. As in the other zoning case discussed in this chapter, the Supreme Court refused to set aside the Illinois court's decision.

As indicated earlier in this book, Hasidic Judaism bears many of the aspects of cultism, as too do Jehovah's Witnesses, at least in some parts of our nation. This may well explain the unfriendly action these groups encountered in the *Lubavitch* and *Lakewood* cases. Realistically, the difference between them in zoning litigation may be that memories of the

Holocaust suffered by European Jewry under Nazism still haunt the American conscience, including that of the judiciary, while the comparatively minor sufferings of Jehovah's Witnesses do not.

If one can be allowed to mix metaphors, *Larkin v. Grendel's Den,* decided in December 1982, can be described as a second coming to strict separationists that shortly thereafter turned out to be a mirage in the desert of accommodationism.

The case involved a constitutional challenge to a Massachusetts zoning statute aimed at protecting churches and schools from the evil consequences of proximity to restaurants that served intoxicating liquors. As originally enacted in 1954, the statute imposed an absolute ban on liquor licenses within five hundred feet of a church or school. In 1968, however, the sinful purveyors of intoxicating liquors had achieved sufficient political influence to obtain amendment of the law so as to permit licenses "if the governing body of such church assents in writing." Understandably, members of some church governing bodies might find it embarrassing to sign an assent form, so in 1970 the law was again amended to permit licensing unless the governing body of a church or school itself filed a written objection.

This seemed to have worked quite well, since in 1979 there were twenty-six liquor licensees within five hundred feet of the Holy Cross Armenian Catholic Church located in the Harvard Square of Cambridge. However, the governing body of the church decided that enough was enough, and accordingly filed a written objection to the issuance of a license to Grendel's Den that would have allowed it to serve intoxicating liquors in its restaurant located only ten feet from the church building.

In its suit against the License Commission the restaurant asserted a variety of grounds to support its claim: that the statute violated (1) the Equal Protection Clause of the Fourteenth Amendment, (2) the Due Process Clause of the same amendment, (3) the Establishment Clause of the First Amendment, and (4) the Sherman Anti-Trust Act. The Establishment Clause ground was urged with respect to all three aspects—purpose, effect, and entanglement. The Sherman Anti-Trust Act claim was based upon the contention that the veto power accorded to churches tended towards according them monopolization powers, effected through conspiracy with present licensees to exclude future competitors by exercise of the veto privilege.

The License Commission contested the plaintiffs' claims, and in addition cited the provision in the Twenty-first Amendment authorizing states to forbid the transportation of intoxicating liquors within their boundaries.

In a comparatively short opinion in favor of Grendel's Den, with the dissent only of Rehnquist, the Court, speaking through Burger, ruled the following:

(1) The Twenty-first Amendment reserves to the states a power relating to liquor sales but that power may not be exercised in a way that impinges upon the Establishment Clause of the First Amendment.

(2) The deference normally accorded courts to legislative zoning judgments is not merited when the important decision-making power is delegated to a religious institution.

(3) Because the Court ruled the Massachusetts statute invalid on Establishment Clause grounds, it did not find it necessary to consider the anti-trust contention.

(4) For the same reason, it did not pass upon the equal protection and due process contentions.

(5) Burger, instead, elected to rule unconstitutionality under the Establishment Clause.

What is just short of amazing about this case is not so much that the Court's decision was in favor of Grendel's Den, as how it justified that decision, and who concurred with it. In reaching the decision, Burger applied the tripartite purpose-effect-entanglement test. Since, he said, the purpose of the statute, as described by the District Court, was to protect "spiritual, cultural, and educational centers from the 'hurly-burly' associated with liquor outlets," there could be little doubt it embraced a valid legislative secular purpose. But effect and entanglement were different. As to the former, Burger pointed out that the statute did not require the churches to meet any specific standards; the church could employ their veto power for achieving religious ends, as for example, favoring liquor licenses for members of the congregation or adherents to its faith. The effect, therefore, was clearly the advancement of the congregation's religion. Moreover, the statute advanced religion by the mere appearance of a joint exercise of legislative authority by church and state.

A statute that violates one part of the purpose-effect-entanglement test is as invalid as a statute that violates all three. In *Epperson v. Arkansas* and *Stone v. Graham*, the Court invalidated respectively statutes forbidding the teaching of evolution and posting of the Ten Commandments in public schools on the sole ground that their purposes were to advance religion; in neither case did the Court find it necessary to consider effect or entanglement. Having determined that the zoning regulation in the *Grendel's Den* case violated the effect ban, it was therefore unnecessary for Burger to proceed further into the arena of entanglement.

Yet that is what he did. In fact, he did more than that. He entered through the portico of political entanglement and did so with a bang. The statute, he said:

> ... substitutes the unilateral and absolute power of a church for the reasoned decisionmaking of a public legislative body acting on evidence and guided by standards, on issues with significant economic and political implications. The challenged statute thus enmeshes churches in the processes of government and creates the danger of "[p]olitical fragmentation and divisiveness along religious lines." Ordinary human experience and a long line of cases teach that few entanglements could be more offensive to the spirit of the Constitution.

This quotation should be contrasted with the following extract from Footnote 11 in Rehnquist's opinion in *Mueller v. Allen*, barely six months later:

> The Court's language in *Lemon I* respecting political divisiveness was made in the context of Pennsylvania and Rhode Island statutes which provided for either direct payments of, or reimbursement of, a proportion of teachers' salaries in parochial schools. We think, in the light of the treatment of the point in later cases discussed above, the language must be regarded as confined to cases where direct financial subsidies are paid to parochial schools or to teachers in parochial schools.

Grendel's Den, by the widest stretch of one's imagination, cannot be deemed a parochial school. How Burger could concur without reservation to Footnote 11 can perhaps be better explained by social scientists than by lawyers.

But that is not all. Not only did Burger place reliance on political entanglement but he went out of his way (since the effect criterion could have disposed of the case) to add a new facet to the entanglement aspect:

> Turning to the third phase of the inquiry called for by *Lemon v. Kurtzman, supra*, we see that we have not previously had occasion to consider the entanglement implications of a statute vesting significant governmental authority in churches. [Such a] statute enmeshes churches in the exercise of substantial governmental powers contrary to our consistent interpretation of the Establishment Clause; "[t]he objective is to prevent, as far as possible, the intrusion of either [Church or State] into the precincts of the other." *Lemon v. Kurtzman supra*. . . . The Framers did not set up a system of government in which important, discretionary governmental powers would be delegated to or shared with religious institutions.

(The last sentence would seem to invalidate New York's *agunah* statute considered in Chapter 8.)

In his dissenting opinion, Rehnquist referred to a statement made by Holmes that "great" cases make "bad" law. He suggested that a third class of cases—silly cases—also make bad law. For Rehnquist, the evolving legislative treatment of the grant of liquor licenses—from absolute ban, to affirmative church assent, to written church veto—was just the sort of refinement that the Court should encourage rather than forbid in the name of the First Amendment. The statute, he said, did not sponsor or subsidize any religious group or activity; nor did it encourage, much less compel, anyone to participate in religious activities. To say that it "advances" religion was to strain the meaning of that word.

How does one react to the *Grendel's Den* decision? It could hardly be deemed a monumental landmark in litigation relating to the proximity of beer saloons to churches. As the Court noted, twenty-seven states continue to prohibit liquor outlets within prescribed distances of institutions such as churches and schools. The Court's decision, said Burger, is not to be construed as expressing an opinion as to the constitutionality of any statute other than that of Massachusetts. As far as is known, no other state has a set-up of the church veto challenged in the *Grendel's Den* case. This would seem to indicate that the decision is of little practical importance. It certainly did not affect the decision in *Mueller v. Allen*. Nevertheless, it may in some post-Burger court turn out to be a constitutional lantern illuminating the dark road leading back to a second coming of strict separation of church and state.

The Burger Court

	Tenure
Warren E. Burger, Chief Justice	1969–
Hugo L. Black	1937–1971
William O. Douglas	1939–1975
John M. Harlan	1955–1971
William J. Brennan, Jr.	1956–
Potter Stewart	1958–1981
Byron R. White	1962–
Thurgood Marshall	1967–
Harry A. Blackmun	1970–
William H. Rehnquist	1971–
Lewis F. Powell, Jr.	1972–
John Paul Stevens	1975–
Sandra Day O'Connor	1981–

Table of Cases

Index

301